# BACK
# HOME
# AGAIN

A

CULINARY COLLECTION

FROM THE

JUNIOR LEAGUE OF INDIANAPOLIS, INC.

The Junior League of Indianapolis is an organization of women committed to promoting voluntarism and to improving the community through the effective action and leadership of trained volunteers. Its purpose is exclusively educational and charitable.

Copies of **BACK HOME AGAIN** may be obtained by using order blanks in the back of the book or by writing:

**JLI Publications**
**BACK HOME AGAIN**
**3050 N. Meridian**
**Indianapolis, Indiana 46208**

For your convenience, credit card orders are accepted. Specify Mastercard or Visa and include card holders name, mailing address, card number, expiration date and signature.

Credit card telephone orders accepted
**1-317-923-7004**
Copies of our original best seller, **WINNERS,** may also be obtained at the above address.

**Design and Art**
Nancy P. Meers
Image Concepts Incorporated

**Photography**
Tony English
Tony English Photography

**Editorial Consultant**
Audrey P. Stehle

Printed in the United States of America by
Shepard Poorman Communications Corporation
Indianapolis, Indiana

First Printing: 30,000 copies
October, 1993

ISBN 0-9614447-1-1

Library of Congress Catalogue Card Number
93-78959

Recycled Paper

The old song "Back Home Again in Indiana", dear to the hearts of Hoosiers, was one inspiration for this cookbook. Its lyrics recall stately sycamore trees, the fragrance of newly mown hay and moonlight on the Wabash River. Such nostalgic images evoke memories of home, of the warmth of love and friendship. And such memories inevitably include gatherings large and small centered around food and the table — in the kitchen, the dining room, on the patio or at a picnic in the park.

Preparing and sharing food has been, since the dawn of time, essential not only to preserving life but to establishing community and companionship. Our major milestones are celebrated with food, and meal times are central to our daily lives. Dining, whether elegantly or simply, draws people together, filling them with nourishment and surrounding them with the glow of hospitality and comfort. Cooking is an act of caring, of welcoming family and friends and providing for them the pleasure of being at home.

Indianapolis graciously welcomes guests and travelers to their city which at the crossroads of four interstates is a center of cultural and world renowned sporting events, bringing visitors back home again year 'round. **BACK HOME AGAIN** reflects the warmth of Hoosier hospitality, featuring recipes and menus that will form the foundation of delightful gatherings and fond memories.

Although **BACK HOME AGAIN** celebrates traditional Midwestern friendliness, it emphasizes up-to-date, contemporary cuisine. This book is a collection of sophisticated and innovative dishes that address today's desire for lighter, fresh ingredients and uncompromising tastes and quality. Our recipes will challenge the most exacting chefs, yet enable even novice cooks to prepare up-scale, exciting foods. The menus you select and prepare will be the highlight of the warm reception your guests receive when you welcome them into your home.

# COMMITTEE MEMBERS

The Junior League of Indianapolis, Inc., extends its heartfelt thanks and appreciation to the committee members and their families. Without their sacrifices and generosity, the accomplishment of this book would not have been possible.

### Chairmen:

| | | | |
|---|---|---|---|
| Connie Brown* | 1990-1992 | Angie Tuckerman* | 1992-1993 |
| Julie Fox* | 1992-1994 | Kathy Volker* | 1993-1994 |
| Elisabeth Palmer* | 1992-1993 | | |

### Committee Members:

| | | |
|---|---|---|
| Mary Arnold | Marcie Hammel | Lisa Peter |
| Ann Arthur* | Kelly Hammond | Sylvia Purichia |
| Pam Baxter* | Amy Hart-Ramey* | Kim Purucker |
| Michelle Bentley | Mary Hauck | Carole Reeves* |
| Sheryl Bierbower | Jane Hawks* | Marla Relford |
| Joan Blackwell | Jan Hogan | Julianne Robinson |
| Patricia Borgogni | Woodie Howgill | Debra Rolfsen |
| Linda Borth | Susan Hoyt | Therese Rooney |
| Mary Bridewesser | Paige Hunkin | Elizabeth Ruddell |
| Angela Burkhart | Kathy Hursh* | Beth Rush* |
| Patricia Burton | Lisa Jacobs | Anita Russell |
| Ellen Butz | Mary Keller | Amy Scher |
| Jeanne F. Carmody | Kathy Martindill | Eve Shirley |
| Susan Casper* | Barbara McGowan* | Stacy Singer* |
| Celeste Cohen | Laurie Merritt | Diane Strader |
| Margo Cory | Anne Miller | Suzanne Thomas* |
| Kim Dant | Peggy Miner* | Ann Toon |
| Janet Dorger | Marty Moheban | Brenda Walker |
| Lisa Fennig | Cindy Newcomer | Carole Walters |
| Beth Finn* | Carolyn Nierman* | Melissa Warriner* |
| Jo Ellen Flynn | Cami O'Herren | Kathleen Washburn |
| Susan Fountain | Kim Parker | Molly Williams |
| Ilene Garrett* | Kris Payne | |

### Finance Development:

| | |
|---|---|
| Karen Glaser* | Candis Shelton* |
| Linda Goad* | Barbara Danquist* |

* denotes 2 years +

# TABLE OF CONTENTS

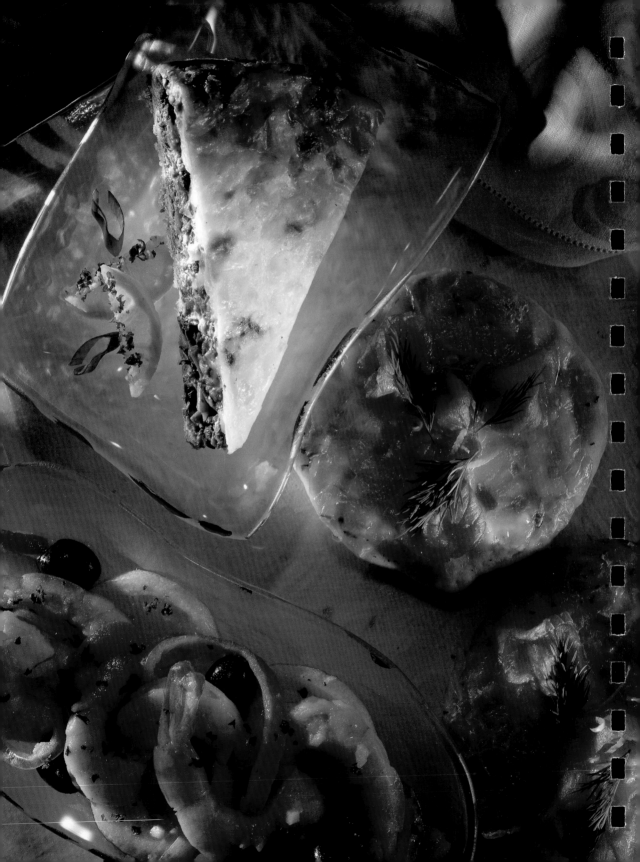

# A Warm Welcome

*Appetizers*

*Beverages*

*Soups*

# A WARM WELCOME

# Savory Gruyere Cheesecake

Preheat oven to 350 degrees.

Combine bread crumbs and melted butter in a small bowl.

Butter a 10-inch springform pan.  Press crumbs onto bottom and side of pan.

Bake 8 to 10 minutes.  Set aside to cool.  Reduce oven temperature to 325 degrees.

Beat cream cheese, cream, salt, nutmeg and red pepper together until smooth in a large bowl.  Beat in eggs one at a time.

Divide mixture between two bowls.  Stir Gruyere cheese into one bowl.  Stir spinach and green onions into the other.  Pour spinach filling into cooled crust.

Melt three tablespoons butter in a medium skillet.  Sauté mushrooms over medium-high heat until all moisture evaporates, stirring frequently.  Season with salt and pepper.

Spoon mushrooms over spinach filling.  Carefully pour Gruyere filling over mushrooms.

Set pan on baking sheet.  Bake for one hour.

Turn oven off; cool cheesecake in oven one hour with door ajar.

Serve warm directly from the oven or at room temperature.

*Decidedly different and definitely delicious.*

¾ cup toasted fine bread crumbs (Italian or French)

3 tablespoons unsalted butter, melted

3 (8-ounce) packages cream cheese, softened

¼ cup whipping cream

½ teaspoon salt

¼ teaspoon ground nutmeg

¼ teaspoon ground red pepper

4 eggs

1 cup shredded Gruyere cheese

1 (10-ounce) package frozen chopped spinach, thawed and squeezed dry

3 tablespoons minced green onions

3 tablespoons unsalted butter

½ pound mushrooms, cleaned and finely chopped

Salt and pepper

**Serves:  10 - 12**

¾ cup (1 ½ sticks) unsalted butter, divided

2 cups coarsely chopped onion

1 ½ cups water

2 teaspoons salt

1 ½ cups all-purpose flour

6 eggs

1 cup grated Parmesan cheese

Milk

Grated Parmesan cheese

**Yield: 2 dozen**

# PARMESAN PUFFS

Preheat oven to 400 degrees.

Sauté onions in 1/4 cup butter until golden, not browned. Set aside.

Bring water to a boil and add 1/2 cup butter; add salt and flour. Turn heat to low; stir until a ball forms and pulls away from the side of the pan.

Remove from heat and add eggs, one at a time, stirring well with each addition. Blend 1 cup Parmesan cheese and then onions into dough mixture.

Drop dough by large tablespoonfuls onto a greased baking sheet, approximately two inches apart. Brush top with milk. Sprinkle with Parmesan cheese. Bake 40 minutes or until puffy and golden.

# Miniature Cheese Tarts

Preheat oven to 425 degrees.

In a food processor, combine pastry ingredients until crumbly. Roll dough 1/8-inch thick on floured board.

Cut dough into small rounds and place in lightly greased miniature muffin pans.

Combine half-and-half, eggs, salt, pepper, hot pepper sauce and Worcestershire.

Place diced cheese in each tin; gently spoon in cream mixture, filling 1/2 to 3/4 full. Sprinkle with red pepper if desired.

Bake 20 to 25 minutes or until browned.

*A favorite appetizer quiche that will disappear in no time.*

Pastry:

¼ pound (1 stick) butter, cold, cut into small pieces

2 cups all-purpose flour

½ teaspoon salt

3 tablespoons shortening

4 - 5 tablespoons cold water

Filling:

1 ⅓ cups half-and-half

2 eggs

Salt and pepper

Dash of hot pepper sauce

Dash of Worcestershire sauce

1 pound sharp Cheddar cheese, diced

Ground red pepper, optional

**Yield: 5 dozen**

# COCKTAIL BISCUITS

4 ½ cups unbleached all-purpose flour

3 tablespoons baking powder

1 ½ teaspoons salt

1 ½ cups (3 sticks) unsalted butter, cold, cut into pieces

6 tablespoons solid shortening

1 ½ cups milk

3 cups finely chopped mushrooms

6 shallots, minced

¼ cup (1 stick) unsalted butter

Salt and pepper

1 ½ cups finely chopped smoked ham

6 green onions, finely chopped

**Yield: 6 dozen**

Prepare dough in 3 batches: In a food processor, place 1 1/2 cups flour, 1 tablespoon baking powder and 1/2 teaspoon salt; process a few seconds. Add 1/2 cup butter and 2 tablespoons shortening; process until resembles coarse meal. Add 1/2 cup milk while processor is running. Process until blended. Repeat twice.

Wrap dough; chill several hours.

Preheat oven to 400 degrees.

In a large skillet, sauté mushrooms and shallots in 1/4 cup butter until lightly browned. Season with salt and pepper. Cool.

Remove dough from refrigerator. Knead in mushroom mixture, then ham and green onions.

Flour hands and shape dough into 1-inch balls. Place on greased baking sheets. Firmly indent each ball with a thumbprint.

Bake 15 minutes or until golden. Serve warm.

Can be frozen. Great spread with Banana Chutney.

*An easy cocktail party finger food.*

# Banana Chutney

Mix all ingredients in a large, heavy saucepan. Bring to a boil; simmer about 15 minutes or until thick.

Heat jars in boiling water. Drain well. Ladle mixture into clean, hot jars. Cover tightly and cool. Store in refrigerator up to 1 week.

Pour over cream cheese and serve with a good crisp cracker as an appetizer or use as an unusual and delicious topper for Cocktail Biscuits.

2 cups peeled and chopped banana (about 6)

½ pound onions, coarsely chopped

½ pound pitted dates, finely chopped

1 ½ cups sugar

1 cup apple cider vinegar

2 tablespoons finely chopped crystallized ginger

½ teaspoon salt

½ teaspoon curry

½ cup golden raisins

5 half-pint glass jelly jars

**Yield: 5 half-pints**

**Cups:**

- 10 (6-inch) wheat tortillas

  Vegetable oil

**Dressing:**

- 1 tablespoon dark rum or tequila
- 1 ½ teaspoons Dijon mustard
- 1 ½ teaspoons red wine vinegar
- 1 tablespoon fresh orange juice
- ½ teaspoon grated orange rind
- ¼ cup vegetable oil

**Salsa:**

- 1 (15-ounce) can black beans, drained
- 2 - 3 jalapeño peppers, seeded and minced
- 1 tablespoon chopped green onions
- 1 navel orange, peeled and chopped
- 2 tablespoons finely chopped red bell pepper

**Yield: 40**

# BLACK BEAN SALSA IN TORTILLA CUPS

Preheat oven to 400 degrees.

Cut tortillas in 2 to 3-inch rounds; brush with oil on both sides. Press rounds into miniature muffin pans; bake 6 minutes or until crisp.

Whisk together all dressing ingredients in a bowl. Add salsa ingredients; mix well.

Place one heaping spoonful of salsa into each tortilla cup.

*A wonderfully different South-of-the-border specialty.*

# Pesto Cheese Stuffed Mushrooms

1 - 2   pounds large mushrooms

1   tablespoon olive oil

1 - 2   cloves garlic, crushed

½   cup fresh, or 1 tablespoon dried, basil leaves

3   tablespoons ricotta cheese

2   tablespoons bread crumbs

2   tablespoons grated Parmesan cheese

Pinch of ground red pepper

1   tablespoon chopped pine nuts

**Serves:  10 - 15**

Preheat oven to 400 degrees.

Clean mushrooms; remove stems and chop.  Set caps aside.

In a large skillet, heat olive oil; sauté mushroom stems and garlic 2 to 3 minutes; add basil and cook about 1 minute.  Remove from heat.

Add ricotta cheese, bread crumbs, Parmesan cheese, red pepper and pine nuts.  Fill mushroom caps.

Bake 12 to 15 minutes or until lightly browned.

*Absolutely delicious and so quick and easy.*

# Marvelous Marinated Mushrooms

1   pound large mushrooms

½   cup wine vinegar

⅔   cup vegetable oil

1   teaspoon tarragon or oregano leaves

1   clove garlic, minced

1   tablespoon lemon juice

½   teaspoon salt

½   teaspoon sugar

½   teaspoon pepper

Clean and quarter mushrooms.  Combine mushrooms with remaining ingredients in zip-closure plastic bag.  Marinate overnight.  Drain and serve.

*Easy and elegant for entertaining.*

*Basic Pizza Dough:*

- 1 tablespoon sugar

- 1 cup warm water
  (110 - 115 degrees)

- 1 envelope (¼-ounce) active
  dry yeast

- 3 ¼ cups bread, whole wheat
  or unbleached all-purpose
  flour

  *(can be a mixture of
  flours), reserve ¼ cup*

- 1 teaspoon salt

- ¼ cup olive oil

  *Choice of toppings
  (recipes follow)*

**Serves: 8 - 10**

# Fresh Pizzettes
# with Choice of
# Three Toppings

In a small bowl, dissolve the sugar in warm water. Sprinkle yeast over water; mix gently until smooth. Let stand in a warm place about 5 minutes or until foamy.

Combine flour and salt in a large mixing bowl. Make a well in the center; add the yeast mixture and 1/4 cup oil. Using a wooden spoon, mix until dough forms a ball, turn out onto a floured surface. Use the reserved flour as necessary to eliminate stickiness. Knead until dough is smooth, elastic and shiny - do not over knead.

Shape the dough into a ball and place in a well oiled bowl. Turn dough to coat all sides. Cover and let stand in a warm place until it has doubled in size, approximately 45 to 90 minutes.

Punch down the dough. Press out the air bubbles and re-shape into a ball. Coat again with oil, cover, and place in refrigerator until risen, approximately 35 to 60 minutes. (The dough can be frozen at this point.)

Preheat oven to 500 degrees. Place oven rack in second-to-top position.

Let dough come to room temperature. Divide into 18 portions, roll out into approximately 3-inch rounds. Place on large baking stone or baking sheet. Prick with fork; brush with olive oil. Add topping. Bake as directed for each topping.

*Definitely worth the effort.*

# Smoked Salmon and Brie Pizzette Topping

Prepare dough as directed. Bake 6 minutes; remove from oven.

Top crusts with cheese, salmon and onion. Drizzle with oil; bake 4 minutes longer or until golden and puffy.

Remove from oven; brush again with olive oil.

Garnish with fresh dill if desired. Serve immediately.

*A terrific combination and pleasing to the palate.*

*Basic Pizza Dough or purchased pizza dough*

1 *pound Brie cheese, rind discarded, cut into small pieces*

12 *ounces smoked salmon, cut into small pieces*

1 *small red sweet onion, thinly sliced, separated into rings*

*Olive oil*

*Fresh dill sprigs, optional*

**Serves: 8 - 10**

Basic Pizza Dough or
purchased pizza dough

1 cup olive oil, divided

2 cups shredded mozzarella

1 cup shredded Fontina
cheese

2 cups firmly packed fresh
basil leaves

3 cloves garlic

½ cup pine nuts

1 cup freshly grated
Parmesan cheese, divided

¼ cup freshly grated Romano
cheese

Olive oil

Fresh basil leaves,
optional

**Serves: 8 - 10**

# PESTO AND PINE NUT PIZZETTE TOPPING

Prepare dough as directed.  Sprinkle with mozzarella and Fontina cheeses; drizzle with 1/2 cup olive oil.

Bake 10 to 15 minutes or until golden brown.

Meanwhile, process the basil, garlic and pine nuts in a food processor until finely chopped.  With machine running, pour in remaining 1/2 cup oil in a thin steady stream.  Add 1/2 cup Parmesan cheese and the Romano; process briefly to combine. Place in a bowl and cover until ready to use.

Remove pizza crusts from baking stone.  Brush lightly with oil. Spoon on pesto; sprinkle with remaining Parmesan.  Serve immediately.

Garnish with fresh basil leaves if desired.

# Goat Cheese, Sun-Dried Tomatoes and Roasted Garlic Pizzette Topping

Preheat oven to 300 degrees. Toss garlic with 3 tablespoons olive oil and place in a small baking dish. Bake covered approximately 30 minutes or until tender, but not brown. Cool; chop. Increase oven temperature to 500 degrees.

Prepare dough as directed. Top with mozzarella and goat cheese. Sprinkle with garlic, tomatoes, parsley, salt and pepper. Drizzle with oil.

Bake 10 to 15 minutes or until golden brown. Sprinkle with Parmesan. Serve immediately.

Basic Pizza Dough or purchased pizza dough

| | |
|---|---|
| 10 - 12 | cloves garlic |
| 3 | tablespoons olive oil |
| 2 | cups shredded mozzarella cheese |
| 2 | cups crumbled goat cheese |
| 12 | oil-packed sun-dried tomatoes, well drained, slivered |
| ¼ | cup minced fresh parsley |
| | Salt and freshly ground pepper |
| | Olive oil |
| ¼ | cup freshly grated Parmesan cheese |

**Serves: 8 - 10**

2 ¼ cups unbleached all-purpose flour

2 teaspoons baking powder

1 teaspoon salt

1 teaspoon freshly ground pepper

½ teaspoon baking soda

1 cup shredded Provolone cheese

⅓ cup oil-packed sun-dried tomatoes, drained, chopped (oil reserved)

¼ cup chopped fresh parsley

1 ¼ teaspoons basil leaves

2 eggs

3 tablespoons vegetable oil

1 teaspoon sugar

1 ¼ cups buttermilk

**Serves: 8 - 10**

# PROVOLONE, SUN-DRIED TOMATOES AND BASIL BREAD

Preheat oven to 350 degrees. Grease three 5 x 3-inch loaf pans.

Combine flour, baking powder, salt, pepper and baking soda in a large bowl. Using fork, mix in Provolone, tomatoes, parsley and basil.

In another bowl, whisk eggs, oil, sugar and two tablespoons oil reserved from tomatoes. Mix in buttermilk. Add to dry ingredients; stir until just combined.

Divide batter among prepared pans.

Bake until tester inserted in center comes out clean, about 50 minutes. Cool in pans on rack 5 minutes.

Invert onto rack; cool completely. Wrap in foil and refrigerate.

Serve bread at room temperature, thinly sliced.

Use to make bite size sandwiches with Grilled Beef Tenderloin.

Can be prepared three days ahead.

*Tasty as an appetizer or as a crusty accompaniment for soups or salads.*

# BEACH WELLINGTON

Preheat oven to 400 degrees.

In large skillet, brown sausage breaking into small pieces; drain. Add ground beef. Cook and stir to brown; drain well.

Sauté onion in butter; add to the meat. Stir in seasonings, cheeses and egg; mix well. Cover; chill overnight.

Grease baking sheet. Thaw pastry following package directions.

Preheat oven to 400 degrees.

Spread pastry out on a flat surface; place meat mixture in center. Fold pastry over meat; tuck in ends to seal. Place seam side down on baking sheet. Make three or four diagonal cuts on top but not all the way through the pastry.

Bake 35 to 40 minutes or until golden brown and crisp. Cool 10-15 minutes.

Serve with Dill Sauce.

Combine ingredients in a small bowl; mix well.

*Terrific main dish for a supper at the beach.*

½ pound beef or turkey sausage

1 pound ground beef or turkey

1 ½ cups chopped onions

½ cup butter or margarine

2 teaspoons oregano leaves

1 tablespoon parsley flakes

½ teaspoon pepper

½ cup grated Parmesan cheese

½ cup ricotta cheese

1 (8-ounce) package cream cheese, softened

1 egg, beaten

1 (17 ¼-ounce) package (2 sheets) frozen puff pastry

**Serves: 6 - 7**

Dill Sauce:

1 (16-ounce) container sour cream

2 tablespoons dill weed

Dash of hot pepper sauce

4 skinless, boneless chicken breast halves, cut into 1-inch pieces

¾ cup (1 ½ sticks) butter or margarine

2 cups dry Italian bread crumbs

1 cup grated Parmesan cheese

1 teaspoon salt

¼ cup chopped parsley

**Serves:  4 - 6**

# HERB CHICKEN NUGGETS

Preheat oven to 400 degrees.  Line baking sheet with aluminum foil; grease.

In large skillet, melt butter; remove from heat.  Add chicken; let stand 5 minutes.

Combine bread crumbs, cheese, salt and parsley; mix well.  Dip chicken pieces first in butter, then in crumb mixture, turning to coat well.

Place chicken on prepared baking sheet.  Bake 15 to 20 minutes or until crisp and brown.

*Serve on a platter or pack for a picnic.  Serve with Creamy Mustard Sauce.*

# Spicy Chicken Fingers and Creamy Green Salsa

¾ cup milk

2 eggs

2 pounds skinless, boneless chicken breasts, cut into strips

⅔ cup cornmeal

2 tablespoons chili powder

2 teaspoons ground cumin

2 teaspoons parsley flakes

1 teaspoon oregano leaves

½ teaspoon garlic powder

½ teaspoon salt

¼ - ½ teaspoon ground red pepper

¾ cup all-purpose flour

½ cup (1 stick) butter or margarine, melted

**Serves: 6 - 8**

In large bowl, beat milk and eggs; add chicken.  Set aside.

Combine cornmeal and seasonings in a shallow bowl.  Place flour in a separate shallow bowl or plate.  In another shallow container, place melted butter.

Dip chicken pieces first in flour, then butter, then cornmeal mixture.  Place on wax paper; freeze at least 4 hours.

Preheat oven to 400 degrees.

Place frozen chicken on a lightly greased baking sheet.  Bake 30 minutes or until crisp.  Serve with Creamy Green Salsa.

Creamy Green Salsa:

½ cup sour cream

⅓ cup mayonnaise

⅓ - ½ cup prepared green salsa

1 tablespoon lemon juice

⅛ teaspoon chili powder

Combine all ingredients in a small bowl; chill.

**Yield: 1 ¼ cups**

2 pounds raw shrimp, cooked, peeled, deveined

¼ cup vegetable oil

2 cloves garlic, crushed

1 tablespoon dry mustard

2 teaspoons salt

½ cup lemon juice

1 tablespoon red wine vinegar

1 bay leaf, crumbled

½ teaspoon paprika

 Dash of ground red pepper

1 lemon, very thinly sliced

1 medium red onion, very thinly sliced

1 (4-ounce) can whole ripe olives, drained, pitted

2 tablespoons chopped pimiento

2 tablespoons chopped parsley

**Serves: 6 - 8**

# SASSY SHRIMP

Place shrimp in a large container with tight-fitting lid.

Blend oil, garlic, dry mustard, salt, lemon juice, vinegar, bay leaf, paprika and red pepper in a medium glass bowl.

Stir in lemon slices, onion, olives, pimiento and parsley. Add shrimp; toss well to coat. Marinate in refrigerator at least 1 hour or up to 4 hours.

*A savory attraction for any gathering.*

# GRILLED BEEF TENDERLOIN PARTY SANDWICHES

1  (4 - 6 pound) beef tenderloin, trimmed

1  cup teriyaki marinade

1  tablespoon cracked pepper

Party rolls, optional

Horseradish sauce, optional

Purple kale, orange slices, cherry tomatoes, optional

**Serves:  20 - 25**

Place meat in a zip-closure plastic bag; add marinade and seal. Place bag in a shallow pan; refrigerate 8 hours, turning occasionally.

Drain meat, discarding marinade; sprinkle with pepper.

Grill beef on high heat with lid closed for three minutes.  Turn and cook 3 additional minutes.  Reduce heat to low and cook 12 minutes longer or until meat thermometer registers 140 degrees (rare).  Cool to room temperature.  Cover; chill several hours or overnight before slicing.

Serve sliced tenderloin with party rolls and horseradish sauce. Garnish with kale, orange slices and cherry tomatoes.

*A favorite crowd pleaser that disappears in no time at any gathering.*

¼ cup butter or margarine, melted

½ teaspoon basil leaves, crushed

¼ teaspoon oregano leaves, crushed

⅛ teaspoon pepper

1 (16-inch) loaf French bread, split lengthwise

8 ounces pastrami, salami or meat of choice

1 (6-ounce) can tomato paste

⅓ cup chili sauce

¼ cup chopped red bell pepper

¼ cup pitted ripe olives, chopped

2 tablespoons thinly sliced green onion

1 ½ cups shredded mozzarella cheese

1 medium tomato, chopped

¼ cup grated Parmesan cheese

1 cup alfalfa sprouts

**Serves: 16**

# PERFECT PASTRAMI PIZZA BITES

Preheat oven to 400 degrees.

Stir together butter, basil, oregano and pepper. Brush over cut sides of bread. Place bread cut side up on a large baking sheet, top with pastrami.

Stir together tomato paste, chili sauce, red pepper, olives and green onion in a small bowl. Spread over pastrami. Bake 15 minutes.

Top with mozzarella, tomato and Parmesan. Return to oven; bake 3 to 5 minutes longer or until cheese melts. Top with alfalfa sprouts.

Slice each loaf half into 8 pieces to serve.

*Not your ordinary pizza bites!*

# Blue Cheese Spread

1 (8-ounce) package cream cheese, softened

1/3 cup crumbled blue cheese

1/3 cup lowfat yogurt

1/4 cup chopped pecans, toasted

2 tablespoons minced chives

**Serves: 6 - 8**

In medium bowl, beat cream cheese until fluffy. Add blue cheese, yogurt, pecans and chives; mix well. Cover; chill 30 to 60 minutes.

Serve with any wonderful crisp crackers, melba toast or fresh pita crisps.

*Easily prepared and everyone loves it.*

# Fresh Basil Cream Cheese

1 (8-ounce) package cream cheese

1 small clove garlic, minced

1/2 teaspoon freshly ground pepper

1 tablespoon mayonnaise

1 cup loosely packed fresh basil leaves, chopped

Salt

**Serves: 6 - 8**

Combine cream cheese, garlic, pepper and mayonnaise in a food processor. Blend well. Add basil; blend well. Season with salt. Serve immediately at room temperature, or, if refrigerated, bring to room temperature before serving.

Can add sun-dried tomatoes for a festive change. Serve with crackers or crudités.

*Another wonderful dip to use with fresh vegetables.*

8 ounces Roquefort or other
   blue cheese

1 (8-ounce) package cream
   cheese, softened

½ cup butter

1 clove garlic, minced

3 tablespoons Cognac or
   other brandy

   *Fresh pear and apple
   wedges, dipped in lemon
   juice and well drained*

**Yield: 2 ½ cups**

# ROQUEFORT SPREAD

In food processor or blender, process Roquefort, cream cheese, butter, garlic and Cognac until smooth and well blended.

Serve dip with fresh pear and apple wedges or assorted crackers.

*An extra special treat for Roquefort lovers!*

1 large Granny Smith apple,
   shredded

1 (8-ounce) package cream
   cheese, softened

4 ounces Gruyere or
   Monterey Jack cheese,
   shredded

1 tablespoon milk

1 teaspoon prepared
   mustard

¼ cup finely chopped pecans

2 tablespoons chopped
   chives

**Yield: 2 cups**

# GRUYERE-APPLE SPREAD

In food processor or blender, combine cheeses, milk and mustard; blend until smooth.

Add pecans, apple and chives; chill.  Serve with assorted crackers.

*Delicious change of pace.*

# CREAM CHEESE WITH CRANBERRY-AMARETTO CHUTNEY

2 (8-ounce) packages cream cheese, softened

2 cups fresh or frozen cranberries

1 cup sugar

4 teaspoons lemon juice

¼ cup amaretto liqueur

½ teaspoon grated lemon rind

1 tablespoon grated orange rind

Juice of half orange

**Serves: 20**

Line a 2-cup mold with a damp cheesecloth, letting cloth hang over edge. Firmly press cream cheese into prepared mold. Fold cheesecloth over cheese to cover; cover with plastic wrap. Chill 4 to 6 hours.

Combine cranberries, sugar and lemon juice in a small saucepan. Cook over medium heat, stirring constantly, until mixture comes to a boil. Reduce heat and simmer 20 minutes.

Remove from heat; add amaretto, lemon rind, orange rind and juice. Cool. Unmold cheese onto serving plate. Remove cheesecloth. Spoon cranberry chutney over cheese.

*A tangy, tart taste!*

1 (2-pound) ripe Brie
   cheese, well chilled

½ cup sliced almonds,
   toasted

1 cup Cranberry Chutney

   Crackers

**Serves: 25**

# ALMOND BAKED BRIE WITH CRANBERRY CHUTNEY

Cut rind off the top of the cheese and discard. Cut cheese in half horizontally. Place bottom half on baking sheet, cut side up. Spread almonds on top. Replace top half. Bring to room temperature.

Preheat oven to 275 degrees.

Cover the cheese with one cup chutney. Bake until cheese is just soft but not runny, about 10 minutes.

Serve with crackers.

*A wonderful combination of flavors.*

# CRANBERRY CHUTNEY

Combine cranberries, raspberries, honey, apple, orange, celery, vinegar, water, ginger, mustard and cloves in a large, heavy saucepan. Bring to a boil, stirring frequently. Reduce heat; simmer 1 hour or until mixture thickens and liquid is syrupy, stirring occasionally.

Heat jars in boiling water; drain well. Ladle mixture into clean hot jars. Cover tightly and cool.

Store in refrigerator up to 3 weeks.

*This chutney is also great served over grilled chicken.*

2 cups fresh or frozen cranberries

1 cup whole frozen unsweetened raspberries, thawed

1 cup honey

1 tart apple, peeled, cored and coarsely chopped

1 large orange, peeled, seeded and sliced

½ cup chopped celery

½ cup raspberry vinegar

2 tablespoons water

1 ½ teaspoons grated fresh ginger root

¼ teaspoon dry mustard

⅛ teaspoon ground cloves

2 (10-ounce) glass jelly jars

**Yield:    2 ½ cups**

2 (8-ounce) packages cream cheese, softened

¼ cup (½ stick) butter, softened

1 tablespoon milk

2 cloves garlic, minced

1 teaspoon caraway seed

1 teaspoon paprika

2 teaspoons Dijon mustard

½ teaspoon anchovy paste

Bibb lettuce leaves

Sliced ripe olives

Sliced red onion

Crisp bacon pieces

Capers

Sliced dill pickles

Cocktail rye or pumpernickel bread

**Yield:** 2 ½ cups

# SPICED CHEESE SPREAD WITH PIZZAZZ

In large bowl, beat cream cheese, butter and milk until smooth. Stir in garlic, caraway seed, paprika, mustard and anchovy paste. Cover and chill at least 8 hours.

Mound cheese spread on large platter. Surround with Bibb lettuce leaf "cups" filled with olives, onion, bacon, capers and dill pickles. Serve with bread slices.

*This is a crowd pleaser.*

# CREAMY HERB-CHEESE SPREAD

Preheat oven to 375 degrees.

Spread mustard over the top of the cheese; sprinkle with parsley, chives, dill, fennel seeds and pepper.

Place cheese, mustard side down, in center of pastry. Fold package style, trimming excess pastry. Seal seams. Place seam side down on lightly greased baking sheet. Brush with egg; chill 30 minutes.

Bake 20 minutes; brush with egg again. Bake 10 minutes longer or until golden brown.

Let stand 5 minutes. Cut in wedges; serve with apple and pear slices or assorted plain crackers.

*An elegant appetizer for a small dinner party.*

1   (12-ounce) piece Havarti cheese

1   teaspoon Dijon mustard

1   teaspoon parsley flakes

½   teaspoon chives

¼   teaspoon dill weed

¼   teaspoon fennel seeds

⅛   teaspoon freshly ground pepper

½   (17 ¼-ounce) package frozen puff pastry, thawed (1 sheet)

1   egg, beaten

Apple and pear slices

**Serves:   6 - 8**

6 - 8 ounces pitted ripe olives, drained

10 ounces pimiento-stuffed green olives, drained

4 ounces capers, washed, dried on paper towels

1 teaspoon anchovy paste

2 tablespoons olive oil

3 tablespoons brandy

1 teaspoon Dijon mustard

1 teaspoon thyme

½ teaspoon ground pepper

**Yield: 4 cups**

# OLIVE TAPENADE

Combine all ingredients in a food processor and blend until finely chopped. Place in a container with a tight fitting lid. Cover the top with a thin layer of olive oil; refrigerate up to 2 weeks.

Serve as a spread on fresh bread, Italian flat bread or finger sandwiches.

---

1 small onion, chopped

½ cup (1 stick) butter

1 (10-ounce) package frozen chopped spinach, thawed and squeezed dry

½ pound crab meat

1 cup grated Parmesan or Romano cheese

**Yield: 8 servings**

# CRAB GRASS

Preheat oven to 350 degrees.

In large skillet, sauté onion in butter over medium heat; add spinach, crab and Parmesan cheese.

Spread mixture in a shallow baking dish. Bake until mixture is hot and bubbly, about 15 minutes.

For a subtle change, substitute Provolone or mozzarella cheese.

*Forget about leftovers!*

# WHITE BEAN AND FETA DIP

2 (14-ounce) cans cannellini beans, drained

1 - 2 cloves garlic, crushed

3 tablespoons olive oil

6 tablespoons freshly squeezed lemon juice

1 (14-ounce) can chick peas, drained

2 ounces feta cheese, crumbled

2 tablespoons finely chopped parsley

Freshly ground black pepper

Combine beans, garlic, oil and lemon juice in food processor; puree. Remove mixture to a bowl; set aside.

In food processor, process chick peas until crumbly; add along with remaining ingredients to bean mixture. Mix well.

Cover and refrigerate at least 1 hour. When ready to serve, place dip in center of platter and surround with fresh vegetables, crisp crackers or Toasted Pita Triangles.

Dip can be made well in advance; flavor improves with standing.

*Healthy and delicious, all in one.*

**Yield: 2 cups**

4 - 6  pita bread rounds

2  tablespoons unsalted
butter, softened

½  teaspoon basil leaves

½  teaspoon thyme leaves

Juice of 1 lemon

# TOASTED PITA TRIANGLES

Preheat oven to 400 degrees.

Split each pita in half; spread with butter.

Mix herbs and lemon juice in a small bowl; sprinkle on each pita half.  Cut each half into 8 triangles; arrange on a baking sheet, face up.

Toast in oven 5 to 7 minutes or until crisp.

Cool completely.  Store in an airtight container.

*Savory and crunchy.*

# CAPONATA

Heat oil, add eggplant and sauté for ten minutest.  Add onion, celery, and green pepper.  Cook until vegetables are tender-crisp.  Add more oil if needed.

Stir in remaining ingredients and simmer uncovered for ten minutes, stirring often.  Cool.  Place in container with tight-fitting lid.  Refrigerate up to a week.  Serve at room temperature with crackers.

Freezes well.

*A special treat which can be prepared ahead.*

1  large eggplant, peeled, and cubed

½  cup olive oil

1  cup chopped onion

1  cup chopped green pepper

1  cup chopped celery

1  cup tomato puree

½  cup halved black olives

⅓  cup red wine vinegar

2  tablespoons granulated sugar

1 ½  teaspoons salt

**Yield:  4 cups**

1 (8-ounce) package cream
cheese, softened

½ cup mayonnaise

4 - 6 tablespoons milk, divided

1 tablespoon lemon juice

¼ teaspoon ground
cinnamon

¼ cup chopped celery

¼ cup chopped raisins

2 tablespoons toasted
walnuts

Apple and pear wedges,
dipped in lemon juice and
well drained

**Yield: 2 cups**

# WALDORF DIP

Combine cheese, mayonnaise, 3 tablespoons milk, lemon juice
and cinnamon in a small bowl. Beat until smooth. Stir in celery and raisins.

Add more milk, one tablespoon at a time, until mixture is of
dipping consistency. Cover; chill about two hours.

Sprinkle dip with walnuts. Serve with fruit.

*A familiar taste with a different twist.*

# Party Salsa

In large bowl, combine ingredients; mix well. Refrigerate at least 1 hour before serving.

Can chop ingredients individually in food processor. Add more jalapeños for increased spice.

*A distinctive fresh, garden salsa.*

4 large, firm tomatoes, finely chopped

3 tomatillos or roma tomatoes, finely chopped

1 medium onion, finely chopped

3 green onions, chopped

½ green bell pepper, chopped

1 green jalapeño pepper, finely chopped

2 yellow chilies, finely chopped

3 tablespoons chopped fresh cilantro

1 teaspoon minced garlic

4 drops hot pepper sauce

2 tablespoons red wine vinegar

Salt

**Yield: 7 cups**

1 (6-ounce) can pitted ripe
olives, finely chopped

3 ripe firm tomatoes, finely
chopped, seeded and
drained

1 (4-ounce) can chopped
green chilies

3 - 4 cloves garlic, finely
chopped

Pinch of salt

2 tablespoons wine vinegar

2 tablespoons olive oil

**Yield: 2 cups**

# DRAGON'S BREATH DIP

In medium bowl, mix olives, tomatoes, green chilies, garlic and salt together. Add the vinegar and oil; mix well.

Serve with taco or tortilla chips.

*A zesty salsa for the palate!*

# IRRESISTIBLE GAZPACHO DIP

| | |
|---:|:---|
| 3 | tablespoons oil |
| 1 ½ | tablespoons cider vinegar |
| 1 | teaspoon salt |
| 1 | teaspoon garlic salt |
| ¼ | teaspoon pepper |
| 1 | (4-ounce) can chopped black olives, undrained |
| 1 | (4-ounce) can chopped green chilies, undrained |
| 2 - 3 | tomatoes, chopped |
| 4 - 5 | green onions, chopped |
| 3 - 4 | avocados, pitted, peeled and chopped |

Blend oil and vinegar in a medium bowl; add salt, garlic salt and pepper; mix well. Add olives, green chilies, tomatoes, green onions and avocados. Put avocado pits in dip to keep from browning. Cover and refrigerate several hours to chill.

Serve with tortilla chips.

*Quick and easy. Make ahead and chill.*

2 pounds Brie cheese, chilled

2 tablespoons all-purpose flour

1 tablespoon butter or margarine

3 tablespoons minced shallots

1 ½ cups (or more) fresh pink grapefruit juice

White pepper

¼ cup chopped fresh chives

1 teaspoon grated grapefruit rind

Pumpernickel, sourdough, or rye bread, cut into 1-inch cubes

**Yield:  4 cups**

# BRIE AND CHIVE FONDUE

Remove rind from cheese.  Break cheese into pieces; place in a large bowl.  Add flour and toss to coat.

Melt butter in heavy saucepan over medium heat.  Add shallots; sauté until golden brown, about 4 minutes.  Add 1 1/2 cups grapefruit juice.  Simmer until liquid is reduced to one cup, about 15 minutes.  Reduce heat to medium-low.

Add small amount of Brie to saucepan and stir constantly until cheese melts, about five minutes.  Repeat, adding small amounts of cheese at a time.  Season with pepper.  Stir in chives and grapefruit rind.

Pour cheese mixture into a fondue pot.  Set pot over candle or canned heat.  Serve with bread cubes.

Can be prepared one day ahead prior to adding chives and grapefruit rind.  Cover and refrigerate if made ahead; reheat over low heat, stirring frequently.

Cooked shrimp, blanched asparagus spears, Belgian endive leaves and boiled new potatoes also make good dippers.

*The preparation time is well worth the mouth-watering results.*

# PICADILLO ALMOND DIP

Crumble beef and pork in a large, deep skillet. Cook and stir over medium heat to brown.

Add salt, pepper and enough water to cover meat. Bring to a boil; reduce heat and simmer for 30 minutes.

Drain excess liquid from meat; add remaining ingredients except tortilla chips. Bring to a boil; simmer 45 minutes, or until mixture is very thick.

Serve hot with tortilla chips.

*A hearty, flavorful dip.*

½ pound ground beef

½ pound ground pork

1 teaspoon salt

¼ teaspoon pepper

Water

4 medium tomatoes, peeled, diced

2 - 3 cloves garlic, minced

3 green onions, minced

1 (6-ounce) can tomato paste

2 jalapeño peppers, rinsed, seeded, diced

Dash of oregano

¾ cup chopped pimiento

¾ cup raisins

¾ cup whole blanched almonds

Tortilla chips

**Yield: 6 cups**

6 lemons

1 lime

1 ½ cups sugar

2 ½ cups water

4 cups vodka

**Yield:  2 quarts**

# LEMON LIQUEUR

Scrub the lemons and lime; finely peel the rind with a vegetable peeler.

Put the lemon and lime rind in a clean jar; pour in 2 cups vodka.

Seal the jar and let it stand in a cool, dark place for three days.

Make a syrup by combining the sugar and water in a saucepan; bring to a boil.  Remove from heat; cool.  Add the lemon-vodka mixture; mix well.  Pour through a coffee filter to strain.

Mix the filtered liquid, the rind, and the remaining 2 cups vodka.  Seal; let stand 2 more days.  Strain through a coffee filter.  Pour into clean bottles and seal tightly.

Let stand for at least 1 week before tasting.

*This liqueur is wonderfully refreshing and will be well worth your patience.*

# BLUEBERRY LIQUEUR

1 cup blueberries
1 cup water, divided
4 cups brandy
1 ½ cups sugar

**Yield:  1 ½ - 2 quarts**

Rinse and gently crush the berries to release the juices.

Combine the berries with juice and 1/2 cup water in a saucepan Bring to a boil; simmer gently 10 minutes.  Cool completely. Pour into a large, clean glass jar; add brandy.  Seal tightly.  Store at least 1 week in a cool, dry, dark place.

Strain and reserve the liquid.  Press berries through sieve to extract as much additional juice as possible; combine reserved liquid and juice.  Combine sugar and remaining 1/2 cup water in a large saucepan.  Boil until syrup begins to thicken. Add reserved blueberry liquid.  Pour into bottles and seal.

Store in a cool, dark place.

1 (6-ounce) can frozen
orange juice concentrate

3 cups dry white wine

1 ½ cups cold water

⅓ cup Triple Sec or other
orange-flavored liqueur

**Serves: 4 - 6**

# MAGNOLIA BLOSSOMS

Combine all ingredients and chill for several hours. Serve over ice.

*A refreshing summer cocktail.*

½ gallon orange juice

1 quart ginger ale or orange
soda

2 cups Amaretto liqueur

½ gallon orange sherbet

**Serves: 15 - 20**

# AMARETTO PUNCH

Mix all ingredients in a container with a tight fitting lid. Cover and chill.

When ready to serve, pour chilled punch mixture in a large punch bowl. Ladle into punch cups to serve.

*A festive punch for any special occasion. Great for a couples shower, baby shower or a brunch. Men love this too!*

# Claret Cup

1 bottle Bordeaux or Claret wine

½ bottle white aperitif wine

3 ounces Curacoa

Mint leaves, optional

Strawberries, optional

**Serves: 6 - 8**

Mix wines and Curacoa in a large container with tight fitting lid. Cover and refrigerate to chill completely.

Pour in a punch bowl to serve. Garnish with mint leaves and freshly cut strawberries. Ladle into small cups to serve.

*A beautiful holiday punch.*

# Sparkling Cider Punch

2 quarts cranberry juice cocktail, chilled

1 quart apple cider or juice, chilled

1 (750-milliliter) bottle dry red wine, chilled, optional

1 (1-liter) bottle ginger ale, chilled

Small ice cubes, optional

Orange and apple slices, optional

**Serves: 10 - 20**

Combine cranberry juice, apple cider, and red wine in a large punch bowl. Slowly add ginger ale. Add small ice cubes and fruit slices if desired. Ladle into small cups to serve.

Makes about 20 six ounce servings without wine, 25 with wine.

*A refreshing and easy punch for a crowd.*

2 medium oranges

10 whole cloves

4 cups fresh orange juice

2 whole cinnamon sticks

8 cups prepared lapsang soochong tea

2 cups pineapple juice

1 whole nutmeg, broken into pieces

¼ cup honey

Ground cinnamon or nutmeg

**Serves: 10 - 12**

# ORANGED SPICED TEA

Pierce oranges all over with a large fork. Insert whole cloves into holes; place in a large saucepan. Add orange juice and cinnamon sticks. Bring mixture to a boil, simmer five minutes. Remove from heat. Cover and set aside to steep about 15 minutes.

Add tea, pineapple juice and nutmeg. Place over low heat and warm slowly. Remove and discard oranges. Add honey; stirring to blend well.

To serve, pour into large warmed mugs. Garnish with nutmeg or cinnamon.

*That back home again taste and a perfect take along drink for cold winter activities!*

# HOT BUTTERED RUM

1   pound (4 sticks) butter, softened

½   (16-ounce) package light brown sugar

½   (16-ounce) package confectioners' sugar

2   teaspoons ground cinnamon

2   teaspoons ground nutmeg

1   quart vanilla ice cream, softened

    Rum

    Whipped cream, optional

    Cinnamon sticks

**Yield:  25 cups**

Combine butter, sugars, cinnamon and nutmeg. Beat until light and fluffy.   Add ice cream, stir until well blended.

Spoon mixture into 2-quart freezer container; cover tightly and freeze.

When ready to serve remove from freezer to thaw slightly.

Place 3 tablespoons butter mixture and 1 jigger of rum into a large mug.  Fill with boiling water; stir well.  Top with whipped cream, if desired.  Serve with cinnamon stick stirrers.  Unused butter mixture can be refrozen.

*A wonderful warm-up after a brisk winter walk.*

¾ cup sugar

1 ½ cups milk

1 teaspoon vanilla extract

1 ½ cups cold brewed coffee

¾ cup whipping cream

Unsweetened whipped
cream


**Serves: 4 - 6**

# CAFÉ GLACÉ

Combine sugar and milk in a saucepan; bring to a boil. Cook
and stir until sugar is dissolved. Remove from heat. Add
vanilla; let stand to cool.

Combine milk mixture, coffee and cream; mix well. Pour into
a metal pan and freeze until hard.

Put frozen mixture in blender or food processor; process until
mixture is mushy. Thaw slightly to make this process simpler.

Pour into tall glasses to serve. Top with whipped cream and
serve immediately.

*Perfect for a luncheon gathering.*


1 (4-ounce) bar sweet
cooking chocolate

1 (14-ounce) can sweetened
condensed milk

1 cup whipping cream

Hot brewed coffee


**Serves: 10 - 12**

# COCA MOCHA

Melt chocolate with sweetened condensed milk in top of double boiler over low heat. Stir occasionally. Cool.

Whip cream until soft peaks form. Fold into cooled chocolate
mixture. Cover tightly and refrigerate up to one week.

For each serving, place 1/4 cup chocolate mixture in a large cup
or mug. Fill with hot brewed coffee. Stir and serve immediately.

*The perfect finale!*

# GINGER PEACH SOUP

1 ½ pounds fresh peaches

2 ½ tablespoons fresh lemon juice, divided

1 ½ cups buttermilk

⅔ cup apple juice

½ teaspoon peeled, grated ginger root

1 teaspoon honey

Fresh peach slices or unsprayed rose petals, optional

**Serves: 4**

Peel peaches and cut in half; remove and discard pit. Brush peaches with 2 tablespoons of lemon juice to prevent discoloration while working.

Place peaches in a food processor; process until pureed and smooth. Scrape peach puree into a medium bowl. Stir in buttermilk, apple juice, ginger root and honey. Cover and refrigerate until cold.

Spoon mixture in chilled shallow soup bowls; garnish with fresh peach slices or rose petals, if desired.

May substitute 1-pound frozen, unsweetened peaches for fresh peaches.

If using frozen peaches, thaw only until slushy, then puree using all the juice from the peaches and adding the lemon juice to the puree.

*Creamy and refreshing!*

2 large tomatoes, peeled, chopped

1 (46-ounce) can tomato juice

1 small onion, chopped

3 large garlic cloves, peeled, minced

½ cup chopped fresh parsley

2 teaspoons coriander

1 ½ teaspoons Worcestershire sauce

⅛ teaspoon ground red pepper

Salt

Freshly ground pepper

1 large green bell pepper, chopped

1 cucumber, unpeeled, chopped

6 scallions, chopped

**Serves: 10**

# GAZPACHO

In a large bowl, combine tomatoes, juice, onion, garlic, parsley, coriander, Worcestershire sauce and red pepper. Add salt and pepper to season. Cover and refrigerate at least 8 hours or overnight to allow flavors to develop.

When ready to serve, ladle soup into chilled soup bowls; garnish with green bell pepper, cucumber and scallions.

*A favorite for all times.*

# CHILLED GORGONZOLA SOUP

Heat oil in a large saucepan; add celery and onion. Sauté until transparent. Add chicken broth; bring mixture to a boil. Simmer 15 minutes.

Puree mixture in food processor or blender. Return to saucepan. Bring to a boil. In a small bowl, combine cornstarch and water; add to chicken broth. Cook, stirring constantly, until mixture thickens.

Stir in Monterey Jack cheese and about half of Gorgonzola. Heat, stirring, until cheese is completely melted and soup is smooth. Set pan in ice water to cool.

When cool, stir in half-and-half and chill. To serve, ladle into individual serving bowls. Garnish with chopped pears and remaining crumbled Gorgonzola.

*Sophisticated beginning to an elegant dinner.*

1   tablespoon vegetable oil

2   small stalks celery, minced

1   onion, peeled, diced

3   cups chicken broth

1   tablespoon cornstarch

2   tablespoons cold water

2   ounces Monterey Jack cheese, grated

5   ounces Gorgonzola, crumbled and divided

1   cup half-and-half

2   pears, peeled, cored, chopped

**Serves: 4**

¼ cup butter or margarine

¼ cup chopped onion

¼ cup all-purpose flour

2 cups chicken broth

1 teaspoon ground nutmeg

Salt

2 tablespoons chicken bouillon granules

2 cups half-and-half

2 cups fresh or cooked chopped asparagus

Fresh Herb Croutons

Lemon slices, optional


Fresh Herb Croutons

1 stick butter, softened

1 loaf white densely textured, sandwich bread

½ teaspoon salt

Dash of ground red pepper

½ teaspoon paprika

½ teaspoon savory

½ teaspoon thyme


**Serves:  4 - 6**

# CREAM OF ASPARAGUS SOUP WITH FRESH HERB CROUTONS

Melt butter in a large heavy saucepan.  Add onions; sauté until transparent.  Stir in flour; cook for 1 minute.  Blend in broth, nutmeg, salt, chicken bouillon and half-and-half.  Bring to a boil.

Add asparagus; reduce heat and simmer gently 25 minutes.  Remove from heat.  Pour mixture into food processor bowl.  Puree until smooth.  Return to saucepan; bring to a boil to heat.  Ladle into serving bowls.  Garnish with Fresh Herb Croutons and lemon slices.


## Fresh Herb Croutons

Beat butter until fluffy.  Add salt, pepper, paprika, savory and thyme.  Spread over bread slices.  Cut bread into small shapes such as triangles, circles, diamonds or use small decorative cookie cutters to make distinctive shapes.  Place on cookie sheet.  Bake in 225 degree oven for about 1 to 1 1/2 hours or until crisp and toasted.  Cool completely and store tightly covered.

*Add unusual shaped croutons for an interesting presentation.*

# APPLE CARROT SOUP

Combine apples, carrots, dill weed and chicken broth in a large pot. Cover and bring to boil. Reduce heat to low; simmer about 1 hour until carrots are very tender.

Process in small batches in food processor or blender until mixture is smooth.

Stir in cream, salt and pepper. Ladle into soup bowls and garnish with apple slices, if desired. Serve hot or cold.

*A great beginning for a fall meal.*

1   pound Granny Smith apples, peeled, cored, chopped (about 2 cups)

1   pound carrots, peeled, chopped (3 ½ cups)

1   tablespoon chopped fresh dill weed or 1 teaspoon dried

8   cups chicken broth

½   cup whipping cream

    Salt and pepper

    Apple slices, optional

**Serves: 6 - 8**

4 cups chicken stock

1 medium butternut squash, peeled, seeded, chopped

2 large tart apples peeled, cored, chopped

1 small onion, chopped

¼ teaspoon dried rosemary

6 tablespoons butter

6 tablespoons all-purpose flour

¾ cup whipping cream

Salt

Pepper

Chopped fresh apples, optional

**Serves: 6 - 8**

# Squash Apple Bisque

Combine stock, squash, apples, onion and rosemary in saucepan. Cover and simmer over low heat until squash is tender, about 10 to 15 minutes. Cool slightly; puree in processor. Return to pan.

Melt butter in 1-quart saucepan. Stir in flour; cook stirring constantly about 2 to 3 minutes over medium heat. Add squash puree. Simmer, uncovered, 15 minutes over low heat. Add cream, salt and pepper. Stir well and heat gently.

Pour into soup tureen or individual bowls to serve. Garnish with chopped fresh apple pieces, if desired. Serve hot.

# Tangy Tomato Mushroom Soup

1 tablespoon butter

1 tablespoon olive oil

1 medium onion, diced

1 clove garlic, chopped

1 ½ pounds fresh mushrooms, wiped clean, sliced

1 (6-ounce) can tomato paste

4 cups chicken broth

⅓ cup dry vermouth

½ teaspoon salt

½ teaspoon pepper

Grated Parmesan cheese, optional

Homemade croutons such as Fresh Herb Croutons, optional

In a large heavy saucepan, melt butter. Stir in oil, onion and garlic. Sauté until onion is cooked and tender. Remove garlic. Continue to sauté until onion is lightly browned.

Add mushrooms to onion mixture; sauté 5 minutes. Add tomato paste, mix well. Blend in chicken broth, vermouth, salt and pepper. Simmer 10 minutes.

Ladle into serving bowls; garnish with Parmesan cheese and croutons, if desired.

**Serves: 6 - 8**

3 medium fennel bulbs
  (about 2 pounds)

1 large yellow onion

½ cup (1 stick) unsalted
  butter

  Salt

  Pepper

2 (28-ounce) cans Italian
  plum tomatoes, undrained

⅓ cup anise-flavored liqueur
  such as Pernod

2 cups chicken broth

  Grated Provolone cheese,
  optional

**Serves: 8**

# FALL TOMATO FENNEL SOUP

Remove and discard the leafy tops from the fennel bulbs. Coarsely chop the fennel bulbs and onion.

Melt the butter in a large saucepan over low heat. Add chopped fennel and onion. Cover and cook over low heat about 15 minutes or until vegetables are soft. Season with salt and pepper.

Add tomatoes with their liquid to the fennel and onion mixture. Simmer for 30 minutes. Puree mixture coarsely in food processor or blender in small batches.

Return pureed mixture to pan. Add liqueur and chicken broth. Simmer uncovered for an additional 30 minutes. Serve with grated Provolone as a garnish, if desired

*After pureeing the tomato fennel mixture, strain through a sieve to make a more delicate and finer accompaniment for a formal meal.*

# NORTH WOODS WILD RICE SOUP

⅓ cup butter

¼ cup onion, minced

⅔ cup all-purpose flour

10 cups chicken broth

5 cups cooked wild rice

2 cups whipping cream

⅔ cup dry sherry

Salt

Pepper

Chopped fresh parsley, optional

**Serves: 8**

Melt butter in saucepan. Add onion; sauté until light golden brown. Blend flour into butter; cook and stir until smooth and bubbly. Add broth, stirring constantly until mixture thickens.

Add wild rice; simmer for 10 minutes. Add cream and sherry; continue stirring and cook until thoroughly heated. Season to taste with salt and pepper. Garnish with fresh minced parsley to serve.

*A great way to use wild rice or you may use equal amounts of cooked wild and white rice.*

½ cup (1 stick) unsalted butter

1 cup chopped onion

½ cup all-purpose flour

5 ½ cups chicken stock

5 cups peeled and diced butternut squash

1 cup dry white wine

3 bay leaves

1 cup whipping cream

1 pound small uncooked shrimp, peeled, deveined

**Serves: 8**

# SHRIMP BUTTERNUT BISQUE

Melt butter in large heavy saucepan over medium low heat. Add onion; cook until transparent. Add flour; cook and stir 3 minutes or until cooked. Add stock and bring to a boil, stirring constantly.

Add squash, wine and bay leaves. Simmer about 25 to 30 minutes or until squash is tender.

Remove and discard bay leaves. Puree mixture in small batches in blender or food processor. Return to saucepan. Add whipping cream and shrimp. Cook over medium heat stirring often until shrimp turns pink. Serve immediately.

*An unusual combination of ingredients with delicious results.*

# Scallop Tomato Chowder

In medium saucepan over medium-high heat, cook bacon until almost crisp. Add onion, green bell pepper, carrot and parsley. Cover and cook over low heat about 10 minutes, stirring occasionally.

Add tomatoes with juice, clam juice, salt, bay leaf, hot pepper sauce, thyme and chicken broth. Bring to a boil. Simmer covered 30 minutes.

Add potatoes; cover and simmer 30 minutes longer or until potatoes are tender. Remove and discard bay leaf. (At this point soup may be refrigerated up to three days or frozen.)

When ready to serve, reheat if cold. Season with salt and pepper. Stir in scallops and cook for 2 to 3 minutes. Do not overcook or scallops will become tough. Serve immediately.

*Sea scallops may be used, but first cut each one into quarters.*

6 slices bacon

1 large onion, chopped

1 small green bell pepper, chopped

1 carrot, peeled and thinly sliced

1 tablespoon chopped fresh parsley,

1 (28-ounce) can of tomatoes, undrained, chopped

1 (7 ½-ounce) bottle clam juice

½ teaspoon salt

1 bay leaf

2 drops hot pepper sauce

1 tablespoon chopped fresh thyme, or 1 teaspoon dried, crumbled

1 ½ cups chicken broth

2 medium potatoes, peeled, diced (2 ½ cups)

Salt

Pepper

1 pound bay scallops, rinsed, drained and patted dry

**Serves:  4 - 6**

1 pound salmon fillets

White wine

6 cups chicken broth

1 pound potatoes, peeled and cut into ½-inch cubes

¼ pound carrots, peeled and cut into ½-inch cubes

1 pound Brussels sprouts, cleaned and cut in half

4 tablespoons butter

5 tablespoons all-purpose flour

2 cups milk

¼ cup whipping cream

2 ounces shredded Monterey Jack cheese

¼ cup dry white wine

Salt

Pepper

½ tablespoon fresh chopped thyme or ½ teaspoon dried

Fresh thyme, optional

**Serves: 6**

# FRESH SALMON CHOWDER

Place salmon in a medium skillet. Add white wine to cover salmon. Loosely cover skillet and cook gently about 5 to 7 minutes. Set aside to cool in liquid.

Heat the chicken broth over medium heat; add potatoes, carrots and Brussels sprouts. Cook over low heat until vegetables are tender, about 10 minutes. Remove vegetables and set aside to drain; reserve chicken stock.

Melt butter in a medium saucepan. Stir in flour; cook over medium heat about 2 minutes or until bubbly. Add milk and cook stirring constantly until mixture is smooth and thick. Add cream, cheese and wine to sauce. Stir until blended.

Remove salmon from poaching liquid; remove and discard skin. Cut salmon into bite-size pieces. Add to sauce along with reserved vegetables. Slowly add reserved stock until soup is of desired consistency.

Add salt and pepper to taste. Simmer briefly to heat thoroughly. Serve in pretty soup bowls, garnished with fresh thyme.

*Beautiful presentation.*

# Corn and Cheddar Chowder

Melt butter in a large heavy saucepan over medium heat. Add onion, celery and carrot. Sauté until vegetables begin to soften, about 5 minutes.

Stir in mustard, chicken broth, diced potatoes, thyme and bay leaf. Bring mixture to a boil. Reduce heat to low. Cover saucepan and simmer until potatoes are tender, about 10 minutes.

Add corn, half-and-half and milk. Cover and simmer gently about 5 minutes.

Just before serving, reduce heat to very low. Add grated cheese. Heat, stirring until cheese melts.

*You may make this soup up to a day ahead by preparing up to the point where the cheese is added. When ready to serve bring refrigerated soup to a simmer. Reduce heat; add cheese and stir to melt.*

3 tablespoons butter or margarine

1 large onion, chopped

1 celery stalk, chopped

1 carrot, peeled, chopped

2 teaspoons dry mustard

1 ½ cups low salt, canned chicken broth

¾ pound potatoes, peeled, diced

1 teaspoon dried thyme, crumbled

1 bay leaf

3 cups frozen whole-kernel corn, thawed

1 ½ cups half-and-half

1 ½ cups milk

2 cups (8-ounces) grated Cheddar cheese

**Serves: 4 - 6**

3 tablespoons butter

1 cup sliced green onions

1 cup sliced fresh
mushrooms

3 tablespoons all-purpose
flour

3 cups chicken broth

1 cup chopped broccoli

1 cup half-and-half

1 cup shredded Swiss
cheese

Fresh croutons, optional

**Serves: 8**

# BROCCOLI AND CHEESE BISQUE

Melt butter in large heavy saucepan. Sauté onions and mushrooms until tender, but do not brown. Add flour and cook stirring constantly until bubbling and hot.

Remove pan from heat; gradually blend in chicken broth. Return to heat; cook stirring constantly until thickened and smooth. Add broccoli; reduce heat and simmer 10 minutes or until broccoli is tender.

Blend in half-and-half and cheese. Simmer briefly until mixture is heated and cheese melts. Serve immediately. Garnish with fresh croutons, if desired.

*A family favorite.*

# Italian Tortellini Soup

Fry bacon until slightly crisp; drain bacon and reserve drippings.

Using 2 tablespoons drippings, sauté onion until soft and translucent. Add minced garlic and mushrooms; sauté 2 to 3 minutes. Remove from heat.

In a large stock pot, bring chicken stock to a boil. Add tortellini and cook 5 to 7 minutes until tender but firm. Add tomatoes and herbs. Reduce heat to low. Add spinach; cover and simmer 5 minutes or until spinach is wilted.

Add onion and garlic mixture to stock pot; simmer 5 minutes. Serve with grated Parmesan cheese and reserved crumbled bacon.

*A quick and easy meal for families on the go.*

3   slices bacon

1   medium onion, chopped

3   garlic cloves, minced

1   pound mushrooms, thinly sliced

2   quarts chicken stock

10  ounces cheese tortellini

2   (15-ounce) cans tomato bits

2   teaspoons Italian herb blend or 1 teaspoon each thyme and oregano

1   (10-ounce) package fresh spinach, washed, stems removed, chopped

Parmesan cheese, freshly grated, optional

**Serves:   10**

2 tablespoons vegetable oil

1 cup carrots, peeled and
  chopped

1 cup onions, chopped

2 cloves garlic, finely
  chopped

½ cup chopped celery

¼ cup chopped celery leaves

½ teaspoon oregano

½ teaspoon basil leaves

2 teaspoons chili powder

½ cup uncooked lentils

1 pound new potatoes,
  unpeeled, cut into ½-inch
  cubes

2 cups tomato vegetable
  juice

1 ½ cups water

  Grated Cheddar cheese,
  for garnish

**Serves: 4**

# SOUTHWEST POTATO LENTIL SOUP

In large saucepan heat oil. Stir in carrots, onions, garlic, celery and celery leaves. Sauté over medium heat until onion is transparent. Add the oregano, basil and chili powder. Cook about 10 minutes or until the seasoning is well distributed.

Add lentils, potatoes, tomato vegetable juice and water. Bring to a boil over medium heat. Reduce heat to low; cover and simmer 40- 45 minutes until potatoes and lentils are tender. Stir several times while cooking and add small amounts of water to reach desired consistency.

Serve garnished with grated Cheddar cheese, if desired.

*A delicious recipe reflective of the popular Southwestern style.*

# Chicken, Rice and Vegetable Soup

Cut leeks in half lengthwise and rinse well in cold running water, separating layers to remove all sand and grit. Drain well and thinly slice.

Melt butter in large pot over medium-high heat. Add leeks, carrot, mushrooms and celery. Sauté until tender. Add rice and stir to coat with butter.

Add 1 1/2 cups chicken broth. Bring to a boil. Cover; reduce heat and simmer 20 minutes or until rice is tender.

While rice is cooking, heat remaining 4 1/2 cups of chicken broth and 1/2 cup dry vermouth in large saucepan until boiling. Add chicken pieces; simmer uncovered for 15 minutes. Remove chicken; set aside to cool.

Strain broth from cooking chicken through cheesecloth lined strainer into rice and vegetable mixture. Add chopped green beans and simmer until tender about 10 minutes. Shred chicken breasts into bite size pieces and stir into the soup. Ladle into warm soup bowls and garnish with celery leaves, if desired.

*The ultimate in comfort food!*

2 medium leeks, white part only

6 tablespoons unsalted butter

1 medium carrot, peeled and grated

4 medium size mushrooms, wiped clean and thinly sliced

2 small ribs of celery, thinly sliced

¾ cup of uncooked long grain rice

6 cups fresh chicken stock or canned chicken broth, divided

½ cup dry vermouth or white wine

3 skinless, boneless chicken breasts halves

1 cup green beans, trimmed, cut into ½ inch pieces

Celery leaves

**Serves: 4 - 6**

1  (1-pound) eggplant, peeled

5  tablespoons olive oil, divided

2  medium onions, chopped

3  cloves garlic, minced

2  medium zucchini, diced

2  large red bell peppers, cored, seeded, diced

1 - 2  jalapeño peppers, seeded, minced

1  (28-ounce) can plum tomatoes

5  large fresh plum tomatoes, diced

1/2  cup dry red wine

2  tablespoons chili powder

1  tablespoon ground cumin

2  teaspoons oregano

1  teaspoon fennel seeds, crushed

1  cup cooked white beans

1  cup cooked kidney beans

1  large lemon, grated rind and juice

1/3  cup chopped fresh cilantro

Freshly ground black pepper

**Serves: 8 - 10**

#  Spicy Vegetable Chili

Preheat oven to 350 degrees. Cut the eggplant into 1-inch chunks; place in a small, shallow roasting pan. Toss with 2 tablespoons olive oil; cover with foil and bake for 30 to 35 minutes, stirring once. Remove from oven and set aside.

Heat remaining 3 tablespoons oil in a Dutch oven. Add onions and garlic; cook 5 to 8 minutes. Add zucchini, red peppers and jalapeños; cook 5 to 6 minutes stirring once.

Coarsely chop the canned tomatoes; add to Dutch oven with their liquid. Add fresh tomatoes, wine, chili powder, cumin, oregano and fennel seeds. Gently stir in reserved eggplant; simmer 20 minutes over low heat.

Add white and kidney beans, lemon rind and juice, cilantro and pepper; stir to mix well. Simmer 5 to 10 minutes until heated. Serve with a choice of garnishes such as grated Cheddar or Monterey Jack cheese, chopped green onions, sour cream or fresh cilantro.

*This is a fabulous soup which takes advantage of summer's garden bounty.*

Optional Garnishes:
Shredded Cheddar cheese
Monterey Jack cheese
Chopped green onions
Sourcream
Chopped fresh cilantro

# WHITE BEAN AND CHICKEN CHILI

Soak beans following package directions.

Place chicken in large saucepan; add water to cover. Simmer about 30 to 35 minutes or until cooked. Drain chicken reserving stock. Measure and add water to make 6 cups. Set aside. Remove and discard chicken skin and bones. Cut into cubes; set aside.

Heat oil in same saucepan over medium-high heat. Sauté onion until transparent. Stir in garlic, chilies, cumin, oregano, cloves and red pepper. Sauté 2 minutes.

Drain soaked beans; add to vegetable mixture along with stock. Bring to boil; reduce heat. Cover and simmer about 2 hours or until beans are very tender, stirring occasionally.

Add cubed chicken and 1 cup cheese to chili; stir until cheese melts. Season with salt and pepper. Ladle into warm bowls; serve topped with remaining cheese, sour cream, salsa and cilantro, if desired.

*Hearty and delicious!*

1   pound dried Great Northern white beans

2   pounds chicken pieces

1   tablespoon olive oil

2   medium onions, chopped

4   cloves garlic, minced

2   (4-ounce) cans chopped mild green chilies

2   teaspoons ground cumin

1 ½  teaspoons oregano

¼   teaspoon ground cloves

¼   teaspoon red pepper

6   cups chicken broth

3   cups shredded Monterey Jack cheese, divided

    Salt

    Pepper

    Fresh chopped cilantro, optional

    Sour cream, optional

    Salsa, optional

**Serves: 8**

3 pounds chicken pieces

4 quarts water

1 teaspoon celery seeds

1 teaspoon whole black peppercorns

2 garlic cloves, peeled

1 (16-ounce) can whole peeled tomatoes, undrained

1 onion, cut into 1-inch pieces

1 green bell pepper, cut into 1-inch squares

3 sprigs fresh cilantro

½ teaspoon ground cumin

¼ teaspoon ground red pepper

¼ teaspoon ground black pepper

1 garlic clove, minced

1 (10-ounce) package frozen corn

4 green onions, coarsely chopped

Salt

1 cup cooked rice

2 teaspoons minced fresh parsley

Tortilla chips, optional

Grated Cheddar cheese, optional

**Serves: 6 - 8**

# CHICKEN AND TORTILLA SOUP

Combine chicken and water in large stock pot. Add celery seeds, peppercorns and garlic tied in small cheesecloth square. Cover and bring to a boil. Reduce heat and simmer until chicken is tender, about 45 minutes. Remove chicken from broth; set aside to cool.

Strain broth through cheese cloth lined strainer; return to stock pot. Add canned tomatoes, onion, pepper, cilantro, cumin, peppers and garlic. Cover and simmer 30 minutes. Add corn and green onion. Simmer 10 minutes more. Season with salt to taste.

Remove and discard chicken bone and skins. Cut chicken meat into 1-inch pieces. Add to broth with rice and parsley. Ladle into warm bowls and garnish with tortilla chips and cheddar cheese, if desired.

*A change of flavors from the typical chicken soup.*

# Hearty Vegetable Chowder

Combine all ingredients except sour cream and tortillas in 4 or 5-quart Dutch oven. Bring to a boil. Reduce heat and simmer covered 30 minutes or until lentils are tender.

Garnish each serving with sour cream or yogurt and serve with tortilla chips, if desired.

*Great to have on hand for easy suppers on cold winter evenings.*

1 (32-ounce) can tomato juice

2 (14-½-ounce) cans stewed tomatoes

2 cups water

2 medium potatoes, peeled, chopped

1 (15-ounce) can garbanzo beans, drained

1 (15-ounce) can kidney beans, drained

1 cup lentils, rinsed, drained

1 large onion, chopped

1 cup green bell pepper, diced

1 cup red bell pepper, diced

1 (10-ounce) package frozen chopped spinach, thawed

2 carrots, peeled, julienned

2 tablespoons dried parsley

2 tablespoons dried basil

2 cloves garlic, crushed

2 tablespoons ground cumin

Sour cream or yogurt, for garnish

Tortilla chips, for garnish

**Serves: 6 - 8**

2 tablespoons butter or margarine

1 ½ cups chopped onion

1 cup minced carrots

2 cups minced celery

2 quarts beef stock

1 bay leaf

1 teaspoon dill weed

1 pound polish sausage, or Kielbasa, cut diagonally into ¼ inch slices

2 (1-pound) solid heads cabbage, coarsely chopped

2 tablespoons chopped parsley

1 (16-ounce) can plum tomatoes, chopped

2 cups diced potatoes

Salt

Freshly ground pepper

Sour cream, for garnish

**Serves: 6 - 8**

# COUNTRY CABBAGE SOUP

In a large heavy skillet melt butter; sauté onion, carrot and celery. Cover and cook 8 to 10 minutes over medium-low heat until vegetables are translucent. Transfer mixture into stock pot or kettle with beef stock, bay leaf and dill weed; simmer gently.

In the same skillet, sauté sausage pieces until slightly browned and the fat has been released. Remove sausage from skillet and discard the drippings.

Add sausage, cabbage, parsley, tomatoes and potatoes to the soup. Continue to simmer for 30 minutes.

Add salt and freshly ground pepper. Ladle soup into bowls and garnish each with sour cream.

*Add warm buttered French bread and this becomes a meal by itself.*

# CHICKEN-FIFTEEN BEAN SOUP

Sort and wash beans; place in a pan. Add 2 tablespoons salt and cover with water. Soak 8 hours or overnight.

Drain beans; discard water from soaking. Add 2 quarts water. Bring to a boil; reduce to simmer. Add smoked sausage, chicken pieces, onion, carrots, celery, bay leaf and sage. Simmer for 2 hours.

Remove chicken from soup; remove and discard skin and bones. Return chicken meat to beans. Add flavor packet. Simmer for 30 minutes.

*Turkey parts or sausage can be substituted for chicken in this soup; it freezes well. Add cornbread and a green salad for a great supper.*

1 (1-pound) package chicken-15 bean soup mix

2 tablespoons salt

2 quarts water

1 pound smoked sausage, sliced

4 - 8 chicken pieces

1 onion, diced

2 carrots

2 cups chopped celery

1 bay leaf

1 tablespoon sage

1 flavor packet from soup mix

**Serves: 10 - 12**

# RISE AND SHINE

*Muffins*

*Breads*

*Breakfast and Brunch*

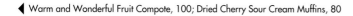 Warm and Wonderful Fruit Compote, 100; Dried Cherry Sour Cream Muffins, 80

# RISE AND SHINE

# Sour Cream Applesauce Bran Muffins

Preheat oven to 400 degrees. Grease one 12-cup muffin pan or use paper baking cups. Set aside.

Sift flour, baking powder, baking soda, salt and cinnamon in a large mixing bowl. In a medium bowl, combine bran, sugar, egg, butter, sour cream, applesauce and raisins. Let stand 2 minutes until bran softens.

Stir into dry ingredients just until flour is moistened. Spoon into prepared muffin pans, filling 2/3 full.

Combine sugar, cinnamon and nuts in a small bowl. Sprinkle over muffin batter before baking.

Bake 20 to 25 minutes.

1 ¼ cups all-purpose flour

1 teaspoon baking powder

½ teaspoon baking soda

½ teaspoon salt

1 teaspoon cinnamon

1 cup bran

½ cup sugar

1 egg

¼ cup butter, melted

½ cup sour cream or yogurt

1 cup applesauce

½ cup raisins

Nut Crunch Topping:

⅓ cup brown sugar

½ teaspoon cinnamon

⅓ cup nuts, chopped

**Yield: 12 muffins**

1 cup all-purpose flour

1 teaspoon baking soda

¼ teaspoon salt

⅓ cup sugar

1 egg

½ cup sour cream

2 tablespoons butter, melted

¼ cup milk

¾ cup dried sour cherries

1 teaspoon grated orange peel

**Yield: 15 - 20 muffins**

# DRIED CHERRY SOUR CREAM MUFFINS

Preheat oven to 400 degrees. Grease muffin pans or use paper baking cups. Set aside.

Combine flour, baking soda, salt and sugar in a large bowl. In a separate bowl, beat egg; add sour cream, melted butter and milk.

Add egg mixture to flour mixture. Stir in cherries and orange peel.

Stir just until dry ingredients are moistened; batter may be lumpy. Spoon batter into prepared muffin pans, filling 2/3 full.

Bake 20 to 25 minutes or until muffins are golden brown and wooden pick inserted in center comes out clean.

# Morning Glory Muffins

Preheat oven to 350 degrees. Grease muffin pans or use paper baking cups. Set aside.

Combine flour, sugar, baking soda, cinnamon and salt in a large mixing bowl. Mix well. Add carrots, apples, raisins, walnuts and coconut. Add to dry ingredients; stir well.

Beat eggs; add oil. Add to dry ingredients; stir to mix just until dry ingredients are moistened. Spoon batter into prepared muffin pans, filling 2/3 full.

Bake 20 to 25 minutes or until top is golden and a wooden pick inserted in the center comes out clean. Remove to a wire rack to cool.

2  cups all-purpose flour

1  cup sugar

2  teaspoons baking soda

2  teaspoons cinnamon

½  teaspoon salt

2  cups peeled, shredded carrots

1  large tart green apple, cored, peeled, chopped

½  cup raisins

½  cup walnuts, chopped

½  cup shredded coconut

3  eggs

⅔  cup oil

**Yield: 18 muffins**

1 cup old-fashioned oats

1 cup whole wheat flour

½ cup all-purpose flour

2 teaspoons baking powder

½ teaspoon salt

2 large eggs

¾ cup brown sugar, packed

¾ cup milk

¼ cup butter, melted

1 teaspoon vanilla

¼ cup raisins

¼ cup walnuts, chopped

**Yield: 12 muffins**

# BROWN SUGAR OATMEAL MUFFINS

Preheat oven to 400 degrees. Grease one 12-cup muffin pan or use paper baking cups. Set aside.

In a large bowl, combine oats, flours, baking powder and salt. Blend well.

Whisk eggs and brown sugar in a medium bowl; beat until smooth. Whisk in milk, melted butter and vanilla. Pour over dry ingredients. Add raisins and walnuts. Fold in with a spatula, just until dry ingredients are moistened. Spoon the batter into prepared muffin cups filling 2/3 full.

Bake 20 to 25 minutes or until springy to the touch and wooden pick inserted in center comes out clean. Remove to a wire rack to cool slightly before serving.

# WONDERFUL DATE SCONES

Preheat oven to 425 degrees. Lightly grease a 16 x 11-inch baking sheet. Set aside.

Combine flour, oats, baking powder, allspice, baking soda and salt in a mixing bowl. Cut in butter using pastry blender or two knives.

Puree banana, buttermilk and 1/4 cup of the dates in a processor. Add to dry ingredients with remaining 3/4 cup dates; mix just to moisten. Gather into ball; knead 12 times on floured board. Pat into 6-inch circle. Brush with milk; sprinkle with sugar.

Cut into 8 wedges with sharp knife. Place 1-inch apart on lightly greased baking sheet. Bake 12 minutes or until golden. Serve warm with butter or cream cheese.

1 ¼ cups all-purpose flour

½ cup quick-cooking oats, uncooked

1 ¼ teaspoons baking powder

½ teaspoon allspice

¼ teaspoon baking soda

¼ teaspoon salt

6 tablespoons cold butter or margarine, cut into pieces

⅓ cup ripe, mashed banana

⅓ cup buttermilk

1 cup chopped dates, divided

1 tablespoon milk

1 tablespoon sugar

Butter or cream cheese, optional

**Yield: 8 scones**

1 ½ cup all-purpose flour

1 teaspoon baking powder

¼ teaspoon salt

6 tablespoons unsalted
butter, room temperature

1 ⅓ cups sugar, divided

2 large eggs

2 teaspoons grated lemon
rind

½ cup milk

1 ½ cups blueberries, fresh or
frozen, thawed, drained

3 tablespoons fresh lemon
juice

**Yield: 1 loaf**

# BLUEBERRY
# LEMON BREAD

Preheat oven to 325 degrees. Grease and flour one 9 x 5-inch loaf pan. Set aside. Combine flour, baking powder and salt in small bowl. Set aside.

In a separate bowl, beat butter with 1 cup sugar until light and fluffy. Add eggs one at a time; beat well after each one. Add lemon rind.

Add flour mixture to butter mixture, alternating with milk, beginning and ending with dry ingredients. Fold in blueberries. (Sprinkle small amount of flour over blueberries to prevent sinking to the bottom of the bowl.)

Spoon batter into prepared loaf pan. Bake for 1 hour and 15 minutes or until wooden pick inserted in center comes out clean. Place on wire rack to cool slightly.

Bring remaining 1/3 cup sugar and 3 tablespoons lemon juice to a boil. Pierce loaf. Spoon mixture over loaf. Let stand in pan 1 hour to cool completely.

# INDIANA PERSIMMON BREAD

Preheat oven to 350 degrees. Lightly grease and flour three 8 x 4-inch loaf pans. Set aside.

Plump raisins in brandy and set aside. Combine sugars, persimmon pulp and oil. Add eggs, one at a time; beat well after each addition.

Sift together the dry ingredients in a medium bowl. Add to egg mixture; blend well. Add raisins and walnuts.

Pour into prepared loaf pans. Bake 1 hour or until a wooden pick inserted in the center comes out clean. Place on wire rack to cool completely.

1   cup seedless raisins

½   cup brandy

½   cup granulated sugar

2   cups dark brown sugar, firmly packed

2   cups ripe persimmon pulp

1   cup vegetable oil

4   eggs

4   cups all-purpose flour, sifted

2   teaspoons baking soda

½   teaspoon salt

1   teaspoon cinnamon

1   teaspoon nutmeg

½   teaspoon powdered ginger

1   cup walnuts, chopped

**Yield:  3 loaves**

1 cup all-purpose flour

½ cup whole wheat flour

½ cup granulated sugar

½ cup brown sugar, firmly packed

2 ¼ teaspoons baking powder

1 teaspoon cinnamon

½ teaspoon salt

½ teaspoon nutmeg

½ cup walnuts, chopped

2 large eggs

⅓ cup vegetable oil

¾ cup peeled and grated apple

½ cup grated zucchini

½ teaspoon vanilla

**Yield: 1 loaf**

# ZUCCHINI AND APPLE HARVEST BREAD

Preheat oven to 350 degrees. Grease one 9 x 5-inch loaf pan. Set aside.

Mix flours, sugars, baking powder, cinnamon, salt, nutmeg, and walnuts with a fork in a large bowl. In a separate bowl, beat eggs with fork until blended. Add vegetable oil, apple, zucchini and vanilla. Mix well with a fork.

Add egg mixture to dry ingredients; stir until dry ingredients are moistened. Pour batter into prepared loaf pan. Bake 55 to 60 minutes or until a wooden pick inserted in center comes out clean.

Place on wire rack to cool in pan for 10 minutes. Remove from pan; cool thoroughly on a wire rack before slicing.

# ORANGE GLAZED CRANBERRY COFFEE CAKE

Preheat oven to 350 degrees. Thoroughly grease one 10-inch tube pan. Set aside. Wash and drain cranberries; spread on towel and set aside to dry thoroughly.

To make coffee cake, sift together flour, sugar, salt, baking powder and baking soda in a bowl. Add toasted nuts, cranberries and orange rind. Stir to combine.

Beat eggs in medium bowl; blend in buttermilk and oil. Add buttermilk mixture to flour and fruit mixture; stir well to blend.

Pour into prepared pan; bake 50 to 60 minutes or until wooden pick inserted in center comes out clean. Place on wire rack to cool slightly. While cooling, make glaze.

To make glaze, combine sugar and orange juice in a small saucepan. Heat until sugar dissolves completely. Pour over warm cake in pan. Cool to room temperature.

To remove from pan, loosen by pressing a small thin spatula between the cake and pan. Place a large plate or platter over pan. Turn upside down. Cover tightly and refrigerate overnight. Place on platter and garnish with orange rind and cranberries.

*Great to serve for morning guests.*

Coffee Cake:

- 1 cup fresh cranberries
- 2 ¼ cups all-purpose flour
- 1 cup sugar
- ½ teaspoon salt
- 1 teaspoon baking powder
- 1 teaspoon baking soda
- 1 cup toasted chopped walnuts or pecans
- 2 tablespoons grated orange rind
- 2 eggs
- 1 cup buttermilk
- ¾ cup vegetable oil

Glaze:

- ½ cup sugar
- ½ cup fresh orange juice
- Fresh orange rind
- Fresh cranberries

**Serves: 8 - 10**

## Coffee Cake:

- 2 cups unbleached flour, unsifted
- 1 teaspoon baking powder
- 1 teaspoon baking soda
- ¼ teaspoon salt
- ½ cup butter
- 1 cup sugar
- 3 eggs, lightly beaten
- 1 cup sour cream
- 1 (16-ounce) package frozen whole strawberries, thawed

## Topping:

- 1 cup dark brown sugar
- ¼ cup butter
- ¼ cup all-purpose flour
- ½ - ¾ cup pecans, chopped

**Serves: 12 - 16**

# STRAWBERRY COFFEE CAKE

Preheat oven to 350 degrees. Thoroughly grease a 13 x 9-inch pan. Set aside.

Combine flour, baking powder, baking soda and salt in small bowl; set aside.

Beat butter and sugar until fluffy. Add eggs; beat well. Alternately add flour and sour cream to egg mixture. Beat at low speed to blend. Fold in strawberries. Pour into prepared pan.

To make topping, beat brown sugar and butter together in a bowl. Add flour and pecans. Stir to make a semi-dry, crumbly mixture. Spread on top of the batter. Bake 30 minutes or until wooden pick inserted in the center comes out clean. The topping should melt and partially sink into the batter.

# PEPPERY CHEESE CORN BREAD

1 ½ cups yellow cornmeal

1 ½ cups unbleached all-purpose flour

¼ cup packed dark brown sugar

1 ½ tablespoons baking powder

1 teaspoon salt

¾ teaspoon ground red pepper

2 cups buttermilk, room temperature

2 eggs

1 stick unsalted butter, melted and cooled

1 ½ cups grated Cheddar cheese

Preheat oven to 425 degrees. Lightly grease a 13 x 9-inch baking pan with vegetable oil; place pan in oven.

Mix cornmeal, flour, brown sugar, baking powder, salt, baking soda and red pepper in a large mixing bowl.

In a small bowl, whisk together buttermilk, eggs and butter. Mix into dry ingredients; stir in grated cheese.

Pour batter into heated pan and bake approximately 25 to 30 minutes, or until wooden pick inserted in center comes out clean. Cool in pan 5 minutes. While still in pan, cut into squares; remove and serve warm.

*Serve this for brunch or as a quick bread with summer vegetables.*

**Yield: 12 - 16 squares**

½ cup butter, softened

¼ cup mayonnaise

1 ½ cups shredded Cheddar cheese

¼ cup green onion, diced

½ teaspoon Worcestershire sauce

2 tablespoons minced red bell pepper

1 large clove garlic, minced

1 ½ tablespoons fresh basil or 1 ½ teaspoons dried

1 teaspoon fresh oregano or ¼ teaspoon dried

¼ teaspoon marjoram, fresh or generous pinch dried

1 loaf French bread

**Yield: 1 loaf**

# EASY CHEESY BREAD

Preheat oven to 350 degrees.

Mix together butter, mayonnaise, cheese, onion, Worcestershire sauce, bell pepper, garlic, basil, oregano and marjoram.

Slice loaf of French bread in half lengthwise. Cut slices at 2-inch intervals but not quite through the bread. Spread cheese mixture evenly over both halves of loaf. Place on baking sheet. Bake 15 minutes or until cheese begins to bubble, or broil bread until cheese bubbles and browns.

*To make plain cheese bread, omit garlic, basil, oregano and marjoram.*

*A savory addition to any casual or informal meal.*

# Herb Cheese Filled Bread

Combine milk, 3 tablespoons butter, sugar and salt in a saucepan. Heat until butter melts; cool slightly. In a large bowl combine yeast, pinch of sugar and warm water; let stand 5 minutes.

Combine milk and yeast mixture. Gradually add 3 cups flour. Turn out onto floured surface and knead 8 minutes. Place dough in buttered bowl, covered, let rise until doubled, about 1 hour.

Preheat oven to 350 degrees.

Beat eggs slightly in a small bowl, reserving 1 tablespoon for glaze. In a large bowl combine softened 3 tablespoons butter, eggs, coriander, pepper and parsley. Stir in cheese.

Grease a 9-inch round cake pan; sprinkle on half sesame seeds.

Punch dough down; roll into a large circle on floured surface. Center dough over prepared pan; fill with cheese mixture. Grasp edges of dough meeting in center; pinch together and twist in a knot. Brush with reserved egg and sprinkle with sesame seeds.

Bake 50 to 60 minutes. Cut in wedges to serve.

1 cup milk

6 tablespoons butter, divided

1 tablespoon sugar

2 teaspoons salt

1 envelope active dry yeast

1 pinch sugar

1/4 cup water (105 - 115 degrees)

3 cups all-purpose flour, unsifted

2 eggs

1/2 teaspoon ground coriander

1/4 teaspoon pepper

1/4 cup parsley, chopped

1 1/2 pounds shredded Muenster cheese

1 tablespoon sesame seeds

**Yield: 1 large round loaf**

# APPLE SWIRL BREAD

**Bread:**

- 1    package dry yeast
- 1    cup warm water (105 - 115 degrees)
- 3    tablespoons granulated sugar
- 2    tablespoons shortening
- 1    egg
- ½    teaspoon salt
- 3 ½    cups all-purpose flour, divided

**Filling:**

- 2    cups finely chopped apple
- ⅓    cup brown sugar, firmly packed
- 1    teaspoon water
- ½    teaspoon ground cinnamon
- ¼    cup almonds, toasted, chopped
- ¼    teaspoon vanilla

**Yield: 1 loaf**

In a large bowl, dissolve yeast in water; stir. Combine sugar, shortening, egg, salt and 1 1/2 cups flour to yeast; beat until smooth. Stir in enough of remaining flour to make a soft dough ball (not sticky). Shape dough into a ball.

Place dough in a large oiled bowl, turning ball to coat with oil on all sides. Cover bowl and let rise in warm place until doubled in size, about 1 hour.

To make filling, combine apple, brown sugar, water and cinnamon in a saucepan. Cover and cook over medium heat for 5 minutes. Remove cover and continue cooking for 10 minutes until all liquid evaporates. Stir in almonds and vanilla. Set aside.

When dough has doubled in size punch down and turn out on a floured surface; knead 4 to 5 times or until smooth and elastic. Roll dough into a 15 x 7-inch rectangle.

Spread apple filling evenly over dough. Roll up jelly roll fashion, starting at short side. Pinch seams and ends together. Place roll, seam side down in a greased 9 x 5-inch loaf pan. Cover pan and let dough rise again about 40 minutes or until doubled in size.

When ready to bake, preheat oven to 350 degrees. Bake 50 to 60 minutes or until loaf sounds hollow when tapped. Remove from pan. Place on wire rack to cool completely.

# Sweet Potato Buns

Preheat oven to 375 degrees. Grease two 8 or 9-inch round baking pans. Set aside.

Combine milk and butter in a small saucepan. Heat until butter melts, stirring occasionally. Cool slightly; add sugar, salt and sweet potatoes. Cool to lukewarm.

Dissolve yeast in warm water in a separate bowl. Mix flour and cardamom in large bowl; add milk mixture, eggs and yeast. Stir in currants and pineapple.

Knead on floured board until elastic and smooth. Place in greased bowl, cover and let rise until doubled, approximately 1 hour. Punch down and let rest 10 to 12 minutes.

Divide dough in half. Pull off and make 9 buns from each half. Place in prepared pans. Cover and let rise until doubled in bulk, about 1 hour. Bake 20 to 25 minutes, or until golden brown.

1   cup milk

⅔   cup butter

½   cup sugar

1   teaspoon salt

1   cup cooked mashed sweet potatoes

1   package active dry yeast

½   cup warm water (105 - 115 degrees)

6   cups all-purpose flour

½   teaspoon cardamom

2   eggs, well beaten

½   cup currants

½   cup crushed pineapple, drained

**Yield:  18 buns**

4 eggs

1 cup milk

1 tablespoon sugar

¼ teaspoon salt

1 teaspoon vanilla

½ teaspoon cinnamon

8 thick slices homemade-style white bread

2 cups cornflake crumbs

Topping:

1 cup orange marmalade

½ cup orange juice

**Serves: 4**

# CRISPY FRENCH TOAST

Whisk eggs, milk, sugar, salt, vanilla and cinnamon in a medium bowl. Dip bread into mixture, coating both sides. Dip in cornflake crumbs, turning to coat with crumbs on each side.

Place toast on a lightly buttered griddle over medium-high heat; cook until golden brown on each side.

Mix orange marmalade and juice in small saucepan; heat over low until warmed through. Serve with french toast.

# Chocolate French Toast

Preheat oven to 200 degrees.

Combine eggs, milk, granulated sugar and salt in a large plate; set aside.

In a small glass measure, microwave chocolate on high 40 to 60 seconds or until melted, stirring once. Remove from microwave; stir in preserves. Divide chocolate mixture and spread over six slices of the bread. Top with remaining slices to make six sandwiches.

Melt one tablespoon of butter in a large non-stick skillet over medium heat. Dip three of the sandwiches in egg mixture; turning to coat. Place sandwiches in skillet. Cook for 4 to 6 minutes, or until golden brown, turning once. Remove to oven-proof platter; keep warm in oven. Repeat with remaining butter, egg mixture and sandwiches.

Mix confectioners' sugar and cocoa in a cup. Sprinkle or sift over the french toast before serving.

3 eggs

⅓ cup milk

1 tablespoon granulated sugar

¼ teaspoon salt

¼ cup semisweet chocolate morsels

2 tablespoons strawberry or raspberry all fruit preserves

12 slices oatmeal or white bread

2 tablespoons butter or margarine

1 tablespoon confectioners' sugar

2 tablespoons unsweetened cocoa

**Serves: 6**

⅓ cup yellow cornmeal

1 ½ cups all-purpose flour

1 teaspoon salt

2 teaspoons baking powder

1 egg

1 ½ cups milk

12 strips bacon, cooked, crumbled

1 tablespoon bacon drippings, reserved

1 tablespoon granulated sugar

**Serves: 4 - 6**

# GOLDEN BACON PANCAKES

In a medium bowl, mix cornmeal, flour, salt and baking powder.

In a separate bowl, whisk together egg and milk. Add reserved bacon drippings. Gradually add liquid mixture to dry ingredients; blend well. Add crumbled bacon. Add more milk if batter needs to be thinned.

Heat griddle to medium-high. Ladle batter onto griddle and cook until golden brown. Serve with maple syrup, fruit topping, fresh fruit and yogurt or other toppings, as desired.

# APPLE PANCAKE PUFF

Preheat oven to 425 degrees.

In a blender or processor, mix eggs, milk, flour, sugar, vanilla, salt, cinnamon and nutmeg. Place butter in a 13 x 9-inch baking dish; heat in oven until butter is melted but not brown. Add apple slices and heat in oven several minutes until they begin to sizzle.

Quickly remove from oven and pour batter over apples all at once; sprinkle with brown sugar and nuts. Return to oven and bake approximately 20 minutes, or until puffed and golden. Cut in squares. Serve immediately.

*Great to serve for weekend or overnight guests.*

|   |   |
|---|---|
| 6 | eggs |
| 1 ½ | cups milk |
| 1 | cup all-purpose flour |
| 2 | tablespoons granulated sugar |
| 1 | teaspoon vanilla |
| ¼ | teaspoon salt |
| ¼ | teaspoon cinnamon |
| ⅛ | teaspoon nutmeg |
| ½ | cup (1 stick) butter or margarine |
| 2 | tart green apples, peeled, cored, thinly sliced |
| 2 | tablespoons brown sugar |
| ¼ | cup chopped walnuts or pecans |

**Serves: 6 - 8**

1 (17 ¼-ounce) package
(2 sheets) frozen puff
pastry, thawed
according to package
instructions

1 pound pork sausage

1 large onion, finely
chopped

2 eggs

2 Granny Smith apples,
finely chopped

¾ cup dried herb stuffing mix

2 tablespoons sesame seeds

**Serves: 14 - 16**

# APPLE AND
# SAUSAGE PUFF

Preheat oven to 400 degrees. Lightly oil a large baking sheet. Set aside.

Roll each pastry sheet into a 14 x 18-inch rectangle; let stand.

In a heavy skillet, cook sausage and onion together until cooked and lightly browned; drain. Place in a large bowl. Add one egg, apples and stuffing mix. Stir to combine well.

Spoon half of sausage mixture down center of each prepared sheet of puff pastry. Spread mixture evenly leaving 2 1/2-inches of pastry at top and bottom and 4-inches on each side free of sausage mixture.

First fold top and bottom edges of pastry over mixture; then make approximately 3-inch cuts at 1/2-inch intervals down each side of pastry. Fold 3-inch cuts alternately crossing one over the next to form a pattern and cover sausage mixture.

Beat remaining egg in a small bowl. Add about 1 teaspoon water. Brush pastry completely with egg glaze; sprinkle sesame seeds over pastry.

Place on baking sheet. Bake 30 minutes, until golden brown. Let stand on wire rack to cool slightly before cutting in slices. Serve hot or at room temperature.

*The sausage apple stuffing, except for the egg, can be prepared ahead and refrigerated until ready to assemble.*

# Sour Cream Waffles

Beat egg yolks in a large mixing bowl; blend in milk, melted butter and sour cream.

Sift together flour, baking powder, baking soda and sugar in a medium bowl. Add dry ingredients to egg yolk mixture; beat well.

In a separate bowl, beat egg whites until soft peaks form. Carefully fold beaten whites into batter until completely blended. Ladle batter into hot waffle iron and bake following manufacturer's directions. Serve with syrup or fruit topping as desired.

*Sure to become a favorite weekend breakfast.*

3   eggs, separated

¾   cup milk

½   cup (1 stick) butter, melted

¾   cup sour cream

1 ½   cups all-purpose flour

2   teaspoons baking powder

½   teaspoon baking soda

1   tablespoon sugar

**Serves: 4 - 6**

2  medium green tart apples,
   peeled, cored, sliced

6  ounces dried pitted prunes

6  dried figs, sliced

⅔  cup (3-ounces) dried
   apricots

⅓  cup water

⅔  cup apple juice

½  cup lemon juice

3  cinnamon sticks

½  teaspoon ground cloves

2  medium pears, peeled,
   cored, sliced

2  medium oranges, peeled,
   seeded, sectioned

1  cup seedless grapes

   Plain yogurt


**Serves: 6**

# WARM AND WONDERFUL
# FRUIT COMPOTE

Combine apples, prunes, figs, apricots, water, apple juice,
lemon juice, cinnamon sticks and cloves in a large saucepan;
bring to a simmer over medium heat. Simmer 5 minutes. Add
pears and continue cooking until pears become tender, about
5 to 10 minutes.

Let stand at room temperature to cool; cover and refrigerate
until ready to use.

Before serving; return mixture to simmer. Stir in orange sections and grapes; cook 2 minutes. Remove cinnamon sticks and
serve warm with a dollop of yogurt.

*Can be made several days ahead of time.*

# COLORFUL FRUIT MELANGE WITH CINNAMON YOGURT

1 ½ cups water

¼ cup honey

1 (8-ounce) package mixed dried fruit

1 cinnamon stick

½ teaspoon ground allspice or 2 whole allspice

½ cup plain lowfat yogurt

1 tablespoon confectioners' sugar

¼ teaspoon ground cinnamon

1 tablespoon toasted walnuts, chopped

**Serves: 4**

Combine water and honey in a medium saucepan. Heat to boiling. Reduce heat; simmer 5 minutes. Cut fruit into bite-size pieces. Add fruit, cinnamon stick and allspice to water. Cover and simmer 10 to 15 minutes until fruit is just tender. Remove from heat. Cool to lukewarm.

Remove cinnamon stick and whole allspice. Spoon into serving dish or bowl. Cover and chill 2 to 3 hours.

When ready to serve, combine yogurt, confectioners' sugar and cinnamon in a small bowl. Spoon yogurt mixture over individual servings of fruit. Sprinkle with toasted walnuts.

*A healthy and flavorful combination to serve for breakfast, brunch or dessert.*

2 medium potatoes, peeled

1 small onion, thinly sliced

2 tablespoons olive oil, divided

1 tablespoon butter or margarine

6 eggs

2 teaspoons water

½ cup (2-ounces) crumbled feta cheese

¼ cup canned roasted red peppers or pimientos, chopped

¼ cup fresh basil, chopped

½ cup olives, sliced

Pepper, to taste

Fresh basil, optional

**Serves: 4**

# SUNRISE FRITTATA

Cook potatoes in saucepan with boiling water to cover, until just tender, about 15 to 20 minutes. Drain; slice thinly.

Sauté onions in 1 tablespoon of oil in a medium skillet. Add potato slices and butter. Cook, turning occasionally, until golden brown, about 3 to 5 minutes.

Whisk eggs and water lightly in a bowl. Stir in cheese, red peppers, basil, olives and pepper. Add remaining tablespoon of oil to skillet. Pour egg mixture over potato mixture. Cover, cook over low heat until eggs are almost set, 5 to 7 minutes.

Remove cover and place under broiler 1 minute to finish cooking top. Loosen eggs from edge of pan with a broad spatula and gently slide onto serving plate.

Garnish with basil sprigs, if desired. Cut into wedges; serve warm or at room temperature.

*An easy supper when time is of the essence.*

# A B C Omelet

In a large, heavy skillet, melt 1 1/2 tablespoons of butter. Sauté apples, but do not brown. Remove apples, set aside.

Combine eggs, milk or half-and-half, salt and pepper; whisk until well blended.

Melt remaining butter in skillet over medium-high heat until butter is foamy. Pour in egg mixture, stirring gently. When mixture begins to set, add apples and Brie. Fold sides of omelet together and slide out of pan onto serving plate.

*A unique entree for Sunday brunch.*

3   tablespoons butter, divided

1   green apple, peeled, cored, thinly sliced

3   eggs, room temperature

3   teaspoons milk or half-and-half

¼   teaspoon salt

⅛   teaspoon pepper

2   tablespoons finely diced Brie cheese

**Serves:  2**

# Basil and Cheese Eggs

Melt butter in a medium skillet. Add eggs; cook over medium heat for 2 to 3 minutes or until eggs just begin to thicken.

Add cream cheese, basil and salt. Stir and cook over medium heat 1 to 2 minutes or until eggs are loosely set. Do not overcook. Serve immediately.

*Boursin cheese adds a unique flavor change from cream cheese.*

3   tablespoons butter

6   eggs, well-beaten

1   (3-ounce) package cream cheese, softened and cut into small pieces

2   tablespoons chopped fresh basil

    Salt

**Serves:  3 - 4**

## Crust:

- 1 cup whole wheat flour
- 3 ounces shredded Cheddar cheese
- 1/4 cup chopped almonds
- 1/4 teaspoon paprika
- 1/3 cup vegetable oil

## Filling:

- 1/2 cup milk
- 1 cup sour cream
- 1/4 cup mayonnaise
- 3 eggs, well beaten
- 1 (9-ounce) package frozen broccoli, thawed, drained
- 1/2 cup shredded Cheddar cheese
- 1 tablespoon onion, minced
- 1/4 teaspoon dill
- 2 drops hot pepper sauce

**Serves: 4 - 6**

# WHEAT CRUSTED BROCCOLI QUICHE

Preheat oven to 400 degrees.

To make crust, combine flour, cheese, almonds, paprika and oil; mix until just crumbly and mixture holds together. Press into bottom and up side of 10-inch pie pan or quiche dish.

Bake 8 to 10 minutes or until crust is golden brown. Reduce oven temperature to 325 degrees.

To make filling, combine milk, sour cream, mayonnaise and eggs; blend well. Stir in broccoli, cheese, onion, dill and hot pepper sauce until well blended. Pour into prepared crust.

Bake 40 to 45 minutes or until knife inserted near center comes out clean. Let stand 5 minutes before cutting into wedges to serve.

# FESTIVE BRUNCH CASSEROLE

Preheat oven to 375 degrees. Lightly butter a 13 x 9-inch baking dish. Set aside.

In large skillet cook sausage. Drain to remove excess liquid and grease; set aside. Heat oil in skillet; sauté onions, garlic and green bell pepper for 2 to 3 minutes. Add cooked potatoes; sauté for 2 minutes. Pour into prepared baking dish. Spoon sausage over potato mixture.

Beat eggs, milk, salt and pepper in a medium bowl. Pour over potatoes and sausage. Sprinkle with shredded cheeses. Bake 45 to 50 minutes or until mixture is golden brown.

1   pound Italian sausage

2   tablespoons vegetable oil

2   cups onions, sliced

1   clove garlic, minced

1   green bell pepper, julienned

2 - 3   medium potatoes, cooked and sliced

4   eggs

2   cups milk

½   teaspoon salt

¼   teaspoon pepper

½   cup shredded Monterey Jack cheese

½   cup shredded Cheddar cheese

**Serves: 8 - 10**

4 tablespoons butter or margarine

¾ cup chopped onion

½ cup diced celery

2 large tart apples, cored, thinly sliced (do not peel)

4 cups cooked turkey or pork

2 cups cooked wild and brown rice

Apple Cream Sauce:

4 tablespoons butter or margarine

2 ½ tablespoons flour

2 cups apple juice or cider

¼ cup whipping cream

1 teaspoon ground coriander

¾ teaspoon grated nutmeg

Salt, optional

Pepper, optional

**Serves: 6 - 8**

# CASSEROLE A LA' NORMANDE

Preheat oven to 350 degrees. Butter a 13 x 9-inch baking dish. Set aside.

Melt butter in medium skillet over medium high heat. Add onion, celery and apple slices. Sauté, stirring occasionally until cooked, 10 minutes. Remove from heat; transfer apple mixture to medium mixing bowl.

Cut cooked turkey or pork into bite-size pieces; add to apple mixture. Stir in cooked rice.

To prepare apple cream sauce, melt butter in a medium pan. Whisk in flour and cook, stirring constantly 1 to 2 minutes. Gradually whisk in cider or apple juice and whipping cream, whisking until smooth. Reduce heat to low and cook, stirring occasionally 5 to 10 minutes more. Add coriander, nutmeg, salt and pepper. Remove from heat.

Add sauce to turkey-wild rice mixture; stir gently to combine. Place mixture in prepared baking dish. Bake until bubbly and golden brown, about 30 - 40 minutes.

Serve with whole berry cranberry sauce or Cranberry Chutney.

*Can be made the night before and refrigerated. Bring to room temperature before baking. To enhance the flavor, add 1/4 cup apple-flavored brandy or liqueur to cream sauce.*

# SCRAMBLED EGGS WITH MUSHROOMS AND HAM

Butter a 13 x 9-inch glass baking dish.  Set aside.

To make cheese sauce, melt butter in a heavy saucepan over low heat.  Add flour, stirring until smooth.  Cook 1 to 2 minutes, stirring constantly.  Gradually add milk. Cook over medium heat, stirring constantly, until mixture is thickened and bubbly.  Stir in salt, pepper, dry mustard and cheeses.  Continue stirring until cheese melts and sauce is smooth.  Set aside.

Sauté ham and green onions in butter or margarine in a large, heavy skillet, until the onion is tender.  Add eggs and cook over medium heat, stirring to form large, soft curds.  When eggs are set, stir in mushrooms and cheese sauce.  Spoon mixture into prepared baking dish.

Prepare the topping by combining the melted butter or margarine and crumbs.  Mix well.  Spread evenly over the egg mixture.  Sprinkle with paprika.  Cover and refrigerate overnight.

When ready to bake, preheat oven to 350 degrees.  Bake 30 to 35 minutes or until heated and golden brown.

*Absolutely delicious and perfect for weekend guests.*

Cheese Sauce:

| | |
|---|---|
| 2 | tablespoons butter or margarine |
| 2 ½ | tablespoons all-purpose flour |
| 2 | cups milk |
| ½ | teaspoon salt |
| ¼ | teaspoon pepper |
| 1 | teaspoon dry mustard |
| 1 | cup shredded Cheddar cheese |
| 1 | cup shredded mozzarella cheese |

| | |
|---|---|
| 1 | pound cubed baked ham |
| ¼ | cup chopped green onion |
| 3 | tablespoons butter or margarine, melted |
| 12 | eggs |
| 4 | ounces mushrooms, sliced |

Topping:

| | |
|---|---|
| ¼ | cup butter or margarine, melted |
| 2 | cups soft bread crumbs |
| ⅛ | teaspoon paprika |

**Serves:  10 - 12**

1 medium onion, chopped

¾ teaspoon dried oregano

3 tablespoons oil

3 medium tomatoes, peeled and chopped

10 (6-inch) corn tortillas

1 cup whipping cream

⅓ cup grated Parmesan cheese

Salt and pepper, to taste

½ cup shredded Monterey Jack cheese

Salsa, optional

**Serves: 4 - 6**

# TORTILLA VEGETABLE CASSEROLE

Preheat oven to 375 degrees. Butter a 1 1/2-quart baking dish or casserole. Set aside.

In a large skillet, sauté onion and oregano in the oil until onion is translucent. Stir in chopped tomatoes; cover and simmer about 5 minutes or until tomatoes are soft and juicy.

Cut tortillas into 1/2-inch wide strips; add to tomato mixture. Combine cream, Parmesan cheese, salt and pepper. Add to tomato mixture. Pour mixture into prepared baking dish.

Bake 30 minutes. Top with Monterey Jack cheese. Return to oven and bake about 5 to 10 minutes or until cheese is melted and mixture is lightly browned.

*Top with salsa, if desired, or serve salsa on the side.*

# WILD MUSHROOM FLAN

Roll out crust on a lightly floured board to 1/8-inch thickness. Pat into bottom and 1-inch up side of a 9 or 10-inch removable bottom tart pan. Bake according to package directions.

Preheat oven to 350 degrees.

In a large skillet over medium heat, sauté leeks, shallots and garlic in butter and oil until golden. Add mushrooms and sauté 2 to 4 minutes longer. Add sherry and herbs; remove from heat. Stir in salt and pepper; set aside to cool.

In a bowl, blend eggs, half-and-half and sugar. Spoon mushroom mixture in cooled pie shell. Pour egg mixture over mushrooms. Bake 30 to 40 minutes, or until set and golden brown. Cut in wedges to serve.

*A perfect brunch recipe.*

½ (15-ounce) package refrigerated pie crusts (1 crust)

¼ cup leeks, minced, cleaned

2 tablespoons minced shallots

2 large cloves garlic, minced

4 tablespoons butter

2 tablespoons olive oil

1 ½ pounds seasonal mushrooms

1 tablespoon dry sherry

¼ teaspoon each dried tarragon, chervil, thyme, basil

1 tablespoon chopped fresh parsley

1 tablespoon chopped fresh chives

¼ teaspoon salt

¼ teaspoon pepper

4 eggs

2 cups half-and-half

1 teaspoon sugar

**Serves: 6 - 8**

# STAPLES AND STANDBYS

◀ Creamy Primavera, 119

# STAPLES AND STANDBYS

# TORTELLINI WITH TOMATO CREAM SAUCE

Melt butter in 1 1/2-quart saucepan. Add onion, carrot and celery. Cook over medium heat about 10 minutes.

Add tomatoes, salt and sugar. Reduce heat to low and simmer gently, uncovered, for about one hour. Stir well several times.

Cool sauce slightly. Puree in food processor or blender; return to saucepan to simmer. Check for seasonings, adding salt if needed.

Cook tortellini following package directions until tender but firm. Drain thoroughly and place on a platter or in a serving bowl. Cover and set aside to keep warm.

Add cream to tomato sauce mixture. Stir and heat for about 1 to 2 minutes. Pour over warm cooked tortellini. Sprinkle with fresh pepper and Parmesan cheese to serve.

¼ pound (½ stick) butter

4 tablespoons finely chopped onion

3 tablespoons finely chopped carrot

3 tablespoons finely chopped celery

2 ½ cups canned Italian tomatoes with their juice

2 teaspoons salt

¼ teaspoon sugar

1 package spinach or cheese tortellini

½ cup whipping cream

Freshly ground pepper

Parmesan cheese

**Serves: 6**

8 ounces angel hair pasta

3 tablespoons olive oil

¼ teaspoon garlic salt

2 tablespoons butter

1 garlic clove, crushed

1 cup chopped tomato
(1 large)

¾ cup sliced zucchini
(about 2 small)

4 ounces fresh mushrooms,
sliced

⅓ cup sliced green onion

2 tablespoons chopped fresh
parsley

1 teaspoon dried basil
leaves

¼ teaspoon salt

¼ teaspoon freshly ground
pepper

1 cup shredded Provolone
cheese

¼ cup grated Parmesan
cheese

¼ cup grated Romano
cheese

**Serves: 4 - 6**

# ANGEL HAIR PASTA WITH ITALIAN CHEESES AND GARDEN VEGETABLES

Cook the pasta according to package directions until tender but firm. Drain, toss with olive oil and garlic salt; cover and keep warm.

Melt butter in a large skillet; sauté garlic about 2 minutes. Stir in tomato, zucchini, mushrooms, green onion, parsley, basil, salt and pepper. Sauté until vegetables are tender, about 7 to 8 minutes.

Arrange pasta on a warm serving platter. Add cheeses to vegetable mixture; stir to combine. Spoon around pasta. Toss gently before serving.

# Angel Hair Flans

Preheat oven to 350 degrees. Butter and lightly flour eight 1/2 cup soufflé dishes or individual ramekins; set aside.

Cook pasta following package directions until tender but firm. Drain completely; set aside to keep warm.

Whisk eggs in a medium bowl; beat in cream, thyme and nutmeg. Add generous amounts of salt and pepper. Stir in 2/3 cup Parmesan cheese.

Divide freshly cooked pasta evenly among prepared soufflé dishes. Pour egg mixture over pasta in dishes. Sprinkle with remaining 1/3 cup Parmesan cheese. Bake until egg mixture is set and golden brown, about 20 minutes. Run small sharp knife around sides of soufflé dishes to loosen. Unmold onto serving plates and serve immediately.

3  ounces angel hair pasta

3  large eggs

1  cup whipping cream

1  teaspoon fresh thyme, minced or ¼ teaspoon dried

½  teaspoons ground nutmeg

   Salt and pepper

1  cup freshly grated Parmesan cheese, divided

**Serves: 8**

8 ounces spinach, red
pepper, parsley or plain
fettucine noodles

⅓ pound Gorgonzola cheese

¼ cup freshly grated Romano
cheese

⅓ cup whipping cream or
half-and-half

White pepper, freshly
ground

Grated Romano cheese,
optional

**Serves: 4**

# FETTUCINE GORGONZOLA

Cook pasta following package directions until tender but firm.
Drain pasta; cover and set aside to keep warm.

In a large saucepan over medium heat, crumble Gorgonzola
cheese; add 1/4 cup Romano, cream and pepper. Add pasta
to cheese mixture in the saucepan. Stir until well mixed and
cook until hot, 3 to 5 minutes.

Serve hot with additional grated Romano cheese, if desired. Use
as a main dish or an accompaniment for steak, grilled burgers or chicken.

*A French Roquefort cheese can be substituted for Gorgonzola.*

# LINGUINE WITH LEMON SAUCE

1 pound fresh linguine

2 tablespoons butter

1 clove garlic, minced

⅛ teaspoon crushed red pepper flakes

1 lemon

6 ounces cooked, smoked ham

2 cups whipping cream

¼ teaspoon salt

2 cups frozen green peas

Fresh Parmesan cheese, grated

**Serves: 4 - 6**

Cook linguine following package directions until tender but firm. Drain well; return to pot.

Melt butter in a large heavy skillet; add minced garlic and red pepper. Cook over low heat until garlic is soft.

Grate rind from lemon. Julienne ham into 1-inch lengths. Add grated lemon rind and ham to garlic-butter mixture. Stir in cream. Heat gently until sauce is slightly reduced, about 10 minutes.

Pour cream sauce over linguine. Simmer gently about 10 or 15 minutes or until sauce thickens. Add frozen green peas and cook about 5 minutes more.

Pour into a heated serving bowl; sprinkle with grated Parmesan cheese to serve.

**Marinara Sauce:**

- 6 tablespoons olive oil
- 4 medium onions, chopped
- 2 garlic cloves, minced
- 5 cups tomatoes, peeled, seeded, diced
- 1 teaspoon sugar
- ½ teaspoon oregano
- ½ teaspoon basil
- ½ teaspoon salt
- ¼ teaspoon freshly ground black pepper

**Pasta:**

- 32 jumbo pasta shells, freshly cooked
- 2 (10-ounce) packages frozen chopped spinach, thawed
- 1 (15-ounce) container ricotta cheese
- 1 cup grated Parmesan cheese, divided
- 2 tablespoons fennel seeds
- 2 tablespoons fresh basil leaves, chopped, or 2 teaspoons dried
- 3 garlic cloves, minced

  Salt, to taste

  Pepper, to taste

- 3 cups Marinara Sauce

  Freshly grated Parmesan, optional

**Serves: 6**

# SPINACH AND CHEESE STUFFED PASTA SHELLS WITH MARINARA SAUCE

To make marinara sauce, heat oil in a heavy, large saucepan over medium heat. Add onions and garlic; sauté until translucent, about 5 minutes.

Add tomatoes, sugar, oregano, basil, salt and pepper. Simmer until thickened, stirring occasionally, about 1 hour.

To prepare pasta, cook pasta shells following package directions until tender but firm; drain well and set aside.

Squeeze spinach dry. Transfer to a large bowl. Add ricotta, 1/2 cup Parmesan, fennel, basil and garlic. Season mixture with salt and pepper; stir to blend well.

Preheat oven to 350 degrees. Spoon 1/2 cup marinara sauce evenly over bottom of 9 x 13-inch baking dish.

Fill each pasta shell with spinach mixture. Place shells, filling side up in a dish. Spoon remaining sauce over shells. Sprinkle with remaining 1/2 cup Parmesan. Cover loosely with foil and bake until heated through, about 30 minutes. Serve with additional Parmesan cheese, if desired.

*Canned Italian plum tomatoes can be substituted for fresh tomatoes in the sauce.*

# CREAMY PRIMAVERA

Melt 3 tablespoons butter in a large, heavy skillet. Add broccoli, carrots and garlic; cook until tender, about 10 minutes. Remove vegetables from butter; set aside.

Cook pasta following package directions until tender but firm. Drain well and set aside.

Melt remaining butter. Blend in flour, oregano and salt; cook 2 to 3 minutes. Gradually add milk, stirring constantly until thickened.

Add cooked vegetables and fettucine, sour cream, cherry tomatoes and Parmesan cheese. Heat thoroughly, stirring occasionally. Serve immediately when heated through.

*A perfect way to use fresh vegetables, and it works just as well with other fresh green or yellow vegetables.*

¼ cup (½ stick) butter, divided

2 cups broccoli flowerettes

1 cup carrots, sliced

1 clove garlic, minced

6 ounces fettucine

¼ cup all-purpose flour

½ teaspoon dried oregano leaves

½ teaspoon salt

1 cup milk

1 cup light sour cream

1 cup cherry tomatoes, halved

¼ cup Parmesan cheese

**Serves: 6**

2 ½ pounds boneless, skinless chicken breasts

2 cups white wine

½ cup soy sauce

1 large onion, chopped

3 cloves garlic, sliced

1 large lemon

¼ pound (½ stick) butter

1 cup whipping cream

¾ cup grated Parmesan cheese

⅓ cup grated Provolone cheese

⅓ cup grated Romano cheese

1 (9-ounce) package fresh angel hair or linguine pasta

2 large ripe tomatoes, cut into bite-size pieces

1 cup parsley, coarsely chopped

1 teaspoon chopped fresh basil leaves

¼ teaspoon ground mace

¼ teaspoon thyme

½ teaspoon ground white pepper

Lemon slices, optional

Parsley, chopped

**Serves: 6 - 8**

# LEMON CHICKEN WITH FRESH PASTA

Place chicken pieces in large shallow baking dish or zip-closure plastic bag.

Combine white wine, soy sauce, onion and garlic in a small bowl. Pour over chicken pieces; cover and refrigerate to marinate several hours or overnight.

When ready to cook preheat broiler to hot; arrange chicken pieces on broiler pan.

Broil chicken pieces about 6 to 8 minutes per side or until chicken is cooked.

Let cool slightly; cut into bite-size pieces. Place chicken in a medium bowl. Squeeze lemon juice over chicken.

Warm the butter and cream over low heat in a heavy saucepan. Add Parmesan, Provolone and Romano cheeses to the hot cream and butter; blend until smooth.

Cook pasta following package directions until tender but firm. Drain well and return to the pan. Add cheese sauce, tomatoes, parsley, chicken, basil, mace, thyme and ground pepper. Mix ingredients gently over low heat. Spoon onto a large serving platter; garnish with reserved lemon slices and chopped parsley, if desired.

# PEANUT CHICKEN AND NOODLES

Cook chicken pieces in 2 quarts of gently boiling water about 10 to 15 minutes. Remove, drain well; set aside to keep warm.

Add vermicelli to same water and cook according to package instructions until tender but firm. Drain well; return to saucepan. Add 1 teaspoon sesame oil.

Combine 1 tablespoon sesame oil, peanut butter, soy sauce, red wine vinegar, garlic, hot red pepper and 3 tablespoons water. Stir until well blended.

Cut chicken into bite-size pieces; add chicken, red pepper strips and cucumber to peanut butter mixture. Toss gently to combine; set aside.

Arrange warm vermicelli on heated serving platter; top with shredded lettuce. Spread chicken and sauce over lettuce. Serve immediately.

*This unique combination combines several interesting flavors... and is simple and easy to make.*

1 pound skinless, boneless, chicken breast halves

4 ounces vermicelli noodles

1 tablespoon plus 1 teaspoon sesame oil, divided

1/4 cup smooth peanut butter

3 tablespoons soy sauce

2 tablespoons red wine vinegar

1 garlic clove, crushed

1/4 teaspoon hot red pepper, crushed

3 tablespoons water

1/4 cup red bell pepper, julienned

1/4 cup cucumber, julienned

2 cups iceberg lettuce, shredded

**Serves: 4**

6 skinless, boneless chicken breast halves, cut into pieces

¼ cup (½ stick) butter

2 cups sliced mushrooms

½ cup chopped onion

2 garlic cloves, minced

¼ cup water

2 tablespoons all-purpose flour

2 cups half-and-half

2 tablespoons instant chicken bouillon granules

¼ cup grated Parmesan cheese

⅓ cup chopped pecans, toasted

8 ounces fettucine, cooked

Toasted Pecans, optional

**Serves: 6**

# CHICKEN PECAN FETTUCINE

Melt butter in medium skillet. Add chicken pieces; cook to brown lightly. Remove from pan; set aside.

Add mushrooms, onion and garlic. Cook until tender. Add water and chicken, cover and cook 10 minutes. Remove chicken pieces; set aside.

Blend flour with 2 tablespoons of half-and-half. Stir to blend. Add flour mixture, remaining cream and bouillon to vegetable mixture. Cook until thick. Stir in cheese and pecans; add chicken and heat thoroughly.

Cook fettucine according to package directions until tender but firm. Drain thoroughly. Spread on a large serving platter. Top with chicken and sauce. Sprinkle with toasted pecans. Serve immediately.

# PASTA WITH CHICKEN, SAUSAGE AND PEPPERS

Heat olive oil in a large skillet. Sauté onion, garlic and pepper until transparent. Add chicken and sausage pieces; cook until browned.

Stir in tomatoes, wine, salt, pepper, basil and sugar. Simmer until meat is cooked. Add cream and heat thoroughly; do not boil.

Cook pasta following package directions until tender but firm. Drain cooked pasta thoroughly; arrange on a warm serving platter. Top with sauce mixture. Serve immediately.

*A fresh green salad, hot bread sticks and wine are the perfect accompaniments for this dish.*

1   tablespoon olive oil

1   onion, thinly sliced

1   clove garlic, minced

1   green or red bell pepper, thinly sliced

½   pound chicken breast, cut into ½-inch strips

½   pound hot Italian sausage, cut into ½-inch strips

1   (14-ounce) can tomatoes, chopped

¼   cup dry red wine

    Salt and pepper, to taste

1   teaspoon chopped fresh basil leaves

¼   teaspoon sugar

¼   cup whipping cream

¾   pound spaghetti

**Serves:  6 - 8 as side dish
4 as main dish**

- ½ pound raw, medium shrimp, peeled, deveined
- 4 tablespoons (½ stick) butter, divided
- 1 teaspoon minced garlic
- 2 tablespoons chopped fresh parsley
- 8 ounces fettucine
- 2 tablespoons white wine
- ½ cup heavy cream
- ¼ cup freshly grated Parmesan cheese
- Pinch red pepper flakes, crushed
- ¼ teaspoon salt
- ⅛ teaspoon freshly ground black pepper

**Serves: 4**

# SHRIMP FETTUCINE

Rinse shrimp well; drain thoroughly and set aside.

Place 1 tablespoon butter in a large skillet; melt over medium heat. Add minced garlic; cook one minute.

Add parsley and shrimp; cook about 2 minutes, stirring constantly until shrimp is pink. Do not overcook. Transfer shrimp mixture to a bowl; set aside.

Cook fettucine following package directions until tender but firm. Drain and set aside.

Heat remaining 3 tablespoons butter in same skillet until melted. Reduce heat to low; add white wine, cream, Parmesan cheese and red pepper flakes. Cook about 2 to 3 minutes or until cheese melts and sauce is smooth. Stir in salt and pepper.

Place well drained fettucine in a warm serving dish. Top with sauce; add shrimp mixture and toss gently to coat thoroughly before serving.

*Our tasters declared this the best pasta dish they had ever tasted.*

# GRILLED CAJUN STEAK AND GARLIC FETTUCINE

2 pounds (1 ½-inch thick) boneless sirloin steak

2 teaspoons oregano

1 ½ teaspoons fennel seed, crushed

1 teaspoon paprika

1 teaspoon salt

1 teaspoon white pepper

½ teaspoon ground red pepper

1 pound fettucine

2 tablespoons butter

¼ cup minced garlic

½ cup Parmesan cheese

Cut steak into serving size portions. Combine oregano, fennel seed, paprika, salt, white and red pepper in a small bowl; stir and mix well. Sprinkle both sides of steak with seasoning blend; pound lightly with meat mallet or dull side of heavy knife to press seasoning into steak. Cover and let stand up to one hour at room temperature or refrigerate several hours.

When ready to cook, heat grill to medium; place steak on hot grill. Cook 6 to 7 minutes per side or to desired doneness.

Cook pasta following package directions until tender but firm; drain well. Melt butter in large heavy skillet. Add garlic and cook, stirring several times until soft and tender. Add drained pasta and Parmesan cheese. Toss to coat with garlic butter mixture.

Spread pasta mixture on large serving platter. Serve with Grilled Cajun steak.

*For a change, cook this zesty steak in a large heated heavy skillet. Brush the skillet lightly with vegetable oil before cooking.*

**Serves: 6**

3 tablespoons butter

¼ cup olive oil

1 large sweet red pepper, cored, seeded, cubed

¼ pound baked Virginia ham, chopped

4 green onions, chopped

½ tablespoon basil leaves

4 tablespoons fresh, chopped parsley

½ teaspoon oregano

2 garlic cloves, minced

2 chicken bouillon cubes

1 cup hot water

1 tablespoon lemon juice

1 pound vermicelli pasta

**Serves: 4 - 6**

# PASTA WITH RED PEPPERS AND HAM

Melt butter in a large skillet over medium heat; add oil. Stir in pepper, ham and onions; sauté until pepper and onion are tender. Add basil, parsley, oregano and garlic. Cook several minutes.

Combine bouillon cubes, water and lemon juice; stir to dissolve cubes. Add to ham and vegetable mixture. Bring to a boil; reduce heat and simmer until slightly thickened.

Cook pasta following package directions until tender but firm. Drain and return to pan to keep warm.

When ready to serve, pour pasta onto serving platter. Top with sauce; toss to combine. Serve immediately.

*This is a perfect quick supper dish, special enough to serve for guests.*

# Fresh Pesto Sauce

Place basil leaves, olive oil, nuts, garlic and salt in food processor; process to puree thoroughly. Add cheese and continue blending. Add butter and blend again.

Place pesto in a bowl and, before serving with pasta, stir in 2 tablespoons hot water in which pasta has been cooked.

Pesto can be made only with fresh basil. You can prepare the sauce (eliminating the cheese and butter) and freeze it for later use. When you are ready to use it, just defrost, add the cheese and butter and serve over hot pasta.

*This classic Italian sauce is rich, flavorful and a perfect way to use basil, fresh from the herb garden when it's plentiful.*

2 cups packed fresh basil leaves

½ cup virgin olive oil

2 tablespoons pine or pignolia nuts

2 cloves garlic, each cut in half

1 teaspoon salt

½ cup freshly grated Parmesan cheese

3 tablespoons butter, cut in 2 or 3 pieces

**Serves: 4**

2 red bell peppers

3 ½ cups whipping cream or half-and-half

1 - 2 teaspoons salt

1 clove garlic, finely chopped

½ teaspoon white pepper

1 pound fettucine or angel hair pasta

1 cup grated Parmesan cheese

**Serves: 4 - 6**

# SWEET RED PEPPER SAUCE FOR PASTA

Preheat broiler until hot. Place peppers on broiler rack. Broil until blackened on all sides. Place in a paper bag; roll top to close. Set aside to steam 10 minutes.

Remove and discard skin, seeds and ribs from pepper. Cut into 1/2-inch strips. Set aside 4 to 5 pepper strips for garnish.

Place cream in a medium saucepan. Stir in salt, garlic, white pepper and pepper strips. Bring to a low boil; reduce heat and simmer gently 12 to 15 minutes. Remove from heat; cool 10 minutes.

Cook pasta following package directions until tender but firm. Drain and return to pot to keep warm.

Puree cream mixture in batches in a food processor or blender. Pour sauce and Parmesan cheese over pasta. Toss gently to coat with sauce; transfer to serving platter. Garnish with red pepper strips to serve.

*A bright and beautiful sauce... just perfect for pasta.*

# FRESH TOMATO SAUCE

Melt butter in a heavy saucepan. Add onion; sauté over medium heat until soft and transparent.

Add tomatoes, salt and basil leaves. Simmer gently 10 minutes.

When ready to serve, pour over freshly cooked pasta; mix well. Sprinkle with grated Parmesan cheese.

*This traditional sauce is particularly good when served with spinach-flavored pasta.*

4 tablespoons unsalted butter

1 medium onion, sliced

2 ½ pounds fresh ripe tomatoes, peeled, seeded, chopped

2 teaspoons salt

1 tablespoon chopped fresh basil leaves

Parmesan cheese, grated

**Yield: 4 cups**

# GARLIC AND FRESH HERB BUTTER

Combine butter, garlic, fresh basil and parsley in food processor bowl. Process to blend all ingredients.

Place butter in container with tight-fitting cover. Refrigerate and store up to 3 weeks. Use with fresh hot cooked pasta or as a spread for bread.

*This no cook sauce is especially nice with fettucine or any broad noodle.*

1 cup butter

8 - 10 cloves elephant garlic

¼ cup firmly packed fresh basil leaves

¼ cup firmly packed fresh parsley

**Yield: 1 ¼ cups**

1 (6-ounce) package long
grain and wild rice

2 teaspoons prepared
mustard

½ teaspoon salt

1 (10-ounce) package
frozen chopped spinach

2 ¼ cups water

½ pound fresh mushrooms,
thinly sliced

½ cup chopped onion

2 tablespoons butter

1 (8-ounce) package cream
cheese, cubed

**Serves: 6 - 8**

# WILD RICE, SPINACH AND MUSHROOM CASSEROLE

Preheat oven to 375 degrees. In a large baking dish, lightly buttered, combine rice mix, mustard and salt.

In a medium saucepan, combine spinach, water, mushrooms, onion and butter. Bring to a boil. Pour over rice mixture. Cover tightly; bake for 30 minutes.

Stir in cheese; bake for 10 to 15 minutes more or until rice is tender but firm. Serve immediately.

*A marvelous dish to serve at a special dinner party.*

# Welcome Autumn Wild Rice Pilaf

In medium saucepan, cook rice according to package directions.

In a large bowl, combine apple, carrot, onion, raisins, parsley and almonds. Add cooked rice; toss together to blend.

In a small bowl, combine butter, poppy seeds, lemon rind, cinnamon and apple juice. Add to rice mixture; toss to combine. Serve immediately or at room temperature.

*A warmly different side dish. Its nutty taste and flavorful combination pleases everyone!*

1 (10-ounce) package long grain and wild rice mix

1 medium to large tart, red or green apple, unpeeled, cored, diced

1 carrot, shredded

1 green onion, minced

¼ cup golden raisins

¼ cup loosely packed, fresh parsley, minced

¼ cup toasted almonds

¼ cup (½ stick) butter, melted

2 teaspoons poppy seeds

1 teaspoon grated lemon rind

½ teaspoon cinnamon

1 tablespoon apple juice

**Serves: 6**

¼ cup (½ stick) butter

1 medium onion, chopped

1 ½ cups long grain rice

½ teaspoon salt

½ teaspoon allspice

½ teaspoon turmeric

¼ teaspoon curry powder

¼ teaspoon ground black
pepper

3 ½ cups chicken stock

¼ cup almonds, slivered

**Serves: 8**

# INDIAN PILAF

Preheat oven to 350 degrees.

Melt butter in a large, heavy skillet over medium heat. Add onion and rice. Cook stirring often until rice is golden colored and onion is tender.

Stir in salt, allspice, turmeric, curry powder and pepper. Pour mixture into ungreased 2-quart casserole or baking dish. Stir well.

Heat chicken stock to boiling. Pour over rice mixture. Cover tightly with casserole cover or aluminum foil. Bake 30 to 40 minutes or until liquid is absorbed and rice is tender. Sprinkle almonds on top to serve.

*A very nice... and distinctive... rice dish.*

# SOUTHWESTERN RICE

Preheat oven to 350 degrees. Butter a 3-quart baking dish. Set aside.

Combine sour cream, yogurt, green chilies, black olives, Worcestershire sauce and garlic in a large bowl.

Spread 1/3 of cooked rice in baking dish. Top with half of the sour cream mixture. Spread Monterey Jack cheese over sauce. Add second layer of rice, remainder of sauce mixture and remainder of rice. Top with Cheddar cheese.

Bake in preheated oven until cheese melts and mixture is lightly browned, about 40 to 50 minutes.

*A perfect make ahead dish for company and family gatherings.*

1   (16-ounce) container light sour cream

1   cup plain yogurt

2   (4-ounce) cans green chilies, chopped

½   cup black olives, chopped

1   tablespoon Worcestershire sauce

1   teaspoon minced garlic

4   cups cooked long grain rice

1   pound Monterey Jack cheese, shredded

¾   cup shredded Cheddar cheese

**Serves: 8 - 10**

5 tablespoons butter or
margarine

4 ounces angel hair pasta,
broken into 1 ½-inch
pieces

1 cup uncooked long-grain
white rice

¾ teaspoon chicken flavored
bouillon granules

2 cups water

1 (10 ½-ounce) can French
onion soup, undiluted

1 ½ teaspoons soy sauce

1 (8-ounce) can sliced water
chestnuts, drained

**Serves: 6 - 8**

# NOODLE AND RICE MEDLEY

Preheat oven to 350 degrees. Lightly oil and 8-inch baking dish. Set aside.

Melt butter in a large, heavy skillet on medium heat. Add angel hair pasta. Cook until golden brown, stirring constantly. Remove from heat.

Stir in bouillon granules, water, soup, soy sauce and water chestnuts; pour in prepared baking dish. Bake, uncovered, at 350 degrees for 40 to 50 minutes, stirring once.

Serve immediately.

*This unusual side dish is especially nice with poultry.*

# Quick and Easy Fried Rice

2 tablespoons butter

½ cup chopped onion

½ cup sliced, fresh mushrooms

1 egg, beaten

2 cups cooked rice

½ cup diced cooked ham

½ cup frozen peas or pea pods

2 tablespoons soy sauce

Melt butter over medium heat in a large, heavy skillet. Stir in chopped onion and mushrooms. Cook, stirring several times, until vegetables are tender.

Stir in egg; scramble to cook. Add rice, ham and peas. Stir gently several times and cook about 2 or 3 minutes longer. Add soy sauce and serve.

*Other cooked meats such as chicken, shrimp or crab meat make nice substitutes. This dish is a perfect accompaniment to grilled steak or chicken.*

**Serves: 2 main dish servings**

**6 side dish servings**

1 cup long-grain rice

2 ½ cups water

½ teaspoon salt

1 teaspoon grated fresh lemon rind

1 - 2 tablespoons fresh lemon juice

1 tablespoon butter

2 tablespoons minced flat-leaf parsley

**Serves: 6**

# ZESTY LEMON RICE

Combine rice, water and salt in a 1 1/2-quart saucepan. Cover tightly and bring to a boil. Simmer 20 to 30 minutes, until moisture is absorbed.

Stir in lemon rind, juice, butter and parsley. Cover and let stand 5 minutes. Fluff gently with a fork before serving.

*Our 9-year old taster said, "This is the best rice I've ever had!"*

# LEBANESE LENTILS AND RICE

In a large pot sauté onion in the olive oil. Add 6 cups of water, salt, pepper and lentils. Cover and cook over medium heat to come to a slow boil. Let mixture boil gently for 20 minutes.

Add rice and remaining 1 cup of water. Turn heat to low; cover and simmer until rice is done about 30 to 45 minutes. The rice and lentils will absorb the water. When finished cooking the mixture should be soupy but thick enough to eat with a fork.

Serve as a side dish to any meat or as a vegetarian entree along with a salad.

*Healthy, hearty, delicious and a great vegetarian meal.*

¼ cup olive oil

1 large red onion, finely chopped

7 cups water, divided

1 ¼ teaspoons salt

¾ teaspoon pepper

1 (1-pound) package lentils, rinsed well

1 cup long grain rice

**Serves: 10 - 12**

6 tablespoons butter or margarine

2 cups chopped onion

2 cups sliced mushrooms

2 cups pearl barley (not quick-cooking variety)

4 cups beef stock

Toasted slivered almonds

**Serves: 10 - 12**

# BARLEY AND MUSHROOM CASSEROLE

Preheat oven to 350 degrees. Lightly butter a 2 1/2 to 3-quart casserole.

In a heavy saucepan, melt butter. Sauté onion until golden and soft. Add mushrooms; sauté until lightly cooked. Add barley; stir to combine. Pour in 2 cups of the stock. Pour mixture into prepared casserole. Cover and bake for 1 hour.

Add remaining stock and stir well; return to oven and bake about 30 minutes, or until stock is absorbed and barley is soft.

Top with almonds; toss gently to serve.

*Men love this hearty, unusual combination; it is perfect for pork or beef.*

# Garlic and Cheese Grits

Preheat oven to 350 degrees.  Butter a 1 1/2-quart casserole or baking dish.

Stir grits into 3 cups briskly boiling water.  Reduce heat to medium-low; cover and cook 5 to 7 minutes until thickened.

Add small amount of cooked grits to beaten egg.  Return grits to mixture in pan; add cheeses, butter and garlic.  Cook over low heat an additional minute or until cheese is melted.

Pour grits into prepared casserole; bake until top is set and lightly puffed, 30 to 40 minutes.  Let stand 5 minutes before serving.

*A wonderful blend of texture and flavor.*

¾  cup hominy grits

3  cups water

1  egg, beaten

1  cup shredded Cheddar cheese

1  cup shredded Monterey Jack cheese,

2  tablespoons butter

1  teaspoon minced garlic

**Serves:  8**

1  (1-pound) package dried
   pinto beans

6  cups water

1  pound smoked pork link
   sausage, cut in ½ inch
   slices

2  medium onions, chopped

1  sweet green pepper,
   chopped

4  garlic cloves, minced

¼  cup Worcestershire sauce

2  tablespoons brown sugar

2  tablespoons ground cumin

1  tablespoon chili powder

1  tablespoon black pepper

1 - 2  teaspoons hot sauce

1  teaspoon salt

1  bay leaf

1  (16-ounce) can tomatoes,
   undrained, chopped

**Serves:  10 - 12**

# SPICY HOT BEANS

Sort and wash beans; place in a large Dutch oven.  Cover with
water 2 inches above beans.  Soak 6 hours or overnight.

Drain beans; return to Dutch oven.  Add 6 cups of water.  Add
remaining ingredients, except tomatoes.  Bring mixture to a boil.
Cover, reduce heat, and simmer for 2 hours, or until beans are
tender; stirring occasionally.

Add tomatoes; stir well and cook 30 minutes longer.  Remove
bay leaf before serving.

*Other meats such as smoked turkey or ham can be used in
place of the sausage.*

# Three Grain Pilaf

1 tablespoon olive oil

1 tablespoon butter or margarine

½ cup chopped onion

1 teaspoon chopped garlic

1 cup orzo or broken capellini

¾ cup bulgur

½ cup long-grain white rice

1 teaspoon salt

1 teaspoon freshly ground pepper

3 cups chicken broth

1 cup minced fresh parsley

1 cup slivered almonds, toasted

In a large saucepan, heat oil and butter. Stir in onion and garlic. Cook 2 to 3 minutes or until soft.

Stir in orzo, bulgur and rice. Stir well and cook about 3 to 5 minutes or until golden brown.

Add salt, pepper and broth. Bring mixture to a boil; reduce heat to simmer. Cover and cook 15 to 20 minutes or until liquid is absorbed and grains are tender. Add water or more broth if mixture becomes dry before grains are tender.

Gently stir in parsley and almonds. Serve immediately.

**Serves: 6 - 8**

# A Garden's Yield

*Salads*

*Salad Dressings*

*Vegetables*

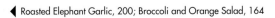
Roasted Elephant Garlic, 200; Broccoli and Orange Salad, 164

# A GARDEN'S YIELD

## Salads

### VEGETABLE SALADS

### MEAT & POULTRY SALADS

### PASTA SALADS

### FRUIT SALADS

## Salad Dressings

## Vegetables

# CROWD PLEASING SALAD

Mix first eight ingredients in a food processor; process briefly. While processor is running, pour oil in slowly. Blend until well mixed.

Toss all salad ingredients except croutons, bacon and pepper slices. Add dressing, croutons and crumbled bacon. May refrigerate covered salad and dressing separately for up to 6 hours before serving.

When ready to serve, add bacon, croutons, pepper slices and desired amount of dressing to salad. Toss and serve.

*Dressing:*

- 6 anchovies or 2 teaspoons anchovy paste
- 1 cup white wine vinegar
- ¾ teaspoon dried oregano
- 1 ½ teaspoons pepper
- 1 tablespoon salt
- 2 tablespoons sugar
- 2 cloves garlic, crushed
- ¼ cup cornstarch
- 2 cups vegetable oil

*Salad:*

- Iceberg lettuce
- Romaine lettuce
- Green onions, chopped
- Parmesan cheese, freshly grated
- Romano cheese, freshly grated
- Mozzarella and Provolone cheese, grated
- Croutons
- Bacon, cooked and crumbled
- Red bell pepper slices

**Serves: 20**

Brush English muffins with dressing. Cut in 1/2-inch cubes. Sprinkle with Parmesan cheese. Bake at 350 degrees. Stir every 5 minutes for 30 minutes or until lightly browned.

*Easy Croutons*

- 6 English muffins
- ½ cup bottled oil and vinegar dressing
- ¼ cup grated Parmesan cheese

1 medium head curly endive lettuce

1 medium head iceberg lettuce

1 medium head romaine lettuce

Garlic croutons

½ cup olive oil

4 teaspoons minced shallot

2 teaspoons minced garlic

½ cup sherry wine vinegar

2 tablespoons lemon juice

4 teaspoons Dijon mustard

10 ounces ripe Brie cheese, room temperature, rind removed

Pepper, to taste

**Serves: 8**

# CONTINENTAL SALAD WITH WARM BRIE DRESSING

Wash, dry, and tear all lettuce into bite-size pieces. Toss with croutons in a large bowl.

Warm olive oil in heavy skillet over low heat. Add shallot and garlic; cook until tender. Blend vinegar, lemon juice and mustard into hot oil mixture. Add cheese and stir until smooth. Add dressing to lettuce; toss well and serve.

*May substitute red wine vinegar for the sherry wine vinegar.*

# Springtime Spinach Salad

Tear spinach into bite-size pieces. Combine spinach, strawberries, jicama and grapes in a large bowl.

To make dressing, place sugar, sesame and poppy seeds, onion, Worcestershire sauce, salt, dry mustard, paprika and vinegar in food processor. With processor running, add oil in a slow, steady stream until thoroughly mixed and thickened. Drizzle over salad. Serve immediately.

*Jicama adds just the right crunch to this springtime salad.*

2 bunches fresh spinach, washed, dried, and trimmed

1 pint fresh strawberries, washed, hulled, halved

1 jicama, peeled, julienned

1 cup seedless green grapes, halved

*Dressing:*

½ cup sugar

2 tablespoons sesame seeds

1 teaspoon poppy seeds

1 tablespoon minced onion

¼ teaspoon Worcestershire sauce

1 teaspoon salt

1 teaspoon dry mustard

¼ teaspoon paprika

½ cup red wine vinegar

1 cup vegetable oil

**Serves: 8 - 10**

2 ½ tablespoons raspberry
vinegar

2 ½ tablespoons seedless
raspberry jam

⅓ cup vegetable oil

7 cups fresh spinach, rinsed,
stemmed, torn into pieces

¾ cup Macadamia nuts,
coarsely chopped, divided

1 cup fresh raspberries,
divided

Kiwifruit, peeled, sliced

**Serves: 6 - 8**

# RASPBERRY
# SPINACH SALAD

Combine vinegar and jam in food processor. Process to blend. Add oil slowly; blend well.

Toss spinach, 1/3 cup nuts, 1/2 cup raspberries and half of kiwifruit with dressing. Top with remaining nuts and fruit. Serve immediately.

*Can use with strawberries in place of raspberries.*

# Savory Spinach Toss

Combine all dressing ingredients in container with tight cover; shake well. Pour into salad bowl.

Place spinach on top of dressing. Do not toss. Cover bowl tightly with plastic wrap and refrigerate. Just before serving, toss spinach with dressing and garnishes.

*Dressing:*

- 2 tablespoons white wine vinegar
- 2 teaspoons Dijon mustard
- 1/2 teaspoon curry powder
- 1/2 teaspoon salt
- 1/3 cup vegetable oil
- 1 tablespoon vermouth
- 1 teaspoon soy sauce
- 1/2 teaspoon sugar
- 1/4 teaspoon freshly ground pepper
- 1 1/4 pounds fresh spinach, washed, dried, torn into bite-size pieces

*Garnishes:*

- 2 tart apples, cored and thinly sliced
- 1/3 cup dry-roasted Spanish peanuts
- 1/4 cup golden raisins
- 1 bunch green onions, thinly sliced
- 1 tablespoon sesame seeds, toasted

**Serves: 8 - 10**

6 cups fresh spinach,
  washed, dried, and
  trimmed

2 cups basil leaves, washed

½ cup olive oil

3 cloves garlic, minced

½ cup pine nuts

4 ounces baked ham,
  julienned

1 cup grated Parmesan
  cheese or Romano cheese

**Serves: 6 - 8**

# SPINACH, BASIL AND PINE NUT SALAD

Combine spinach and basil in a large bowl; toss to combine.

Heat the oil in a large skillet over medium heat. Add garlic and pine nuts; sauté until nuts begin to brown. Stir in ham; cook one minute longer.

Dress the greens with the warm dressing. Sprinkle with the Parmesan cheese. Toss and serve immediately.

*Walnut pieces make a nice substitute in this delicious salad accented with fresh basil leaves.*

# Do Ahead Greens

Mince garlic. Combine garlic, salt, pepper and mustard in a large salad bowl; mash with back of spoon. Add vinegar, oil and lemon juice; whisk to combine.

Place lettuce on top of dressing. Chill for 2 to 3 hours. To serve, toss lettuce with dressing and Parmesan cheese. Top with orange sections. Serve immediately.

1   small clove garlic

½   teaspoon salt

¼   teaspoon pepper

¼   teaspoon dry mustard

1   tablespoon tarragon vinegar

¼   cup vegetable oil

1   tablespoon lemon juice

2   small heads Boston lettuce, washed, dried, torn in small pieces

¼   cup grated Parmesan cheese

3   large orange sections

**Serves:  6**

*Dressing:*

- ¼ cup chili sauce
- ¼ cup honey
- 3 tablespoons white vinegar
- 2 teaspoons Worcestershire sauce
- 2 teaspoons onion, minced
- ½ cup vegetable oil

<br>

- 1 head red lettuce, washed, dried and torn
- 1 stalk celery, diced (about ½ cup)
- 1 small cantaloupe, peeled, cut into bite-size pieces
- 1 large avocado, peeled, sliced

**Serves: 4 - 6**

# CANTALOUPE AND AVOCADO WITH CHILI DRESSING

To make dressing, combine chili sauce, honey, vinegar, Worcestershire sauce, onion and oil. Whisk to mix well. Toss with salad ingredients. Serve immediately.

# SALAD GREENS WITH HAZELNUTS

Combine shallot, garlic, vinegar, salt and pepper in a small bowl; mix well. Gradually whisk in oil in thin stream. Add apple and toss to coat with oil mixture.

Combine greens in a large salad bowl. Pour apple dressing mixture over and toss well. Garnish with hazelnuts and chives. Serve immediately.

1   medium shallot, minced

1   medium clove garlic, minced

1   tablespoon balsamic vinegar

    Salt, to taste

    Freshly ground pepper, to taste

6   tablespoons olive oil (extra-virgin)

1   medium Granny Smith apple, cored, julienned

6   cups salad greens, washed, dried, torn into pieces (a combination of green leaf, romaine, butter lettuce, kale, arugula, sorrel, watercress, radicchio)

3   tablespoons chopped hazelnuts, toasted, skinned

    Fresh chives, finely snipped

**Serves:  6**

**Dressing:**

- ½ cup mayonnaise
- ½ cup sour cream
- ¼ cup fresh lemon juice
- 2 tablespoons Dijon mustard
- 2 tablespoons olive oil
- 2 tablespoons sugar
- 1 tablespoon white wine vinegar
- 1 tablespoon prepared horseradish
- 1 teaspoon salt
- ½ teaspoon celery seeds
- ½ teaspoon pepper

- 8 cups, (1 ½-pounds) cabbage, shredded
- ½ red bell pepper, julienned
- ½ green bell pepper, julienned
- 1 carrot, peeled, shredded
- 2 tablespoons fresh parsley, chopped
- 2 teaspoon grated lemon rind
- Salt and pepper, to taste

**Serves: 8 - 10**

# LEMONY COLESLAW

Combine dressing ingredients in bowl; whisk to blend. Refrigerate dressing until cold. (Can be prepared one day ahead.)

Combine cabbage, bell peppers, carrot, parsley and lemon rind in large bowl. Toss with desired amount of dressing. Season to taste.

*This is a generous amount of dressing. Store any leftover dressing in the refrigerator up to 7 days.*

*Refreshing taste to a traditional salad.*

# SUMMER CORN SALAD

Cook fresh corn kernels in boiling water to cover 5 minutes. Frozen corn should be cooked according to package directions. Drain and cool. Combine corn and the next six ingredients. Set aside.

Combine garlic and remaining ingredients, stirring well. Toss gently with vegetables. Chill eight hours.

*Perfect as a star addition to summer meals.*

3  cups fresh corn kernels

1  large onion, chopped

2  medium zucchini, unpeeled, cubed

1  bunch green onions, sliced

1  red bell pepper, chopped

1  green bell pepper, chopped

¼  cup parsley, minced

1  clove garlic, minced

¼  teaspoon salt

⅛  teaspoon pepper

2  teaspoons sugar

1  teaspoon ground cumin

2  teaspoons Dijon mustard

½  teaspoon hot pepper sauce

⅔  cup vegetable oil

⅓  cup white vinegar

**Serves: 8 - 10**

1 pound fresh green beans,
   washed and trimmed

½ cup water

¼ cup white wine vinegar

¾ cup vegetable oil

½ cup red onion, diced

½ teaspoon dried savory,
   crumbled

2 teaspoons lemon rind,
   grated

¾ cup blue cheese, crumbled

½ cup pecans or walnuts,
   chopped, toasted

1 head leaf lettuce, washed
   and dried

**Serves: 4 - 6**

# SAVORY FRESH
# GREEN BEAN SALAD

Combine beans and water in a saucepan. Bring to a boil;
cover and reduce heat. Cook approximately 5 minutes or until
tender-crisp.

Drain beans and rinse under cold water; drain again. Dry well,
chill.

Combine vinegar, oil, onion, savory and lemon rind in a jar.
Shake well to blend. Combine beans with desired amount of
dressing. Cover and chill.

To assemble salad, place lettuce on plates. Top with beans,
crumbled cheese and toasted nuts.

# FETA AND MINT GREEN BEAN SALAD

1 ½ pounds fresh green beans

½ cup fresh mint leaves, chopped

¾ cup olive oil

¼ cup white wine vinegar

¾ teaspoon salt

¼ teaspoon pepper

½ teaspoon crushed garlic

1 cup walnuts, coarsely chopped, toasted

1 cup sliced red onion

1 cup feta cheese, crumbled

Blanch green beans in boiling water to cover for 4 to 5 minutes. Drain and rinse under cold running water. Drain and chill. Add mint to green beans, toss to combine; set aside.

Combine oil, vinegar, salt, pepper and garlic in a small bowl; set aside.

Combine green beans, walnuts, red onion and feta cheese in a large salad bowl. Pour dressing over bean mixture; toss to coat. Chill until ready to serve.

*Green beans sitting in vinaigrette dressing tend to lose their bright green color. Plan to serve this dish just after preparing so it will look its best.*

**Serves: 4**

1 pound fresh mushrooms, wiped clean

½ cup olive oil

3 tablespoons lemon juice

1 tablespoon Dijon mustard

½ teaspoon salt

¼ teaspoon ground pepper

1 head leaf lettuce, washed and dried

**Serves: 4**

# LEMON MARINATED MUSHROOM SALAD

Slice mushrooms and place in a medium bowl. Combine olive oil, lemon juice, mustard, salt and pepper in a jar; cover tightly and shake well to blend.

Pour prepared dressing over mushrooms, tossing to coat. Let stand at room temperature for 1 hour, or chill for 2 hours stirring occasionally.

Line serving plates with lettuce leaves and spoon mushrooms on top to serve.

# Snow Peas in Basil Vinaigrette

Combine lime juice and vinegar in a small bowl. Add shallot; let stand for 5 minutes. Whisk in oils, garlic, basil, salt and pepper. Set aside.

Bring 3 quarts of water to a boil. Add snow peas; cook 30 seconds. Drain and rinse in cold water until snow peas cool. Drain well; pat dry on paper towels.

Toss snow peas with dressing and almonds just before serving. Serve warm or cold.

2 tablespoons fresh lime juice

2 tablespoons balsamic vinegar

1 shallot, finely chopped

2 tablespoons vegetable oil

1 tablespoon olive oil

1 clove garlic, finely chopped

1 tablespoon chopped fresh basil leaves

¼ teaspoon salt

Black pepper, to taste

1 ½ pounds snow peas

¼ cup chopped toasted almonds

**Serves: 6**

1 tablespoon Dijon mustard

4 tablespoons red wine vinegar

1 teaspoon sugar

½ teaspoon salt

½ teaspoon pepper, freshly ground

2 tablespoons fresh parsley, minced

½ cup olive oil

4 large, ripe tomatoes, cut into ¼-inch slices

1 pound fresh mozzarella, shredded

¼ cup fresh basil leaves, chopped

¼ cup fresh parsley, chopped

½ cup Nicoise olives, chopped

½ cup vinaigrette

Freshly ground pepper, to taste

**Serves: 6**

# LAYERED MOZZARELLA AND TOMATO SALAD

In a medium bowl, combine mustard, vinegar, sugar, salt, pepper, and parsley; whisk to blend. Continue to whisk while slowly adding olive oil until mixture thickens. Adjust seasoning to taste.

On a large serving platter, alternate overlapping slices of tomato and mozzarella cheese. Sprinkle basil, parsley and olives over all. Drizzle vinaigrette over salad. Grind black pepper generously over tomatoes and cheese to serve.

*Summer garden tomatoes are a must for this salad... and are well worth waiting the year for!*

# Easy but Elegant Asparagus and Tomato Salad with Dijon Vinaigrette

4 green onions, minced

Dash of Worcestershire sauce

2 teaspoons Dijon mustard

Salt, to taste

Freshly ground pepper, to taste

3 tablespoons white wine vinegar

½ cup olive oil

½ pound fresh asparagus

1 small ripe tomato, thinly sliced

½ ripe avocado, peeled, thinly sliced

6 - 8 fresh mushrooms, thinly sliced

Bibb lettuce leaves

**Serves: 4 - 6**

Whisk together minced onions, Worcestershire sauce, Dijon mustard, salt, pepper and vinegar in a small bowl. Add olive oil in a steady stream, whisking to blend and emulsify. Set aside.

Trim woody ends off asparagus stalks. Peel asparagus stalks if needed; cut into 2-inch lengths. Blanch briefly in boiling water. Drain and rinse with cold water to stop cooking. Spread on paper towel to dry thoroughly.

Combine salad dressing, asparagus, tomato and avocado; toss thoroughly to coat vegetables. When ready to serve, arrange Bibb lettuce leaves on salad plates. Top with tomato mixture.

*To insure a rich flavor, use very ripe tomatoes.*

1/4 cup tarragon white wine vinegar

1 teaspoon Dijon mustard

1/2 - 1 teaspoon garlic salt

3/4 cup vegetable oil

3 medium zucchini, cubed

1 green pepper, thinly sliced

1/4 cup chopped green onion

Lettuce leaves, washed and dried

Tomato wedges

**Serves: 6 - 8**

# ZESTY ZUCCHINI AND PEPPER SALAD

Combine vinegar, mustard and garlic salt in a large bowl; mix well. Gradually whisk in oil. Add zucchini, green pepper and green onion to dressing; toss to combine.

To serve, arrange salad greens on plates. Add zucchini mixture and tomato wedges.

# Quintessential Broccoli Salad

Combine prepared vegetables in large bowl. Set aside.

Combine oil, vinegar, sugar and salt in a jar with tight fitting lid; shake well to mix. Pour dressing over vegetables and toss to mix well.

Line serving plates with lettuce leaves. Arrange vegetable mixture over lettuce leave; garnish with crumbled bacon. Serve immediately.

*Add or substitute sliced water chestnuts, chopped green onions and chopped celery for any of the other ingredients.*

4 small summer squash or zucchini, unpeeled, thinly sliced

½ pound fresh mushrooms, cleaned, thinly sliced

1 (6-ounce) jar marinated artichoke hearts, drained, cut into thirds

1 small red bell pepper, cored, seeded, thinly sliced

1 small yellow bell pepper, cored, seeded, thinly sliced

1 bunch fresh broccoli, cut into bite-size pieces, blanched

¾ cup olive oil

⅔ cup white wine vinegar

¼ teaspoon sugar

2 teaspoons salt

1 head leaf lettuce

Bacon, cooked, crumbled, for garnish

**Serves: 8**

1  small bunch broccoli

3 - 4  navel oranges, peeled,
     sliced

1  small red onion, thinly
   sliced

1  head romaine lettuce,
   washed, dried, torn,
   chilled

3  tablespoons fresh lemon
   juice

2  teaspoons Dijon mustard

¼  cup olive oil

   Freshly ground pepper,
   to taste

**Serves: 6 - 8**

# BROCCOLI AND
# ORANGE SALAD

Cut broccoli into flowerettes; peel and cut the stems into bite size pieces.  Drop broccoli stems into boiling, lightly salted water.  Bring to a boil; add flowerettes and bring to a second boil.

Drain broccoli into a colander; briefly cool under cold running water.  Drain well, pat dry.  Chill thoroughly.

To serve, combine broccoli, orange slices, onion slices and romaine lettuce in a large bowl.

Combine remaining ingredients in a small bowl or jar with a tightly fitting lid.  Shake to blend well.  Pour over salad, toss well and serve.

*All vegetables can be prepared well in advance.  Toss with dressing just prior to serving time.*

# New Potato Salad with Peas and Mint

3 pounds new potatoes, scrubbed, not peeled

1 ½ cups frozen tiny peas, thawed

½ cup sour cream

½ cup mayonnaise

1 tablespoon freshly grated lemon rind

½ cup fresh mint, chopped

Salt and pepper, to taste

**Serves: 6 - 8**

Cook potatoes in large pot of boiling water 15 to 20 minutes or until just tender when pierced with a knife. Drain and pat dry. Allow potatoes to cool slightly; cut into 1/2-inch cubes.

Spread peas on paper towel; dry thoroughly. Add to potatoes.

Whisk together sour cream, mayonnaise, lemon rind, mint; salt and pepper to taste.

Add dressing to potato cubes and peas; toss gently to combine. Taste for seasoning and add salt and pepper if necessary. Refrigerate at least 2 hours or longer. Garnish with sprigs of fresh mint and serve.

*The key to this dish is fresh potatoes and the correct seasoning.*

5 pounds red potatoes, unpeeled

⅓ cup red wine vinegar

2 tablespoons country style Dijon mustard

2 teaspoons salt

1 teaspoon freshly ground black pepper

½ cup vegetable or olive oil

3 cups chopped celery

1 cup minced red onion

½ cup chopped fresh parsley

¼ cup chopped fresh tarragon or 2 teaspoons dried

**Serves: 16 - 20**

# PERFECT PICNIC POTATO SALAD

Place potatoes in a large saucepan; add water to cover. Bring to boil. Cover and cook just until potatoes are tender when pierced with a fork, about 20 to 30 minutes.

Drain potatoes and cool until easy to handle. Peel and cut into one-inch or larger pieces.

Whisk vinegar, mustard, salt and pepper in a large bowl. Gradually whisk in oil. Add warm potatoes and toss. (Can be made ahead to this point. Cover and refrigerate up to 24 hours.)

When ready to serve, cool to room temperature; add celery, onion, parsley and tarragon. Toss gently to combine.

*The name says it all about this salad.*

# New Potato Salad

Arrange potatoes in a large shallow baking dish; add 1 teaspoon salt and water to cover. Bake in a 350 degree oven for 1 hour and 15 minutes or until potatoes are tender. Drain.

When cool, slice potatoes in half leaving skin on. (Cooking potatoes this way makes the skin stay perfect when slicing.)

Combine potatoes, green beans, mushrooms and green onions in a very large bowl; toss gently and set aside.

Combine remaining 1/2 teaspoon salt, pepper, seasoning blend, parsley and dressing. Add to vegetables; toss gently.

Cover and refrigerate to chill at least one hour. Best served cold. Garnish with freshly chopped fresh dill, if desired.

*A salad with a fresh light approach.*

2 pounds whole new potatoes (about 20 medium)

1 ½ teaspoons salt, divided

1 pound fresh green beans, steamed, cut in half

1 pound fresh mushrooms, sliced

4 green onions, chopped

1 teaspoon coarse black pepper

½ teaspoon Creole seasoning blend

2 tablespoons chopped parsley

1 ½ cups bottled creamy buttermilk-type dressing

Fresh dill, optional

**Serves: 12 - 14**

6 skinless, boneless chicken breast halves, cooked, cut into strips

2 tablespoons olive oil

2 cloves garlic, minced

¾ cup cider vinegar

¼ cup honey

1 tablespoon chopped fresh basil leaves or 1 teaspoon dried basil

3 tablespoons chopped fresh parsley

2 teaspoons Dijon mustard

1 teaspoon dry mustard

¾ cup vegetable oil

9 - 10 ounces fresh tortellini

1 medium red bell pepper, seeded, chopped

1 medium green bell pepper, seeded, chopped

2 ribs celery, sliced

1 medium red onion, chopped

Salt, to taste

Pepper, to taste

**Serves: 8**

# CHICKEN AND TORTELLINI SALAD

Heat olive oil in a large skillet; add garlic. Sauté over medium heat until golden brown. Add chicken. Sauté 1 minute, stirring constantly. Remove garlic and chicken to a large bowl. Set aside.

In a small bowl, combine vinegar, honey, basil, parsley and mustards. Slowly whisk in vegetable oil, blending until dressing is creamy.

Pour dressing over garlic and chicken in bowl. Cover and marinate for several hours in the refrigerator.

Cook tortellini in boiling water until tender but firm. Drain and rinse quickly in cold water to stop the cooking process. Drain well.

To assemble salad, combine marinated chicken and dressing, drained tortellini, chopped bell peppers, celery, onion, salt and pepper in a large bowl; toss well. Chill and serve.

# Szechwan Chicken Salad

Halve pineapple lengthwise, cutting through leafy crown. Remove pineapple in one piece from shells. Refrigerate shells. Remove core from pineapple. Cut enough pineapple into chunks to make 2 cups (save remaining fruit for another use.)

In a large bowl, combine pineapple chunks, chicken, green onion and red bell pepper.

In small bowl, whisk together mayonnaise, red pepper flakes, ginger root and salt. Slowly add oil; whisk until blended. Add half the dressing to chicken mixture; toss gently to coat chicken and vegetables with dressing.

Cover salad and remaining dressing. Refrigerate until ready to serve. Just before serving, blend in remaining dressing and cashews. Spoon salad into shells.

1   fresh, ripe pineapple

2   boneless chicken breasts, cooked, chilled, cut in 1-inch chunks

½   cup green onion, cut in 1-inch pieces

1   red bell pepper, diced

1   cup mayonnaise

1   teaspoon red pepper flakes

1   teaspoon fresh ginger root, minced

½   teaspoon salt

1   tablespoon sesame oil

½   cup cashew nuts, toasted

**Serves: 4**

1 ½  cups water

1  cup long grain white rice

2  cups cooked diced turkey
   or chicken

¾  pound ripe plum tomatoes,
   seeded, diced

1  cup thinly sliced green bell
   peppers

1  cup frozen corn, thawed

½  cup olive oil

6  tablespoons chopped fresh
   cilantro

3  tablespoons white wine
   vinegar

1  tablespoon Dijon mustard

1  large jalapeño pepper,
   seeded, minced

1 ¼  teaspoons ground cumin

¾  teaspoon salt

¼  teaspoon pepper


**Serves:  6**

# SOUTHWEST TURKEY
# AND RICE SALAD

Bring 1 1/2 cups water to boil in heavy medium saucepan; add rice. Cover and cook over low heat until rice is tender, about 15 to 20 minutes. Transfer rice to large bowl. Add turkey, tomatoes, green pepper and corn. Toss to combine.

Whisk together oil, cilantro, vinegar, mustard, jalapeño pepper, cumin, salt and pepper. Pour dressing over salad; mix gently. Cover and refrigerate to chill before serving. Can be prepared up to 3 hours ahead.

*An excellent way to use leftover grilled or roasted turkey.*

# Papaya and Avocado with Grilled Mustard Chicken

To make marinade, whisk together marinade ingredients in a small bowl.  Place chicken breasts in a large glass dish or zip-closure plastic bag.  Add marinade, turning chicken pieces to coat all sides.  Cover and refrigerate 2 to 4 hours.

Combine dressing ingredients in a small glass jar; shake well to combine.  Reserve.

Divide lettuce among six chilled salad plates.  Peel and slice papaya and avocados, dividing each among the six plates.  Garnish with toasted almonds.

Preheat barbecue grill to medium-high.  Place marinated chicken on the grill; brush with marinade and cook about 5 minutes per side or until chicken is golden and cooked to desired doneness.  (Use non-stick spray or oil the grill to prevent sticking.)

When chicken is cooked, transfer to a cutting board.  On an angle cut into 1/2-inch thick pieces.  Fan slices of chicken over prepared salad greens; drizzle with salad dressing to taste.

*A one-dish salad perfect for summer guests.*

Marinade:

- ⅓ cup olive oil
- ⅓ cup white wine
- Rind of 1 lime, grated
- 3 tablespoons fresh lime juice
- ⅓ cup Dijon mustard
- ⅓ cup fresh parsley, finely chopped
- ⅓ cup fresh basil, finely chopped
- ¼ teaspoon ground black pepper
- ½ teaspoon salt
- 6 boneless, skinless chicken breast halves

Dressing:

- 1 shallot, chopped
- 2 tablespoons honey
- ¼ cup fresh lime juice
- ⅔ cup olive oil

Salad:

- 1 large head of red leaf lettuce, washed and drained
- 1 ripe papaya
- 2 ripe avocados
- 2 ¼ ounces slivered almonds, toasted

**Serves:  6**

8 cups  spinach, romaine or leaf lettuce, washed, dried, torn

1 pound cooked turkey breast, cut into strips

1 large grapefruit, cut into sections

1 large orange, cut into sections

1 (8-ounce) can red kidney beans, rinsed, drained

1 bunch green onions, cut in 1-inch pieces

¼ cup vegetable oil

½ teaspoon basil leaves

½ teaspoon salt

2 tablespoons cider vinegar

**Serves:  4 - 6**

# WARM TURKEY SALAD

In large bowl, toss salad greens, turkey, fruit sections and kidney beans.  Set aside.

In large, heavy skillet heat oil over medium heat.  Add onions, basil and salt.  Cook until onions are tender.

Pour hot onion mixture over salad.  Sprinkle with vinegar and gently toss until salad is coated with dressing mixture.

*Quick, easy and a great way to use leftover Thanksgiving turkey.*

# CALYPSO SHRIMP SALAD

To make dressing, whisk dressing ingredients together in a small bowl; cover and chill.

To make salad, combine salad ingredients except almonds. Toss with desired amount of dressing; cover and refrigerate until serving time. Arrange salad on plates and sprinkle with almonds to serve.

*Serve with cantaloupe, avocado, artichoke, pineapple, or papaya, or substitute crab or chicken for shrimp.*

Dressing:

- ³/₄ cup mayonnaise
- ¹/₂ cup sour cream
- Juice of 1 lemon
- ¹/₄ teaspoon curry powder
- Dash of hot pepper sauce
- 6 dashes white wine Worcestershire

Salad:

- 2 cups small shrimp, cooked
- 1 cup celery, diced
- ¹/₂ cup green onions, minced
- Juice of 1 lemon
- ¹/₄ cup chopped green bell pepper
- ³/₄ cup chopped fresh pineapple
- ³/₄ cup seedless white grapes
- 2 tablespoons capers, drained
- ³/₄ cup slivered almonds, toasted

**Serves: 4 - 6**

12 ounces orzo (rice shaped pasta)

2 cups mayonnaise

¼ cup half-and-half

1 tablespoon salt

2 tablespoons lemon juice, freshly squeezed

2 teaspoons white pepper

4 cups cooked, cubed chicken

2 cups green grapes, halved

2 cups cucumber, seeded, chopped

1 cup celery, chopped

½ cup pecans, toasted

**Serves: 25**

# COMPANY'S COMING CHICKEN SALAD

Cook orzo following package directions to desired tenderness. Rinse in cold water; drain well.

In large bowl, combine mayonnaise, half-and-half, salt, lemon juice and white pepper. Stir in orzo, chicken, grapes, cucumber and celery. Cover tightly and refrigerate several hours or overnight before serving. To serve, garnish with toasted pecans.

*Great for special occasion luncheons with croissants or muffins.*

# Slivered Chicken with Lime and Basil

Bring chicken stock to boil in a large saucepan. Reduce heat to low; add chicken breasts and cook eight to ten minutes at a low simmer or until barely firm to the touch. Let cool in stock at least one hour.

While chicken is cooling, combine lime juice, garlic, basil, tarragon, shallots, oil, sugar, salt and pepper for marinade in a large bowl.

Drain cooled chicken; remove and discard skin and bones. Slice meat into strips about 1/2-inch wide. Place in marinade. Cover and refrigerate 24 hours.

To serve, drain chicken and arrange on lettuce lined platter. Garnish with tomato wedges and fresh basil.

3 quarts chicken stock

8 whole chicken breasts

Marinade:

2 cups fresh lime juice (about 16 limes)

9 garlic cloves, lightly crushed

½ cup tightly packed fresh basil leaves or ¼ cup dried

1 tablespoon fresh tarragon or 1 teaspoon dried

6 large shallots, minced

2 cups olive oil

¾ teaspoon sugar

Salt and freshly ground pepper, to taste

Lettuce leaves, washed, drained and chilled

Tomato wedges, for garnish

Fresh basil leaves, for garnish

**Serves: 16**

3 whole boneless, skinless chicken breasts, cooked and diced

2 tart, green apples, cored, cut into 1-inch pieces

1 ½ cups fresh pineapple, cored, cut into 1-inch pieces

1 ½ cups green or red seedless grapes

3 tablespoons chutney, chopped

½ cup mayonnaise

1 ½ teaspoons curry powder

1 ½ cups macadamia nuts, coarsely chopped

Bibb and leaf lettuce, washed and drained

Macadamia nuts, optional

**Serves: 6 - 8**

# CHICKEN SALAD MACADAMIA

Combine chicken, apples, pineapple and grapes in a large bowl.

Stir together chutney, mayonnaise and curry powder in a small bowl. Add to chicken mixture; toss to combine. Cover; refrigerate 4 hours or overnight.

When ready to serve, taste for seasonings; add 1 1/2 cups macadamia nuts and salt, if necessary. Arrange salad on lettuce leaves. Top with macadamia nuts, if desired.

*Cool island breezes will come to mind when you serve this delicacy.*

# GINGERED CHICKEN SALAD

Combine mayonnaise. sour cream. sugar. lemon rind. lemon juice, ginger and salt.  Stir well.

Add chicken, grapes and celery.  Toss to coat well with dressing.  Cover and chill at least two hours.

Arrange chicken salad on lettuce lined plates with a wedge of cantaloupe, if desired.

¾ cup mayonnaise

½ cup sour cream

1 ½ tablespoons sugar

¾ teaspoon lemon rind, grated

1 ½ tablespoons fresh lemon juice

¾ teaspoon ground ginger

¼ teaspoon salt

3 cups cooked, cubed chicken

1 ½ cups seedless green grapes

1 cup celery, sliced

2 small cantaloupes, peeled, seeded, cut into wedges

Leaf lettuce, for garnish

Cantaloupe wedges, for garnish

**Serves:  8**

½ cup dry white wine,
   Chardonnay or other

1 ¼ cups golden raisins

8 ounces fuselli or corkscrew
   pasta

1 ½ cups whole Greek or ripe
   olives

3 tablespoons olive oil or
   vegetable oil

3 tablespoons lemon juice

2 tablespoons chopped fresh
   herbs ( tarragon, basil
   leaves or chives)

1 tablespoon chopped
   shallots or green onion

1 tablespoon Dijon mustard

½ teaspoon salt

½ teaspoon pepper

½ cup pine nuts or walnut
   pieces, toasted

# WINE COUNTRY
# VINEYARD PASTA SALAD

In a small saucepan, heat the wine over medium heat just until
warm. Add raisins. Let stand 15 to 30 minutes to plump.
Drain; reserving wine. Set both aside.

Cook the pasta in lightly salted boiling water according to package directions until tender but firm. Pour into colander; rinse
under cold water. Drain well.

In a large serving bowl, combine cooled and well drained
pasta, raisins and olives; toss gently to combine. Set aside.

In a jar with a tight fitting lid, combine reserved wine, oil, lemon
juice, fresh herbs, shallots or green onion, mustard, salt and pepper. Cover and shake to mix well.

Add toasted nuts to pasta mixture. Pour desired amount of
dressing over mixture; toss to coat. Cover and chill until
ready to serve or up to 6 hours.

*This is definitely not "the same old pasta salad."*

# SUMMER SHRIMP PASTA SALAD

3 tablespoons olive oil, divided

½ pound bow tie pasta

3 cups fresh basil leaves

2 tablespoons fresh lemon juice

¼ cup extra virgin olive oil

Salt and pepper, to taste

1 ½ pounds large shrimp, uncooked, peeled, deveined

2 cups frozen tiny peas, thawed

2 ripe tomatoes, seeded, cut into ¼-inch cubes

2 whole fresh basil leaves, for garnish

Tomato wedges, for garnish

**Serves: 8**

Bring 2 large pots and 1 small pot of water to a boil. Add 1 tablespoon olive oil to one of the large pots. Add pasta to this boiling water. Follow package directions and cook until pasta is tender but firm.

Place basil leaves in food processor. Add remaining 2 tablespoons olive oil. Process until smooth. Remove to a small bowl. Add lemon juice, olive oil, salt and pepper. Stir well; set aside.

Place shrimp in second large pot of boiling water; cook 2 minutes or until shrimp are pink and opaque. Do not overcook! Drain and rinse shrimp with cold water to stop cooking. Pat dry with paper towels.

When pasta is cooked, drain well. Combine with cooked shrimp in large bowl; toss with basil puree, peas and tomatoes. Adjust seasoning to taste. Garnish with basil leaves and tomato wedges to serve.

*To easily thaw, pour boiling water over peas in a colander; drain well and pat dry.*

*Garlic vinaigrette:*

- 2 garlic cloves, peeled
- 2 green onions, trimmed, cut into 2-inch lengths
- 1 tablespoon fresh parsley, minced
- ¼ teaspoon red pepper flakes
- 2 ½ tablespoons fresh lemon juice
- 2 tablespoons red wine vinegar
- ½ tablespoon Dijon mustard
- ½ teaspoon sugar
- 2 twists of the pepper mill
- ¼ cup vegetable oil
- ¼ cup olive oil

<br>

- ¼ pound cheese tortellini
- 1 (14-ounce) can artichoke hearts, rinsed, drained, quartered
- 1 pound small shrimp, cooked, peeled, deveined
- 2 cups mushrooms, quartered
- ¼ teaspoon dried Italian seasoning blend, crushed
- 14 cherry tomatoes, halved

  Fresh lettuce leaves

**Serves: 6 - 8**

# TORTELLINI AND VEGETABLES IN GARLIC VINAIGRETTE

To make garlic vinaigrette, combine all the vinaigrette ingredients except the oils in food processor. Process until well blended. With the machine running, slowly add the oils. Store in a covered jar in the refrigerator.

To prepare salad, cook tortellini according to package directions until tender but firm. Rinse under cold water; drain and pat dry. Combine tortellini, artichokes, shrimp, mushrooms, 3/4 cup prepared vinaigrette and seasoning blend. Stir to coat. Cover and chill at least 4 or up to 24 hours.

To serve, stir in tomatoes and remainder of the dressing. Serve on lettuce lined plates as a salad.

*Serve as an appetizer or antipasto with wooden picks for easy pick up.*

# MEDITERRANEAN PASTA SALAD

To make dressing, combine brandy, mayonnaise, garlic, capers, salt, tarragon and pepper in a jar. Cover tightly with lid and shake to mix well.

Cook pasta according to package directions until tender but firm. Drain well.

In large bowl, combine pasta, oranges, chicken, green pepper, green onion, cheese, olives and walnuts. Toss with dressing; chill well before serving.

*Fresh pineapple chunks are the perfect addition to this tasteful combo.*

Dressing:

1 tablespoon brandy

³/₄ cup mayonnaise

1 clove garlic, minced

1 teaspoon capers

½ teaspoon salt

½ teaspoon tarragon

¼ teaspoon white pepper

8 ounces shell pasta

1 small can mandarin oranges, drained

2 cups cooked, chopped chicken, about 4 breasts

1 green pepper, chopped

3 green onions, chopped

1 cup feta cheese, crumbled

¼ cup ripe olives, chopped

¼ cup walnut pieces

**Serves: 6**

*Raspberry Puree:*

- ¼ cup raspberry vinegar
- ¾ cup sour cream
- 1 cup raspberries

- 1 head Bibb lettuce, washed, dried and chilled
- 1 small head romaine lettuce, washed, dried and chilled
- 4 pears

  Juice of 1 lemon
- ¼ - ½ pound Brie, thinly sliced, bite-sized
- ¼ cup raspberries, washed, drained

**Serves: 4 - 6**

# PEAR AND BRIE SALAD

To make raspberry puree, mix vinegar, sour cream and raspberries in a blender or food processor. Process to blend. Strain through fine mesh colander if you wish to remove seeds. Set aside.

Arrange chilled greens on serving plates. Peel, quarter, core and slice pears. Brush lightly with lemon juice.

Arrange pears on greens in a decorative pattern. Top with 3 to 4 bite-size Brie pieces. Drizzle with raspberry puree and accent with whole berries to serve.

# Apple Asiago Salad with Dijon Vinaigrette

To make vinaigrette, combine oil, vinegar and mustard in jar with tight-fitting lid. Cover tightly. Shake to blend thoroughly.

Core apples; cut into 1/4-inch thick slices or small wedges.

Set aside 1/4 cup of vinaigrette dressing. Toss apples with remaining dressing. When ready to serve combine lettuce, apples, cheese and walnuts. Toss gently with remaining vinaigrette. Arrange on well chilled plates to serve.

Dijon Vinaigrette:

- ½ cup olive oil
- 3 tablespoons red wine vinegar
- 2 teaspoons Dijon mustard

- 4 - 5 firm, tart Granny Smith apples
- 2 heads Bibb lettuce, washed, dried, torn
- ¾ cup Asiago cheese, shredded
- ¾ cup walnuts, coarsely chopped, toasted

**Serves: 6 - 8**

# Summer Melon and Berries with Raspberry Vinegar

Arrange washed and dried lettuce on well chilled salad plates.

Cut cantaloupe and honeydew into bite-size pieces. Cut strawberries into halves.

Combine fruits in a large mixing bowl. Toss gently with vinegar.

When ready to serve, arrange lettuce on well-chilled plates. Top with desired amount of fruit. Serve immediately.

- 1 large cantaloupe, peeled, seeded
- 1 large honeydew melon, peeled, seeded
- 1 quart fresh strawberries, washed and drained
- ½ pound red seedless grapes, washed and drained
- ⅓ - ½ cup sweet raspberry vinegar
- 1 head of Boston or romaine lettuce, washed, dried and chilled

**Serves: 8 - 10**

4 large nectarines or peaches, sliced

½ pound bing cherries, seeded, halved

2 pints blueberries

¼ cup sugar or more depending on sweetness in fruit

¼ cup Grand Marnier or other orange-flavored liqueur

1 pint raspberries

**Serves:  8**

# FRESH SUMMER FRUIT WITH GRAND MARNIER

Gently toss nectarines, cherries and blueberries in a large bowl.  Sprinkle with sugar.  Add Grand Marnier; stir well.  Serve in pretty glass bowls.  Top with raspberries just before serving.

*A multi-colored delight, and also delicious!*

¼ cup fresh lime juice

¼ cup honey

¼ cup vegetable oil

½ teaspoon celery seed

¼ teaspoon dry mustard

Dash of salt

**Yield:  ¾ cup**

# GOLDEN SALAD DRESSING

Combine all ingredients in a jar with a tight fitting lid.  Cover and shake to blend well.  Chill before serving.

# RASPBERRY VERMOUTH VINAIGRETTE

½ cup dry vermouth

½ cup raspberry vinegar

4 ounces red currant jelly

1 teaspoon dry mustard

1 ½ cups vegetable oil

**Yield: 3 cups**

Whisk together vermouth, vinegar, jelly and dry mustard in a medium bowl until smooth. Slowly add oil, whisking well after each addition. Beat until dressing is smooth.

*A perfect dressing for mixed greens topped with slices of fresh pear, Brie cheese and fresh raspberries.*

# TARRAGON DRESSING

½ cup vegetable oil

¼ cup fresh lemon juice

3 tablespoons white wine tarragon vinegar

2 tablespoons sugar

2 tablespoons minced onion

1 clove garlic, minced

1 teaspoon salt

½ teaspoon dry mustard

Freshly ground black pepper, to taste

**Yield: 1 cup**

Combine all ingredients in a jar with a tight fitting lid. Shake well.

Serve with crisp salad greens, artichoke hearts, sliced radishes, avocado slices and other combinations of fresh vegetables.

1 large orange, peeled,
   quartered

¼ cup cider vinegar

3 tablespoons vegetable oil

1 small clove garlic, minced

2 - 3 sprigs parsley

½ teaspoon fresh basil
   leaves, minced

   Salt and pepper, to taste


**Yield: 1 cup**

# CITRUS SALAD DRESSING

Process orange in food processor until pulp is pureed. Add remaining ingredients; process until well blended. Store in refrigerator. Shake well to serve. Best if made 2 to 3 days in advance.

*Perfect with fresh crisp greens or summer fruits.*

⅓ cup pine nuts

½ cup coarsely chopped
   fresh parsley

¼ cup white wine vinegar

10 fresh basil leaves

1 garlic clove, crushed

1 teaspoon sugar

⅓ cup freshly grated
   Parmesan cheese

1 cup olive oil


**Yield: 2 cups**

# BASIL VINAIGRETTE

Combine pine nuts, parsley, vinegar, basil, garlic, sugar and Parmesan cheese in the blender or food processor. Add oil in a slow stream with the processor running. Continue mixing until all ingredients are well blended.

*Best if made with garden-fresh basil, but dried basil works if you must substitute.*

# Artichokes in Cream with Toasted Pecans

Preheat oven to 300 degrees. Lightly grease a 13 x 9-inch baking dish; set aside. Arrange artichoke hearts in prepared dish.

In a small saucepan melt butter over medium heat. Add flour, cook 1 to 2 minutes, stirring constantly. Slowly add half-and-half. Continue cooking and stirring until mixture begins to thicken. Season with salt, pepper, nutmeg and hot pepper sauce.

Pour sauce over artichoke hearts. Sprinkle with pecans. Top with bread crumbs and Romano cheese. Bake 20 to 30 minutes until bubbly and golden. Serve immediately.

*A very tasty combination.*

2 (14-ounce) cans artichoke hearts, drained

2 tablespoons butter or margarine

2 tablespoons flour

1 cup half-and-half

¼ teaspoon salt

¼ teaspoon freshly ground black pepper

¼ teaspoon freshly ground nutmeg

2 drops hot pepper sauce

½ cup pecan pieces, lightly toasted

½ cup dry bread crumbs

3 tablespoons grated Romano cheese

**Serves: 4 - 6**

1 pound fresh asparagus, peeled, trimmed

¼ teaspoon salt

2 tablespoons butter or margarine

2 tablespoons balsamic vinegar

2 tablespoons crumbled Blue cheese

2 tablespoons walnuts, lightly toasted

*Serves: 4*

# ASPARAGUS WITH BLUE CHEESE AND WALNUTS

Lay asparagus flat in a 10-inch skillet. Add about 1-inch of water and 1/4 teaspoon salt. Cover pan and bring to a boil. Reduce heat to low. Cook until stalks are tender-crisp, about 5 minutes. Drain and place on warm serving dish.

In a small saucepan, melt butter; whisk in vinegar. Pour over asparagus. Top with blue cheese and walnuts. Serve immediately.

*Eye-appealing dish.*

# GREEN BEANS AND FONTINA IN GARLIC SAUCE

1 pound small green beans, washed, trimmed

¼ pound Fontina cheese

1 large clove garlic

½ teaspoon Dijon mustard

¼ cup lemon juice

½ cup olive oil

¼ teaspoon salt

¼ teaspoon pepper

**Serves: 4 - 6**

Cook green beans in lightly salted, boiling water until just tender; about 2 minutes. Refresh under cold running water; drain and blot well on towel to remove all water.

Cut cheese into 1/4 by 2-inch strips. Combine beans and cheese strips in a large serving bowl.

In a food processor, combine garlic, mustard and lemon juice. Process to blend. With processor running, slowly add oil. Pour sauce over beans and cheese. Toss well; add salt and pepper to taste. Serve at room temperature.

*Tangy and flavorful, especially with garden-fresh summer green beans.*

2 tablespoons olive oil

3 green onions, chopped

1 pound green beans, washed, trimmed

2 tablespoons balsamic vinegar

1 tablespoon Dijon mustard

2 tablespoons sesame seeds, lightly toasted

**Serves: 4 - 6**

# CRUNCHY GREEN BEANS

In a large skillet over medium heat combine olive oil and onions. Sauté until onion is golden. Add green beans; sauté until tender-crisp, about 3 to 5 minutes.

In a small bowl whisk together balsamic vinegar and mustard. Add to green beans in skillet; gently toss to coat. Remove from heat and place in serving bowl. Sprinkle with sesame seeds and serve immediately.

*A unique treat.*

# BROCCOLI PARMESAN

1  bunch broccoli, washed

2  tablespoons olive oil

2  cloves garlic, minced

1  red pepper, cut in julienne
   strips

¼  cup freshly grated
   Parmesan cheese

1  lemon, cut in wedges

**Serves:  4**

Break broccoli into florets.  In a covered sauce pan, steam broccoli in a small amount of water until tender-crisp.  Drain well.  Place in a warm serving dish.

In a small skillet over medium-high heat, combine olive oil, garlic and red peppers.  Sauté 2 to 3 minutes or until garlic and peppers are lightly cooked.

Spoon pepper mixture over broccoli; sprinkle with Parmesan cheese.  Serve with lemon wedges.

*In place of lemon wedges, sprinkle small amount of balsamic vinegar over broccoli.*

3 slices bacon

2 tablespoons cider vinegar

2 tablespoons brown sugar

½ cup water

1 teaspoon salt

1 medium head cabbage,
red or white, shredded

2 apples, cored, peeled,
sliced (2 cups)


**Serves: 6**

# GERMAN STYLE SWEET AND SOUR CABBAGE

In a large deep skillet. cook bacon. Remove and set aside. Leave 2 tablespoons of bacon drippings in skillet.

Add vinegar, brown sugar, water and salt to drippings; cook over medium heat. Stir in cabbage and apples and mix well. Cover and cook over low heat, stirring occasionally for 5 to 10 minutes. Serve warm.

*Great for a chilly winter night.*

# BROCCOLI STRUDEL

In a large skillet, sauté onions, broccoli and mushrooms with 1/2 cup butter. Add cheese, salt, pepper, paprika, lemon juice, almonds, eggs and dill weed; cook and stir until blended. Remove from heat.

Preheat oven to 375 degrees.

Working on a large piece of waxed paper, layer 6 sheets of phyllo dough, buttering each one. Keep remaining dough moist as package directions indicate. Place 1/4 of vegetable mixture on half of the phyllo rectangle. Roll as a jelly roll. Repeat with remaining dough and vegetable mixture to make 4 rolls.

Place rolls seam side down on a baking sheet. Brush with melted butter. Using a sharp knife, cut diagonally halfway through layers to make 1 to 2-inch pieces.

Bake 20 to 30 minutes or until puffed and golden brown. Cut in slices to serve.

| | |
|---|---|
| 2 | cups green onions, chopped |
| 3 | heads broccoli, washed, chopped |
| 1 | pound mushrooms, wiped clean, sliced |
| ½ | cup butter, melted |
| 1 | pound shredded Swiss cheese |
| ½ | teaspoon salt |
| ¼ | teaspoon pepper |
| 1 | teaspoon paprika |
| 4 | tablespoons fresh lemon juice |
| 4 | ounces slivered almonds, lightly toasted |
| 6 | eggs, slightly beaten |
| 1 | teaspoon dill weed |
| 24 | sheets phyllo dough, thawed |
| 1 ½ | cups butter, melted |

**Serves: 8 - 12**

A GARDEN'S YIELD

1 pound Brussels sprouts

3 tablespoons olive oil

1 tablespoon Dijon mustard

1 lemon, juiced

Pepper, to taste

¼ cup fresh dill, chopped or
1 tablespoon dried dill
weed

1 teaspoon grated lemon
rind

Salt, to taste

**Serves: 4**

# BRUSSELS SPROUTS WITH DIJON DILL SAUCE

Trim ends of Brussels sprouts; remove outer leaves. Make a cross-wise cut in each stem end. Rinse and drain.

Place enough water in a saucepan to barely cover Brussels sprouts. Bring water to a boil; add salt and Brussels sprouts. Stir, cover and return to boil; reduce heat and simmer about 10 minutes or until tender. Drain well; set aside.

In a small bowl, whisk together olive oil, mustard and lemon juice. Place Brussels sprouts in a serving bowl; toss with dressing mixture. Before serving, sprinkle with fresh dill and grated lemon.

# GINGER GLAZED CARROTS

Cook carrots in lightly salted boiling water to cover until tender-crisp. Drain well.

In a skillet over medium heat, melt butter. Add sugar and brandy; stir to blend. Add cooked carrots; toss to coat. Reduce heat; simmer several minutes. Remove from heat and place in serving dish.

Garnish with crystallized ginger and chopped parsley. Serve warm.

2 cups carrots, peeled, sliced

2 tablespoons butter or margarine

1 - 2 teaspoons sugar

2 tablespoons ginger brandy

Salt, to taste

1 tablespoon chopped crystallized ginger

¼ cup chopped fresh parsley

**Serves: 4**

2 medium heads cauliflower

4 tablespoons butter or margarine

¼ cup golden mustard seed

2 ½ cups plain yogurt

Salt, to taste

Freshly ground pepper, to taste

**Serves: 6 - 8**

# CAULIFLOWER IN TOASTED MUSTARD SEED SAUCE

Break cauliflower into florets. Cook in small amount of salted water until tender-crisp, approximately 4 minutes. Drain and cool under running water. Spread on a paper towel; blot dry. Place in a large bowl to cool.

Melt butter or margarine in a small skillet over medium heat. Add mustard seeds to the butter. Immediately cover the skillet. Cook until seeds start to pop. Remove from heat promptly and let stand, covered until popping stops, approximately 5 minutes.

Add toasted mustard seeds to cauliflower. Toss to coat. Stir in yogurt, salt and pepper. Cover and chill thoroughly at least several hours or overnight.

# STIR FRY CAULIFLOWER WITH THYME

1 small head cauliflower

4 tablespoons vegetable oil

1 teaspoon whole yellow
    mustard seeds

¼ teaspoon thyme

½ teaspoon salt

4 tablespoons water

Fresh ground pepper,
to taste

**Serves: 4**

Break cauliflower into bite-size florets.

Heat oil in a large wok or skillet over medium-high heat. When heated, add mustard seeds; stir until they begin to pop. Stir in thyme.

Add cauliflower; stir and cook about 2 to 3 minutes. Sprinkle in salt and water. Cover; cook 2 to 4 minutes or until cauliflower is tender-crisp.

Remove cover and cook to reduce liquid. Sprinkle with pepper and serve.

*Healthy, simple and refreshingly light.*

*Spread:*

- ½ cup butter or margarine, softened
- ½ teaspoon lime rind, grated
- 3 tablespoons fresh lime juice
- 1 - 2 teaspoons ground red pepper

- 6 fresh ears of corn, cleaned
- 1 teaspoon sugar
- 2 tablespoons half-and-half

**Serves: 6**

# FRESH CORN WITH LIME BUTTER SPREAD

To make spread, blend butter, lime rind and juice and pepper. Stir well; set aside.

Boil water in a pan large enough to hold corn. Add corn, sugar and half-and-half when water begins to boil. Cook 3 to 6 minutes after returning to boil. Remove corn; brush with lime butter spread; serve immediately.

*A fresh accent for succulent, sweet summer corn.*

# HERBED CORN CAKES

Sift flour, baking powder, and salt into a medium bowl.

Whisk milk, egg and oil in another bowl to blend. Add liquid ingredients to dry ingredients; mix with fork just until blended.

Add corn, cheese, shallots, parsley, hot pepper sauce, red and black pepper; stir to blend. Let stand 30 minutes.

Fry bacon in a large skillet until crisp. Drain and chop. Pour off and reserve all but a thin coating of bacon drippings.

Heat skillet over medium-high heat. Stir bacon into batter. Pour scant 1/4-cup portions of batter into lightly greased hot skillet. Fry until golden brown on both sides. Top with chopped chives; serve immediately.

1   cup all-purpose flour

1   teaspoon baking powder

½   teaspoon salt

⅔   cup milk

1   egg

1   tablespoon vegetable oil

1   cup fresh corn kernels (may use thawed frozen corn)

½   cup shredded Monterey Jack cheese

¼   cup shallots, minced

2   tablespoons chopped fresh parsley

2 - 3   dashes hot red pepper sauce

¼   teaspoon ground red pepper

¼   teaspoon ground black pepper

5   slices of bacon

Chopped fresh chives

**Serves: 4 - 6**

1 bulb of elephant garlic per person

1 - 2 tablespoons olive oil

¼ teaspoon salt

1 - 2 tablespoons butter

1 loaf French bread or dark rye slices, toasted

Pepper, freshly ground

**Serves: 1**

# ROASTED ELEPHANT GARLIC

Preheat oven to 300 degrees.

Peel outer skin from each garlic bulb, leaving cloves intact. Put garlic heads, base down, in a baking dish. Drizzle with olive oil and sprinkle with salt.

Bake 30 to 35 minutes. Remove from oven; add enough water to just cover the bottom of the baking dish. Cover with a lid or aluminum foil and bake for another 45 to 60 minutes or until garlic cloves are soft.

To serve, place garlic cloves and hot buttered toast on serving plate. Squeeze each garlic clove to make the inside pop out. Spread on toast; add freshly ground pepper.

*Puree baked garlic cloves through a sieve; add just enough oil to form a smooth paste. This can be stored up to 2 weeks in refrigerator.*

# Ginger Garlic Sugar Snap Peas

1 pound sugar snap peas

2 tablespoons vegetable oil

1 tablespoon sesame oil

1 tablespoon finely minced ginger

2 cloves garlic, minced

1 medium red bell pepper, julienned

¼ teaspoon salt

¼ teaspoon black pepper

**Serves: 4**

String peas by beginning at the tip of the pea and pulling down; omit this if peas are young. Cut stem ends and leave beans whole. Wash in colander; shake and drain well.

In a large skillet, heat oils. Add ginger and garlic; sauté and stir about 1 minute. Add peas and gently toss over medium heat for 2 to 4 minutes. Be sure to keep peas tender-crisp; do not over cook.

Stir in red pepper and seasonings. Cook until tender-crisp. Remove from heat and serve immediately.

*Since sugar snap peas are seasonal, snow peas may be substituted.*

2 red bell peppers

1 green bell pepper

1 yellow bell pepper

1 tablespoon balsamic
vinegar

Ground black pepper,
to taste

3 tablespoons extra virgin
olive oil

1 clove garlic, minced

**Serves: 6**

# ROASTED SWEET PEPPERS

Char peppers under hot broiler until blackened on all sides.
Transfer to paper bag; roll top of bag and let stand 10 minutes
to steam. Peel, seed and remove inside ribs; reserve any
juices.

Rinse peppers and pat dry. Cut into 1-inch strips. Arrange on
serving dish alternating colors.

Combine vinegar and ground pepper in a small bowl. Slowly
add oil, whisking constantly. Add garlic. Pour dressing over
peppers turning to coat. Serve at room temperature as a
salad.

½ cup soft bread crumbs

¼ cup grated Romano
cheese

2 tablespoons butter

¾ cup chopped peppers
(green, yellow, red)

½ cup green onions,
chopped

2 cups zucchini, sliced

2 cups tomatoes, peeled and
quartered

¼ teaspoon salt

¼ teaspoon pepper

**Serves: 6 - 8**

# PEPPERS AND ZUCCHINI

Preheat oven to 400 degrees. Combine cheese and bread
crumbs in a small bowl. Set aside.

Melt butter in medium oven-proof skillet. Sauté peppers with
onions 2 to 3 minutes. Add zucchini and tomatoes; sauté 2 to
3 minutes longer.

Sprinkle cheese and bread crumbs over vegetables. Place in
oven and cook until crumb topping is golden and mixture is
bubbly.

*Simple, very pretty, colorful and highly nutritious.*

# BAY LEAF ROASTED NEW POTATOES

Preheat oven to 375 degrees. Butter a 13 x 9-inch baking dish. Set aside.

Quarter new potatoes; place in prepared baking dish.

In a small bowl combine lemon juice, oregano, basil, lemon rind, salt and pepper. Gradually whisk in oil. Pour oil mixture over potatoes and toss to coat. Add bay leaves.

Place baking dish in center of oven. Cook potatoes turning several times, until golden brown and tender. Should bake approximately 40 to 50 minutes.

Remove and discard bay leaves; serve immediately or at room temperature.

*These potatoes have a delightfully sweet light flavor.*

2 pounds red new potatoes, washed

¼ cup fresh lemon juice

1 ½ teaspoons oregano

½ teaspoon dried sweet basil, crushed

1 teaspoon grated lemon rind

½ teaspoon salt

¼ teaspoon pepper

½ cup olive oil

10 small dried bay leaves

**Serves: 6 - 8**

4 medium baking potatoes

1 tablespoon olive oil

3 medium tomatoes, sliced

1 small onion, thinly sliced

¼ cup grated Parmesan cheese, divided

1 cup shredded Provolone cheese, divided

½ cup shredded mozzarella cheese, divided

½ teaspoon oregano

1 teaspoon salt

¼ cup butter or margarine

**Serves: 6**

# POTATOES ITALIAN

Preheat oven to 375 degrees. Lightly oil a 9 x 9-inch baking pan. Set aside.

Peel and slice potatoes 1/4-inch thick. Place in prepared baking dish.

Layer vegetables, sprinkling each layer with cheeses and seasonings and ending with a layer of cheese and seasonings.

Dot with butter or margarine. Bake about 50 minutes or potatoes are tender and top is brown and toasty.

*A new baked potato dish that's bound to be a sure-fire hit.*

# HOLIDAY MASHED POTATOES

Combine potatoes and salted water to cover in a large saucepan. Cover; cook until tender. Drain potatoes in a large colander. Place in large mixing bowl.

Mash or beat until smooth. Add cream cheese and butter or margarine. Beat until smooth. Stir in sour cream.

In a small bowl blend milk, eggs, onions and seasonings. Add to potato mixture; whip until mixture is light and fluffy.

Pour into a buttered 9-inch round baking dish; cover and refrigerate several hours or overnight. Can also be frozen, if desired.

When ready to bake, preheat oven to 350 degrees. Bake 45 to 50 minutes or until puffed and golden brown.

*Any left overs are super for potato pancakes.*

12   medium potatoes, peeled, quartered

1   (8-ounce) package cream cheese, cubed

¼   cup butter or margarine

½   cup sour cream

½   cup milk

2   eggs, slightly beaten

4   green onions, finely chopped

1   teaspoon salt

¼   teaspoon pepper

¼   teaspoon nutmeg

**Serves: 8 - 12**

2 pounds sweet potatoes, baked, cooled and peeled

1 teaspoon grated orange rind

2 cups whole fresh cranberries or whole berry cranberry sauce

1/4 cup flour

1/4 cup brown sugar

1/2 cup oats

1 teaspoon ground cinnamon

1/3 cup butter or margarine

**Serves: 8**

# CRANBERRY SWEET POTATOES

Preheat oven to 350 degrees. Lightly butter a 1 1/2-quart baking dish. Set aside.

Mash sweet potatoes in a large bowl. Add orange peel; stir to mix well. Stir in cranberries or cranberry sauce. Set aside.

In a bowl blend flour, brown sugar, oats, cinnamon and butter or margarine; mix until crumbly.

Add 3/4 to 1 cup crumb mixture to sweet potatoes. Spoon mixture into prepared dish. Top with remaining crumb mixture. Bake for 35 minutes until heated through.

*A real holiday favorite considered a classic for winter holiday dinners.*

# Sweet Potato Soufflé with Praline Topping

Preheat oven to 350 degrees. Butter a 2-quart baking dish. Set aside.

In a large saucepan, boil potatoes in water to cover until tender. Drain and cool slightly; peel and quarter potatoes.

In a large bowl, combine sweet potatoes, butter, sugars, salt, vanilla, cinnamon, eggs and milk. Beat to combine. Pour into prepared baking dish.

To make topping, combine brown sugar, pecans, flour and butter or margarine in a small bowl. Mix until crumbly. Sprinkle mixture over potato mixture. Bake for 35 to 40 minutes or until golden brown and slightly firm.

*A family favorite especially during winter holiday season.*

2   pounds sweet potatoes, scrubbed

¼   cup butter or margarine, melted

¾   cup granulated sugar

¾   cup brown sugar

½   teaspoon salt

1   teaspoon vanilla

1   teaspoon ground cinnamon

3   eggs

½   cup milk

Topping:

½   cup brown sugar

½   cup pecans, chopped

⅓   cup all-purpose flour

⅓   cup butter or margarine, melted

**Serves:  6**

3 tablespoons butter, divided

¼ cup pine nuts

1 pound fresh spinach,
washed, stemmed,
thoroughly dried

½ pound fresh mushrooms,
wiped clean, sliced

1 clove garlic, minced

½ teaspoon salt

¼ teaspoon pepper

**Serves: 4**

# SPINACH AND MUSHROOM SAUTÉ

In a large skillet over medium heat, melt 2 tablespoons butter. Add pine nuts and sauté until golden. Remove nuts from skillet. Set aside.

Add remaining 1 tablespoon of butter to skillet and melt. Adjust heat to medium-high. Add spinach and mushrooms; sauté until liquid evaporates, stirring frequently.

Add garlic, salt and pepper; stir constantly.

Remove from heat, add pine nuts and serve immediately.

*Green and glorious describes this best.*

# Herbed Cherry Tomatoes

Preheat oven to 425 degrees. Butter a 2-quart baking dish. Place tomatoes in prepared dish.

In a small skillet over medium-high heat, sauté oil, onion and garlic 1 to 2 minutes or until cooked.

Stir in bread crumbs; sauté 1 to 2 minutes longer. Remove from heat. Add parsley, thyme, salt and pepper; stir to combine. Spoon over tomatoes. Bake for 6 to 8 minutes or until tomatoes are hot.

*Nice presentation and great for a garnish.*

1 ½ pints cherry tomatoes, washed and drained

2 tablespoons olive oil

1 medium onion, minced

1 - 2 cloves garlic, minced

½ cup soft bread crumbs

¼ cup fresh parsley, chopped

½ teaspoon thyme

¼ teaspoon salt

⅛ teaspoon pepper

**Serves: 6**

# GLORIOUS BAKED SUMMER VEGETABLES

4 tablespoons (½ stick) butter or margarine, divided

1 pound carrots, sliced in ¼-inch rounds

1 pound zucchini, sliced in ¼-inch rounds

1 pound yellow squash, sliced in ¼-inch rounds

2 medium sized onions, thinly sliced

1 pound mushrooms, quartered

½ teaspoon salt

1 cup fresh parsley, lightly chopped

1 ½ cups shredded Swiss cheese, divided

½ cup grated Parmesan cheese, divided

12 cherry tomatoes, halved

Preheat oven to 350 degrees. Lightly butter a 3-quart baking dish.

In a large skillet over medium heat, melt 2 tablespoons butter or margarine. Add carrots; sauté 4 to 5 minutes or until tender crisp. Remove from heat; place carrots in a bowl.

Add a small amount of butter or margarine into same skillet over medium heat. Sauté zucchini and yellow squash 2 minutes until tender crisp. Remove from heat; spoon squash into separate bowl.

Melt remaining butter or margarine in skillet. Sauté onions and mushrooms 3 to 4 minutes. Remove from heat.

In prepared baking dish arrange a layer of carrots; sprinkle with salt and parsley. Top with about 1/2 cup Swiss and 3 tablespoons Parmesan cheese.

Repeat procedure next with zucchini and yellow squash, then mushroom and onion mixture.

Arrange cherry tomatoes on top; sprinkle with remaining Parmesan cheese. Bake for 30 minutes or until vegetables are cooked and lightly browned.

*Can be prepared ahead.*

# Oven Roasted
# Winter Vegetables

Preheat oven to 400 degrees. Lightly coat a 13 x 9-inch baking dish with olive oil.

Clean potatoes well by scrubbing. Steam in small amount of water for about 20 minutes until tender. Drain well.

Cut leeks in half; wash several times to remove grit.

Cut each potato into 2 or 3 large slices. Arrange around ends of prepared baking dish. Set leeks next to potatoes; then arrange carrots, onions, red peppers and mushrooms over and around the leeks and potatoes.

Drizzle vegetables with olive oil; sprinkle with thyme, salt and pepper.

Roast 1 to 1 1/2 hours or until vegetables are cooked and tender when pierced with a fork. Baste about every 15 minutes with pan juices.

Serve hot or at room temperature.

*This gloriously colored vegetable dish is a perfect accompaniment for roast chicken or turkey. For smaller quantities simply cut down on the amounts of each vegetable.*

6 small red potatoes

4 small leeks

4 large carrots, peeled, cut in large pieces

2 medium red onions, peeled, quartered

2 sweet red peppers, cored, seeded, cut in wide strips

½ pound shiitake mushrooms, wiped clean, stems removed

1 - 2 tablespoons olive oil

½ teaspoon thyme

¼ teaspoon salt

¼ teaspoon freshly ground black pepper

**Serves: 6 - 8**

# THE BUTCHER SHOP

*Beef*

*Veal*

*Lamb*

*Pork*

*Poultry and Game*

*Marinades and Chutney*

◀ Herbed Pork Roast with Vegetable Sauce, 235; Lime and Sesame Roasted Cornish Hens, 254; Welcome Autumn Wild Rice Pilaf, 131

# THE BUTCHER SHOP

# Tenderloin of Beef with Peppercorns

Preheat oven to 425 degrees. Cut down entire length of tenderloin going only two-thirds deep. Spread meat open and press with hands to flatten. Spread mustard and scatter green peppercorns evenly over open meat pressing into meat lightly. Sprinkle one tablespoon of ground peppercorn blend evenly over open meat.

Place sage leaves in a row down center. Press beef back to original shape and tie with string. Rub outside of tenderloin with butter. Press remaining peppercorn blend onto outside surface. Salt to taste. Place seam side down in shallow roasting pan.

Slip bay leaves underneath strings on top of beef tenderloin. Roast 45 to 55 minutes for rare. Let stand 10 minutes before carving. Serve with pan juice, if desired.

1   (3 - 4-pound) beef tenderloin

3   tablespoons Dijon mustard

1 ½  tablespoons green peppercorns

3   tablespoons peppercorn blend, coarsely ground

8   fresh whole sage leaves

2   tablespoons unsalted butter, softened

4   bay leaves

Salt, optional

**Serves:  6 - 8**

1　(2 - 3-pound) beef
　　tenderloin, trimmed

4　tablespoons butter or
　　margarine, softened

¼　cup finely chopped green
　　onion

2　tablespoons soy sauce

1　teaspoon Dijon mustard

¾　cup dry sherry

　　Freshly ground black
　　pepper, to taste


**Serves: 6**

# SHERRIED BEEF
# TENDERLOIN

Preheat oven to 400 degrees. Place tenderloin on rack in shallow roasting pan, folding tail under. Rub with 2 tablespoons softened butter. Insert meat thermometer in thickest part. Roast, uncovered, in 400 degree oven for 20 minutes.

Sauté onion in remaining 2 tablespoons butter until soft. Stir in soy sauce, mustard, sherry and generous amount of pepper. Bring to a boil, then reduce to a simmer.

Baste beef with prepared sauce after meat has roasted 20 minutes. Repeat basting every 10 minutes and roast until thermometer registers 130 to 140 degrees. Remove meat; cover and let set for 10 minutes before carving.

Pour pan drippings into remaining sauce and boil over high heat to desired consistency. Spoon over carved meat before serving.

*You may whisk additional butter into sauce before serving.*

# Medallions of Beef with Fennel Sauce

4  (6-ounce) filet mignon
   steaks

4  tablespoons flour

4  tablespoons unsalted
   butter or margarine

½  cup Marsala or dry sherry

½  cup dry red wine

½  cup beef stock

1  teaspoon fennel seeds

1  tablespoon tomato paste

   Salt, to taste

   Pepper, to taste

**Serves: 4**

Preheat oven to 200 degrees. Arrange steaks on waxed paper or large plate. Dust lightly with flour. Heat butter in large skillet over medium-high heat. Add meat; cook 4 minutes on each side or until browned. Remove meat to heat proof platter and place in preheated oven to keep warm.

Add Marsala to skillet; stir continuously to deglaze pan over high heat until liquid is reduced by half. Add red wine, stock, fennel and tomato paste. Simmer until reduced by half. Season to taste.

Return meat to skillet and cook in sauce 3 minutes over medium-high heat. Place filets on warm serving plates; spoon sauce over each filet.

½ cup coarsely cracked pepper

½ teaspoon ground cardamom

1 (5 - 6-pound) boneless well-trimmed rib eye beef roast

1 tablespoon tomato paste

1 clove garlic, crushed

1 teaspoon paprika

1 cup soy sauce

¾ cup vinegar

1 ¼ cups water, divided

1 ½ tablespoons cornstarch

**Serves: 10 - 12**

# ROAST PEPPERED RIB EYE OF BEEF

Combine pepper and cardamom; rub over entire surface of roast and press in with heel of hand. Place in shallow baking dish.

Combine tomato paste, crushed garlic and paprika; gradually stir in soy sauce and vinegar. Pour marinade mixture over roast in a zip-closure bag. Refrigerate several hours or overnight. Turn bag over several times to coat meat for even marinating.

Remove roast from bag and marinade; let stand at room temperature 1 hour. Wrap in foil and place in shallow pan. Roast at 300 degrees for 2 hours for medium-rare. Open foil; ladle drippings into a bowl; set aside and reserve. Place roast uncovered in 350 degree oven while making gravy.

Strain reserved drippings; skim off excess fat. In medium saucepan, add 1 cup water to 1 cup drippings. Heat to a boil. Combine cornstarch with remaining 1/4 cup water; stir to dissolve well. Whisk into hot dripping mixture. Slice roast and serve with au jus on the side.

# Summer Beef and Chicken Kabobs

In large glass baking dish or zip-closure bag, combine all marinade ingredients. Add beef and chicken to marinade; turn to coat evenly. Cover and marinate up to 24 hours in refrigerator, turning occasionally.

Add prepared vegetables to meat during the last three hours of marinating. Assemble skewers, alternating meat with squash, zucchini, onions, peppers and mushrooms.

Grill over hot coals for 3 minutes or longer per side, depending on degree of doneness desired. Turn and baste often with the marinade. Serve immediately.

*Great for a summertime barbecue or served on a bed of rice pilaf.*

Marinade:

- 2 large cloves garlic, crushed
- 1 cup vegetable oil
- ¼ cup soy sauce
- ¼ cup Worcestershire sauce
- ¼ cup Dijon mustard
- ¼ cup fresh lemon juice
- 1 - 2 teaspoons coarsely ground black pepper

- 1 (1-pound) boneless chicken breast, skinned, cut in 1 ½-inch cubes
- 1 (2-pound) sirloin tip roast of beef, cut in 1 ½-inch cubes
- 1 yellow squash, sliced in ½-inch rounds
- 1 zucchini, sliced in ½-inch rounds
- 2 Bermuda onions, cut in chunks
- 1 green bell pepper, cut in 1 ½-inch pieces
- 1 red bell pepper, cut in 1 ½-inch pieces
- 1 yellow bell pepper, cut in 1 ½-inch pieces
- 1 pound mushrooms, stems removed

**Serves: 8 - 10**

3 tablespoons all-purpose flour

1 ¼ teaspoons salt

½ teaspoon ground allspice

½ teaspoon ground cinnamon

½ teaspoon pepper

2 pounds beef stew meat, cut in 1-inch cubes

4 - 5 tablespoons vegetable oil

2 large onions, halved, sliced

1 cup pitted dried cherries, quartered

2 tablespoons sugar

2 tablespoons red wine vinegar

2 tablespoons water

1 cup dry red wine

1 cup beef broth

½ pound mushrooms, sliced

**Serves: 6**

# BEEF STEW WITH DRIED CHERRIES

Combine flour, salt, allspice, cinnamon and pepper in large zip-closure bag. Add beef to bag and toss to coat meat pieces evenly with seasoned flour.

Heat 2 tablespoons oil in heavy large skillet. Add half of beef cubes and brown over medium-high heat about 5 minutes. Add more oil and repeat with remaining beef cubes. Remove meat from skillet and transfer to Dutch oven.

Add remaining oil to skillet if needed. Sauté onions and dried cherries about 10 to 12 minutes, stirring frequently. Mix in sugar, vinegar and water. Cook until onions are brown, stirring frequently for about 8 minutes.

Add onion mixture to Dutch oven. Add wine, broth and mushrooms; stir to blend. Cover tightly and bake in 350 degree oven for 2 hours or until tender. If stew appears too thin, uncover during last 30 minutes to allow sauce to evaporate and thicken.

*A tasty version of an American favorite.*

# JALAPEÑO AND BEER-BAKED BEEF

Preheat oven to 425 degrees.

Arrange short ribs in a single layer in 2 large baking pans or place beef brisket in one large pan. Sprinkle onions around ribs or brisket.

Combine all remaining ingredients except beer and cilantro in large saucepan. Simmer over medium heat until slightly thickened, stirring occasionally, about 10 minutes. Cool slightly. Stir in beer. Pour mixture over beef. Cover pans with foil and bake until meat is very tender, 2 1/2 hours.

Remove ribs or brisket from pan; set aside and keep warm.

Combine all pan juices in heavy medium saucepan. Skim fat from pan juices. Boil over medium heat until liquid is reduced to 2 cups. Spoon sauce over beef. Can be prepared 1 day ahead. Return beef and sauce to pans. Cover and refrigerate.

Remove any hardened fat from surface. Cover pans with foil. Bake in 375 degree oven until meat is heated through, about 45 minutes. Garnish with cilantro.

*A great Southwestern main dish perfect for an after-the-game crowd.*

8  pounds beef short ribs, cut into 3-inch pieces, or 5 - 8-pound beef brisket

2  large onions, coarsely chopped

2  (8-ounce) cans tomato sauce

4  large jalapeño chilies, finely chopped (1/4 cup)

1/4  cup red wine vinegar

1/4  cup brown sugar, packed

2  tablespoons chopped green bell pepper

1  tablespoon dry mustard

4  large garlic cloves, minced

1/2  teaspoon cayenne pepper

1/4  teaspoon cloves

1/4  teaspoon cinnamon

2  cups beer

   Fresh cilantro, chopped

**Serves: 6 - 8**

1   (1 ½ - 2-pound) beef flank
    steak

½   cup vegetable oil

2   tablespoons white wine
    vinegar

3   tablespoons dry vermouth

2   tablespoons whole-grain
    mustard

2   tablespoons minced fresh
    rosemary, or 1 tablespoon
    dried

½   teaspoon ground white
    pepper

½ - 1   teaspoon Dijon mustard

    Fresh rosemary

    Fresh thyme

**Serves: 6**

# GOLDEN GRILLED FLANK STEAK

Place steak in zip-closure bag. In small bowl, combine all marinade ingredients and whisk to emulsify. Pour marinade over steaks, turn to coat sides well. Cover and refrigerate overnight, turning occasionally.

Remove steak from marinade; reserve marinade.. Place steaks on hot grill 4 to 6 inches above hot coals. Cook for 5 to 7 minutes per side or until cooked to desired doneness, basting meat occasionally with marinade.

Slice thinly on the diagonal and garnish with sprigs of rosemary and thyme. Heat remaining marinade to boil; serve with sliced steak.

*This marvelous blend of flavors also complement chicken breasts.*

# BRAISED BEEF WITH BLACK BEANS, SAUSAGE AND TOMATOES

Toss beef cubes with flour in large zip-closure bag. Coat thoroughly.

In a 12-inch skillet, heat the butter and oil. Sauté half of beef cubes until brown. Remove with slotted spoon. Repeat with remaining beef.

Combine 1/2 cup beans, onions, scallions, carrots, pepper, sausage, 2 cups chopped tomatoes, tomato juice, brown sugar, cinnamon, cloves, salt and pepper in a large heavy saucepan or Dutch oven.

Return all the beef to the skillet, add the garlic, vinegar and coffee; allow the mixture to simmer until reduced by half.

Add beef to the vegetable mixture. Bring beef and vegetable mixture to a boil. Reduce heat and simmer uncovered for one hour, stirring frequently until reduced and thickened.

Add remaining drained black beans and the remaining two cups tomatoes. Simmer for 10 minutes.

Ladle into soup bowls or in hollowed out brioches as a main dish.

2 pounds chuck roast, cut in ½-inch cubes

¼ cup all-purpose flour

1 tablespoon butter

1 tablespoon vegetable oil

3 (15-ounce) cans black beans, drained, rinsed, divided

1 cup finely chopped onions

8 scallions, chopped

½ cup finely chopped carrots

2 jalapeño peppers, seeded, finely chopped

4 ounces sausage, such as Kielbasa, chopped

4 cups peeled, seeded, finely chopped tomatoes, divided

4 cups tomato juice

1 tablespoon dark brown sugar

½ teaspoon cinnamon

¼ teaspoon ground cloves

½ teaspoon salt

1 teaspoon freshly ground pepper

2 tablespoons minced garlic

1 tablespoon red wine vinegar

¾ cup brewed coffee

6 - 8 fresh brioches (optional)

**Serves: 8**

1 ½   pounds ground round

1   medium onion, chopped

2   tablespoons vinegar

2   tablespoons brown sugar

½   cup catsup

½   cup chili sauce

2 - 3   tablespoons
       Worcestershire sauce

½   tablespoon dry mustard

½   cup water, if desired

     Salt and pepper, to taste

**Serves: 6**

# BARBECUED HAMBURGERS

Brown ground round in large, heavy skillet. Drain fat. Add onion and cook about 5 minutes.

Add remaining ingredients. Simmer about 15 minutes or until heated completely.

2   pounds lean ground beef

4   tablespoons crumbled blue
    cheese

2   cups red wine
    (Cabernet Sauvignon)

     Butter

**Serves: 4**

# BLUE CHEESE
# STUFFED BURGERS

Divide beef into eight portions. Shape into flat patties. Sprinkle blue cheese over four patties; gently top with remaining beef. Press edges together to seal.

Arrange stuffed burgers in large shallow baking dish. Pour wine over burgers; cover and refrigerate to marinate 4 to 6 hours.

Grill or sauté in butter.

# DILLY CHEESEBURGERS

Preheat grill to medium heat.

Combine ground chuck, zucchini, mushrooms, 1/2 teaspoon dill, salt and pepper; mix well. Divide into four portions and form into patties 1/2-inch thick.

Combine yogurt, mayonnaise and 1/4 teaspoon dill; set aside.

Grill burgers for 10 to 12 minutes turning once. Place cheese slices on burgers to barely melt at end of grilling time.

Place burgers on bun. Top with 1 tablespoon yogurt sauce, tomato slice and lettuce to serve.

1   pound ground chuck

½   cup shredded zucchini

½   cup finely chopped mushrooms

¾   teaspoon dill weed, divided

½   teaspoon salt

⅛   teaspoon pepper

2   tablespoons plain yogurt

2   tablespoons mayonnaise

4   slices cheddar cheese

4   whole wheat sandwich buns

4   lettuce leaves

4   tomato slices

**Serves: 4**

2 pounds veal stew meat, cut in 1-inch cubes

5 tablespoons all-purpose flour

¾ teaspoon freshly grated nutmeg

1 teaspoon salt

¼ teaspoon pepper

5 tablespoons unsalted butter

1 onion, finely chopped

2 cups carrots, diagonally sliced

1 tablespoon chopped fresh dill

2 - 3 cups chicken stock

½ cup heavy cream, room temperature

**Serves: 4 - 6**

# DILLED VEAL STEW

Preheat oven to 350 degrees.

Mix flour, nutmeg, salt, and pepper in a plastic bag. Shake to mix. Add half of veal cubes to flour mixture in bag; shake to coat. Repeat with remaining veal.

Melt butter in large, heavy skillet over medium to high heat.

Brown coated veal cubes in butter in small batches removing veal as it browns lightly. After removing veal, add chopped onion and small amount of additional butter if needed. Adjust temperature and slowly sauté onion about 3 to 5 minutes.

Return veal to skillet with onion. Add carrots, dill and chicken stock to almost cover meat. Bring to a simmer. Cover and place in 350 degree oven for 1 1/2 hours.

Remove from oven. Add cream to veal mixture. Stir to mix well. Serve immediately.

# Veal Medallions with Lime Cream Sauce

Wipe veal scallops with a dry paper towel. Combine flour, salt and pepper. Dust both sides of veal scallops with flour. Set aside.

Sauté veal scallops in butter and oil in a large skillet 4 to 5 minutes on each side or until lightly browned. Transfer veal to a serving platter; set aside and keep warm.

Add wine, lime rind and juice to skillet; stir well. Bring to a boil and reduce mixture to a consistency of a thick syrup.

Stir in heavy cream and peppercorns; heat to a boil. Spoon sauce over veal scallops. Garnish with lime wedges to serve.

12  veal scallops

2  tablespoons all-purpose flour

Salt, to taste

Pepper, to taste

1  tablespoon butter

1  tablespoon olive oil

1 ½  cups dry white wine

1  teaspoon grated lime rind

1  tablespoon fresh lime juice

¼  cup whipping cream

12  whole green peppercorns

Fresh lime wedges or slices

**Serves: 4 - 6**

6  veal chops, (1 ½-inch
   thick)

2  tablespoons butter or
   margarine

1  medium onion, finely
   chopped

2  garlic cloves, minced

4  ounces ham, chopped

2  tablespoons all-purpose
   flour

½  cup milk

1  (10-ounce) package
   chopped frozen spinach,
   thawed, drained

1  ounce Pernod

⅛  teaspoon nutmeg

   Freshly ground pepper


**Serves:  6**

# Spinach Stuffed Veal Chops with Bordelaise Sauce

Cut a pocket in each veal chop.  Arrange on broiler rack.  Set aside.

Sauté onion, garlic and ham in butter in large, heavy skillet until onion is transparent.  Add flour and stir to cook over medium heat.  Add milk, stirring over medium heat until mixture becomes smooth and creamy.

Add spinach, Pernod, dash of nutmeg and pepper.  Simmer 3 to 4 minutes longer.  Cool.

Stuff prepared veal chops with spinach mixture; close with toothpicks.  Broil or grill as desired.

Serve with Bordelaise Sauce.

*Recipe continued on next page*

## Bordelaise Sauce

Melt butter in a heavy 1-quart saucepan over low heat. Add onion; cook until tender. Stir in flour; cook until lightly browned. Add parsley, thyme and pepper. Gradually stir in beef broth, red wine and water. Increase heat to medium-high; stirring constantly until sauce boils and thickens. Spoon over veal chops to serve.

- 3 tablespoons butter
- 1 tablespoon onion
- 3 tablespoons all-purpose flour
- 1 tablespoon chopped parsley
- 1/4 teaspoon thyme
- 1/8 teaspoon freshly ground black pepper
- 1 (10-1/2-ounce) can condensed beef broth
- 1/2 cup red wine
- 1/4 cup water

4  veal loin chops,
   (1-inch thick)

3  tablespoons fresh lime
   juice

1  lime, rind grated

2  tablespoons honey

2  tablespoons vegetable oil

   Fresh papaya slices

   Fresh lime wedges


**Serves:  4**

# GRILLED TROPICAL
# VEAL CHOPS

Place veal chops in a single layer in a shallow baking dish.

In a bowl, combine lime juice, grated rind, honey and vegetable oil.  Blend thoroughly.  Pour over veal chops, turning to coat both sides.  Let stand at room temperature 30 minutes or cover and refrigerate to marinate longer.

When ready to cook, heat grill to medium.  Place veal over hot coals.  Cook 12 to 14 minutes, turning once to cook to desired doneness.

Serve garnished with papaya and lime slices.

# ROAST LEG OF LAMB WITH MUSTARD COATING

Preheat oven to 350 degrees.

Place lamb on roasting rack in large shallow roasting pan.

Place the chopped garlic in a small bowl; add salt and mash to a paste. Whisk in the mustard, soy sauce, thyme, lemon juice and then the oil to make a mayonnaise-like cream mixture.

Spread mustard coating evenly over lamb. Roast in 350 degree oven about 2 hours, or until a meat thermometer registers 145 degrees for medium-rare, 165 degrees for well done. Let the roast stand for 5 to 10 minutes before carving.

1 (3 - 5-pound) leg of lamb, trimmed

2 large garlic cloves, chopped

½ teaspoon salt

2 tablespoons Dijon mustard

1 tablespoon soy sauce

1 ½ teaspoons thyme

2 tablespoons fresh lemon juice

¼ cup olive oil

**Serves: 4 - 6**

1 (5 - 7-pound) leg of lamb, boned and pocketed

½ teaspoon dried thyme

Stuffing:

1 egg

¼ cup milk

1 - 2 cloves garlic, crushed

¼ teaspoon salt

¼ teaspoon pepper

½ pound ground ham

½ cup fresh chopped parsley

¼ cup pine nuts, finely chopped (may substitute almonds)

¼ cup soft rye bread crumbs

**Serves: 8**

# LEG OF LAMB WITH PARSLEY HAM STUFFING

Preheat oven to 325 degrees.

Rub lamb with thyme, inside and out.

Combine egg, milk, garlic, salt and pepper. Add ham, parsley, nuts and bread crumbs. Mix well.

Fill cavity of lamb with stuffing. Tie to reshape and hold stuffing inside. Place the lamb in a shallow roasting pan. Roast at 325 degrees for about 2 hours, or until a meat thermometer registers 145 for medium-rare or 165 for well-done. Let the roast stand 5 to 10 minutes before carving.

*Simple, elegant and easy... with a fabulous flavor.*

# Lamb Chops with Fresh Herbs

4 loin lamb chops (¾-inch thick), trimmed

½ tablespoon fresh chopped oregano

½ tablespoon fresh chopped thyme

½ tablespoon fresh chopped rosemary

1 garlic clove, crushed

Pepper, to taste

**Serves: 2**

Place lamb chops in a shallow baking dish or on a large plate.

Finely mince oregano, thyme, rosemary and garlic together; add desired amount of pepper. Press mixture firmly onto lamb chops. Let stand at room temperature about 30 to 40 minutes.

Preheat broiler. Arrange chops on broiler pan. Place 4 to 6 inches from heat. Broil 5 to 10 minutes or to desired degree of doneness.

12  loin lamb chops,
    (1-inch thick)

    Salt, to taste

    Pepper, to taste

1   cup plain yogurt

1   tablespoon coriander
    seeds, crushed

2   teaspoons ground cumin

1   red onion, finely chopped

2   cloves garlic, chopped

    Rind of 1 lime, grated

    Juice of 1 lime

1   slice ginger root, peeled,
    chopped

¼   teaspoon hot pepper
    sauce

    Freshly ground pepper


**Serves:  6**

# INDIAN LAMB CHOPS IN YOGURT MARINADE

Arrange lamb chops in shallow baking dish; season with salt and pepper.

Combine yogurt, coriander, cumin, red onion, garlic, lime rind and juice, ginger root and hot pepper sauce.  Pour over lamb.  Cover and marinate overnight in refrigerator.

When ready to cook preheat broiler or grill.  Arrange lamb chops on broiler rack or hot grill rack.  Broil or grill about five minutes on each side or to desired degree of doneness.

Top with coarsely ground fresh pepper to serve.

# HERBED PORK ROAST
# WITH VEGETABLE SAUCE

Preheat oven to 450 degrees.

Place pork roast on rack in shallow roasting pan.

Combine salt, pepper, thyme and nutmeg. Rub into meat. Roast at 450 degrees uncovered for 30 minutes.

Reduce oven temperature to 350 degrees. Add carrots, onions, garlic, cloves, celery, parsley, bay leaves and consommé. Cover and roast for 2 1/2 to 3 hours or until meat is tender, basting often.

Transfer meat to heated platter. Skim fat from meat juices. Press pan juices and vegetables through a sieve or process in electric blender or food processor, removing cloves and bay leaves. Heat sauce and serve in a sauceboat to accompany meat.

*Perfect fall dinner party fare!*

1   (4 - 6-pound) loin of pork

2 ½ teaspoons salt

1   teaspoon pepper

1   teaspoon thyme

½   teaspoon ground nutmeg

2   carrots, thickly sliced

2   onions, coarsely chopped

2   large cloves garlic, minced

4   whole cloves

3   celery leaves, chopped

3   sprigs parsley

3   bay leaves

1   (10-½-ounce) can chicken consommé

**Serves:  6**

1 (3 - 4-pound) boneless
pork loin roast

Marinade:

1 cup soy sauce

2 tablespoons fresh lemon
juice

1 tablespoon finely chopped
garlic

1 tablespoon freshly
chopped chives

2 teaspoons tarragon leaves

2 teaspoons basil leaves

1 teaspoon ground sage

1 teaspoon pepper

Jezebel Sauce:

1 (12-ounce) jar pineapple
preserves

1 (10-ounce) jar apple jelly

4 tablespoons Dijon mustard

2 tablespoons prepared
horseradish

**Serves: 8 - 10**

# ROAST LOIN OF PORK WITH JEZEBEL SAUCE

Place pork loin in large zip-closure bag or shallow baking dish.

To make marinade, combine soy sauce, lemon juice, garlic, chives, tarragon, basil, sage and pepper in a small bowl. Pour marinade over pork. Cover tightly. Marinate up to 1 hour at room temperature or overnight in refrigerator, turning several times.

To make Jezebel Sauce, combine pineapple preserves, apple jelly, Dijon mustard and horseradish in a small bowl; mix well. Cover; store in refrigerator.

When ready to cook roast, preheat oven to 325 degrees. Remove pork from marinade; reserve marinade. Place meat in a shallow roasting pan. Insert meat thermometer into center at thickest part of roast. Roast, basting every 30 minutes, for 2 to 3 hours or until meat thermometer reaches 165 to 170 degrees.

Let stand for 15 minutes before slicing. Serve with Jezebel Sauce.

# PORK TENDERLOIN WITH SCALLION MUSTARD SAUCE

¼ cup soy sauce

¼ cup bourbon

2 tablespoons brown sugar

3 (1-pound) pork tenderloins

Scallion Mustard Sauce:

⅓ cup sour cream

⅓ cup mayonnaise

1 tablespoon finely chopped scallions

1 tablespoon dry mustard

Salt, to taste

1 ½ tablespoons vinegar

**Serves: 5 - 6**

Place pork in a large zip closure bag or shallow dish. Combine soy sauce, bourbon and sugar. Mix well. Pour marinade over pork; cover and refrigerate 2 hours or longer, turning occasionally.

Preheat oven to 325 degrees. Remove meat from marinade; place on rack in shallow roasting pan. Roast 30 minutes or up to 1 hour, depending on degree of doneness desired. Baste several times with marinade to enhance flavor and to prevent dryness.

To prepare Sauce, combine sour cream, mayonnaise, scallions, dry mustard, salt and vinegar. Mix well. Refrigerate until ready to serve.

Carve pork into thin diagonal slices. Top with sauce to serve.

*This can also be cooked on an outdoor grill. Heat grill and place tenderloins on rack. Cover and cook about 20 to 30 minutes or to desired degree of doneness.*

*The pork is beautifully enhanced by the creamy Scallion Mustard Sauce.*

4 pork chops, (1 ½-inch thick)

**Blue Cheese Stuffing:**
- ½ cup shredded carrots
- ¼ cup chopped pecans
- ¼ cup crumbled blue cheese
- 1 green onion, minced
- 1 teaspoon Worcestershire sauce

**Sauce:**
- 4 teaspoons all-purpose flour
- ¼ cup plain yogurt
- ½ cup milk
- ¼ cup dry sherry
- ½ teaspoon instant chicken bouillon granules
-  Pepper, to taste
-  Blue cheese

**Serves: 4**

# GRILLED STUFFED PORK CHOPS

Trim excess fat from each chop. Cut a pocket in each from fat side to bone. Set aside.

Mix carrots, pecans, cheese, green onion and Worcestershire sauce. Spoon about 1/4 cup stuffing into each pocket. Close pockets with wooden picks.

In a saucepan, stir the flour into the yogurt. Add the milk, sherry, bouillon and pepper. Cook and stir until thickened and bubbly. Cook for an additional minute. Keep warm.

Grill the chops, covered, over drip pan for about 40 minutes or until no longer pink.

Spoon sauce over chops and sprinkle with extra blue cheese to serve.

*This will steal the heart of every blue cheese lover!*

# CARIBBEAN CHERRY CHICKEN WITH DARK RUM

Preheat oven to 350 degrees.

Sprinkle chicken with salt and paprika. Heat oil and butter in a large skillet. Sauté chicken on both sides until golden brown. Remove chicken, reserving drippings. Put in a shallow baking dish, set aside.

Stir flour, sugar, allspice, cinnamon and mustard into skillet drippings. Add cherries, chicken stock, pineapple, brown sugar and rum. Mix well and bring to boil.

Pour over chicken, cover and bake for 50 minutes or until chicken is tender. Remove cover and bake for ten more minutes. Serve with fresh pineapple as a garnish.

4 chicken breasts, (about ½-pound each)

1 teaspoon salt

½ teaspoon paprika

2 tablespoons vegetable oil

1 tablespoon butter or margarine

1 tablespoon all-purpose flour

1 teaspoon sugar

¼ teaspoon allspice

¼ teaspoon cinnamon

¼ teaspoon dry mustard

2 cups fresh cherries, pitted, halved

1 cup chicken stock

1 cup unsweetened crushed pineapple with juice

2 tablespoons brown sugar

2 tablespoons dark rum

Fresh pineapple wedges or slices

**Serves: 4**

8 skinless, boneless chicken
   breast halves

Horseradish Cream Sauce:

1 cup whipping cream

2 tablespoons mayonnaise

1 tablespoon prepared
   mustard

2 tablespoons horseradish

¼ teaspoon fresh lemon juice

¼ teaspoon Worcestershire
   sauce

⅛ teaspoon seasoned salt

⅛ teaspoon white pepper


¼ cup all-purpose flour

1 teaspoon salt

½ teaspoon pepper

3 tablespoons butter

1 garlic clove, minced

1 cup sliced mushrooms

   Fresh parsley sprigs


**Serves: 8**

# CHICKEN WITH HORSERADISH CREAM

To make Sauce, combine whipping cream, mayonnaise, mustard, horseradish, lemon juice, Worcestershire sauce, seasoned salt and white pepper in a small bowl; blend well. Cover and refrigerate to chill for at least 2 hours.

Combine flour, salt and pepper in a plastic kitchen bag. Add half the chicken; toss and turn to coat each piece. Repeat with remaining chicken.

Melt butter in a skillet. Add chicken pieces; sauté 8 to 10 minutes, or until chicken is cooked. Remove chicken to platter; cover and keep warm.

Add garlic and mushrooms to skillet. Sauté for 2 minutes. Add horseradish cream sauce. Bring to a boil; reduce heat and simmer for 5 minutes. Pour sauce over chicken to serve; garnish with parsley.

# MARINATED CHICKEN IN PEPPER CREAM SAUCE

Arrange chicken breasts in a large shallow baking dish. Combine olive oil, basil, lemon juice, pepper flakes and garlic in a small bowl. Pour over chicken. Cover and refrigerate overnight.

Melt 3 tablespoons butter in a large, heavy skillet. Sauté peppers for 2 minutes. Remove peppers; set aside. Stir in wine and chicken broth. Increase heat to high and boil until sauce is reduced to 2 tablespoons, about 5 minutes. Add cream; reduce heat and cook until sauce is reduced by half, about 4 to 5 minutes.

Melt remaining 2 tablespoons butter in a second large skillet. Sauté mushrooms over medium-high heat until slightly browned. Add reserved peppers, cream sauce and salt. At this point the pepper sauce may be refrigerated for up to 24 hours.

Preheat oven to broil or prepare barbecue grill and heat to medium.

Drain chicken breasts, discard marinade. Broil or grill chicken 4 inches from heat, turning once, cooking until chicken is tender. Cut chicken into 1/2-inch strips. Arrange chicken breasts attractively on serving platter.

Stir Parmesan and 1/4 cup basil into heated pepper sauce. Pour sauce over chicken . Serve with hot cooked fettucine, if desired.

2 pounds boneless, skinless chicken breasts

½ cup olive oil

¼ cup fresh minced basil

3 tablespoons fresh lemon juice

1 tablespoon red pepper flakes, crushed

2 teaspoons garlic, minced

5 tablespoons butter, divided

1 medium red bell pepper, julienned

1 medium yellow bell pepper, julienned

½ cup dry white wine

½ cup chicken broth

2 cups heavy cream

1 cup sliced mushrooms

½ teaspoon salt

¾ cup freshly grated Parmesan cheese

¼ cup chopped fresh basil

Hot cooked spinach or red pepper fettucine, optional

**Serves: 6 - 8**

2 whole skinless, boneless chicken breasts, cut in 1-inch cubes

⅓ cup honey

2 teaspoons curry powder

2 apples, peeled, sliced

3 tablespoons oil

1 celery stalk, diced

¼ cup raisins

3 tablespoons chopped parsley

Hot cooked rice

**Serves: 4**

# STIR-FRIED CHICKEN AND APPLES

Place chicken pieces in a large bowl. Combine honey and curry. Pour over chicken; toss to coat well. Stir in apple slices. Set aside.

Heat oil in a heavy skillet or wok over high heat. Add celery; stir-fry one minute. Add chicken and apple mixture; stir-fry 3 to 4 minutes until chicken is cooked.

Add raisins and parsley; stir well, spoon over hot, cooked rice to serve.

*Other crunchy vegetables such as sugar snap or snow peas can be added to this dish.*

# Chicken with Olives and Raisins

Heat oil in a large heavy skillet. Add chicken pieces and cook to brown lightly on all sides. Remove chicken; set aside.

Add onions and garlic to skillet. Cook until tender. Add tomato paste, water, bouillon and vinegar. Heat 10 minutes. Add chili powder, pepper and cumin; stir to blend well.

Return chicken pieces to skillet. Add raisins and olives. Simmer covered for 30 minutes. Turn chicken pieces and cook an additional 10 minutes.

*This is a nice way to use chicken other than white meat, but you can of course substitute breast pieces if they are your preference.*

2 - 3  pounds chicken pieces

⅓  cup oil

2  medium onions, chopped

6  garlic cloves, chopped

1  (6-ounce) can tomato paste

1  cup water

2  tablespoons chicken bouillon granules

1  teaspoon cider vinegar

½  teaspoon chili powder

¼  teaspoon black pepper

2  teaspoons cumin

¼  cup golden raisins

1  small jar green olives, pitted

**Serves:  6 - 8**

4 skinless, boneless chicken breast halves (about 1-pound), pounded to ¼-inch thickness

2 small eggplants, sliced in ⅜-inch rounds

4 - 5 tablespoons virgin olive oil, divided

Freshly ground black pepper, to taste

¼ teaspoon salt

¼ cup dry sherry

2 tablespoons fresh lemon juice

1 teaspoon fresh thyme, or ¼ teaspoon dried thyme

¼ cup water

3 ounces dried mushrooms, sliced

3 large tomatoes, peeled, cut in ¾-inch thick slices

1 tablespoon red wine vinegar

2 garlic cloves, finely chopped

2 scallions, minced, divided

**Serves: 4**

# MEDITERRANEAN CHICKEN

Blanche the eggplant slices a few at a time in a large pan of boiling water for 30 seconds. Remove slices with a slotted spoon; drain well on a paper towel.

Heat 1 1/2 tablespoons of oil in a skillet over medium-high heat. Sprinkle the chicken cutlets with pepper and 1/8 teaspoon salt. Sauté the cutlets 2 minutes on each side, or until lightly browned. Reduce heat to low. Add sherry, lemon juice, thyme, and 1/4 cup water. Simmer, covered, until the chicken is cooked, about 2 to 3 minutes. Remove the pan from the heat; set aside.

Heat 1 tablespoon of the oil in a second large skillet over medium-high heat. Sauté one-third of the eggplant slices in a single layer until golden brown, turning them once. Repeat the process with the remaining eggplant, adding 1/2 tablespoon of oil each time. Remove the eggplant from the skillet, placing the slices in a single layer in the bottom of an oven-proof serving dish.

Heat 1 tablespoon of oil in the skillet over medium-high heat. Sprinkle the tomato slices with the remaining 1/8 teaspoon of salt. Sauté them until softened, about 2 minutes on each side.

Arrange the tomatoes on top of the eggplant. Remove chicken cutlets from skillet, reserving the liquid. Place the cutlets on top of the layered eggplant and tomato slices. Cover and keep warm.

Bring the liquid in the skillet to a simmer over medium heat. Add the mushrooms, 1/2 cup water, vinegar, garlic and half the chopped scallions. Simmer the mixture over low heat until it is reduced by one-third. Spoon this sauce over the chicken, sprinkle with remaining scallions. Serve immediately.

# Rosemary Chicken and Potatoes

Cut each potato into 6 wedges. In a large baking dish, toss potatoes with 3 tablespoons olive oil, 1/4 teaspoon salt, 1/4 cup tomatoes and pepper. Roast potatoes at 450 degrees until tender, about 25 to 30 minutes, stirring occasionally so tomatoes do not burn.

About 5 to 10 minutes before potatoes are cooked, in a 9-inch cast iron skillet melt 1 tablespoon butter with 1 tablespoon olive oil. Brown chicken breasts pieces, a few pieces at a time over medium-high heat and remove to a warm platter. Set aside.

Brown onion over medium heat in batches in the same skillet, scraping up any bits of chicken. Add onions and chicken breasts to potato mixture. Sprinkle with remaining salt. Top chicken breasts with remaining tomato, butter and rosemary.

Roast about 15 minutes at 450 degrees or until chicken is fully cooked. Remove from oven and allow chicken to rest 5 minutes before serving. Garnish with parsley and scallions.

1   pound red potatoes

4   tablespoons virgin olive oil, divided

½   teaspoon kosher salt

¾   cup canned tomatoes, chopped

¼   teaspoon fresh cracked pepper

5   tablespoons unsalted butter

8   (8 - 10-ounces each) chicken breast halves, with skin

4   large onions, peeled, halved, sliced lengthwise

1   teaspoon fresh or ¼ teaspoon dried rosemary

¼   cup fresh Italian parsley, chopped

2   scallions, thinly cut on a diagonal

**Serves:  6 - 8**

4 - 5  pounds chicken pieces

1  tablespoon sweet
Hungarian paprika

1  teaspoon salt

¼  teaspoon red pepper

½  teaspoon freshly ground
black pepper

¼  teaspoon dry mustard

⅓  cup water

2  tablespoons
Worcestershire sauce

⅓  cup red wine vinegar

¼  cup unsalted butter

Vegetable oil

**Serves:  8 - 10**

# SOUTHERN GRILLED CHICKEN

Arrange chicken in a large shallow glass or ceramic dish. Combine paprika, salt, red and black pepper, mustard and water in a medium saucepan. Bring to boil; remove from heat. Add Worcestershire sauce and vinegar. Stir in butter by bits.

Pour sauce mixture over chicken pieces. Cover and refrigerate for 1 hour or overnight.
When ready to cook, preheat grill. Brush grill rack lightly with oil. If using wood chips, mesquite or other flavorings sprinkle over coals or lava rocks.

Place dark meat on grill rack. Cover and cook on medium-high for 15 minutes, basting and turning as desired to brown evenly.

Add white meat to grill rack. Cook covered 20 to 25 minutes longer basting often and turning once, until skin is crisp and juices run clear when chicken is pricked with a fork.

*Served with crisp baked potatoes and a fresh green salad, this makes the perfect summer cook out meal.*

# Lemon Chicken with Thyme

Combine flour, salt and pepper in a plastic or paper bag; shake to mix. Add chicken and shake to coat lightly. Remove the chicken and reserve the excess seasoned flour.

Heat 1 tablespoon of oil in a large skillet over medium heat. Add the chicken pieces; brown on one side, about 5 minutes. Add the remaining oil, turn the chicken and brown well on the second side, about 5 minutes longer. Transfer the chicken to a large plate; set aside.

Melt the butter in the skillet. Add onion and cook, stirring until softened. Stir in the reserved seasoned flour and cook, stirring until the flour is well blended, about 1 minutes. Add the broth, 2 tablespoons of lemon juice and the thyme. Bring mixture to a boil, stirring constantly.

Return the chicken to the skillet, reduce the heat to medium-low and cover. Cook until the chicken is tender, about 5 minutes.

Remove chicken to serving plates. Stir the remaining lemon juice into the sauce in the skillet; pour over the chicken. Garnish with lemon slices and parsley.

*For a flavor change, substitute lime juice for lemon juice; garnish with limes slices and parsley.*

3 tablespoons all-purpose flour

½ teaspoon salt

¼ teaspoon pepper

4 skinless, boneless chicken breast halves, (¼-pound each)

2 tablespoons olive oil, divided

1 tablespoon butter or margarine

1 medium onion, coarsely chopped

1 cup chicken broth

3 tablespoons lemon juice, divided

½ teaspoon fresh chopped thyme

Lemon slices or wedges

Fresh parsley, chopped

**Serves: 4**

6 skinless, boneless chicken breast halves, (about 4-ounces each)

¼ cup fresh chopped parsley or 1 tablespoon dried parsley

½ teaspoon fresh ground pepper

½ teaspoon grated lime rind

1 cup dry white wine

Vegetable cooking spray

Lime slices

**Serves: 6**

# LIME GRILLED CHICKEN

Arrange chicken pieces in a large shallow baking dish.

Combine parsley, ground pepper, lime rind and wine in a small bowl. Pour over chicken, turning to coat. Cover and refrigerate 1 hour or longer, if desired.

Spray grill rack with cooking spray to coat; place on grill over medium hot coals.

Remove chicken from marinade, reserving marinade. Place chicken pieces on rack; cook 5 minutes on each side or until done, basting with reserved marinade. Garnish with lime slices to serve.

# ORIENTAL CHICKEN ROLLS

Combine the soy sauce, sugar, sherry, vinegar, crushed peppercorns and 3 tablespoons of water in a small bowl. Set aside.

Sprinkle the chicken with salt and crushed peppercorns. Cut scallions, cucumber and red pepper strips to fit inside the breast halves. Place a combination of the strips on each chicken cutlet; roll tightly and fasten, if desired, with a small skewer or wooden picks.

Heat the oil in a skillet. Carefully sauté the chicken rolls over medium-high heat, turning them, until golden, about 4 minutes. Remove the chicken rolls. Pour the sauce into the skillet; stir well. Return the chicken to the skillet. Cover loosely, and simmer for 5 minutes, turning once.

Arrange the chicken rolls on a heated serving platter, remove any skewers or toothpicks. Spoon the sauce over the rolls and serve immediately.

*A unique entree with a flavorful oriental touch.*

4 skinless, boneless chicken breast halves, pounded to 1/4-inch thickness

Sauce:

3 tablespoons soy sauce

1 tablespoon sugar

2 tablespoons dry sherry

2 teaspoons rice vinegar

1/2 teaspoon crushed Szechwan peppercorns, or 1/4 teaspoon crushed black peppercorns

3 tablespoons water

1/4 teaspoon salt

1/2 teaspoon crushed Szechwan peppercorns, or 1/4 teaspoon crushed black peppercorns

3 scallions, blanched for 30 seconds, drained, cooled, and sliced lengthwise in four strips

1 cucumber, peeled, halved lengthwise, seeded, cut in 1/4-inch wide strips, blanched for 30 seconds, drained

1 red bell pepper, seeded, cut into 1/2-inch strips, blanched for 2 minutes, drained

2 tablespoon safflower oil

1 ½ pounds chicken breast
tenders

2 teaspoons chili powder

¾ teaspoon ground cumin

Vegetable oil or cooking
spray

¾ teaspoon freshly ground
pepper

¼ teaspoon salt

1 large lime, juiced

8 extra large (9 or 10-inch)
flour tortillas

1 ½ cups chopped green onion

1 cup chopped fresh cilantro

½ cup light sour cream

2 cups coarsely chopped red
leaf lettuce

3 tomatoes, coarsely
chopped

**Serves: 4 - 6**

# Chicken Fajitas

In a small bowl, combine chicken breast tenders, chili powder
and cumin; toss gently to combine. Let stand for about 10 minutes to allow flavor to develop.

Brush a large skillet with small amount of vegetable oil. Place
over medium-high heat until hot. Add chicken to hot pan; sauté
5 minutes or until chicken is cooked.

Wrap tortillas in aluminum foil. Bake at 350 degrees for 7 to
8 minutes or until softened; set aside.

Combine chicken, pepper, salt and lime juice in a small bowl;
toss well. Add green onions, cilantro and sour cream; toss gently to combine.

To serve, place chopped lettuce on each tortilla; top with
chicken mixture and tomato pieces; roll up.

*For a change of pace, grill the chicken and expand the
quantity to turn this into a quick and easy choice for special
family or company meals.*

# Company Chicken Supreme

Place chicken pieces in a single layer in one or two large shallow baking pans.

Combine sour cream, lemon juice, Worcestershire sauce, celery salt, paprika, garlic, pepper and salt in a large bowl. Pour mixture over chicken, coating each piece well. Cover and refrigerate several hours or overnight.

When ready to cook, preheat oven to 350 degrees.

Remove chicken from cream mixture, coat each piece evenly with bread crumbs. Place chicken pieces in a large shallow pan.

Melt butter in a small saucepan. Spoon half of butter over chicken. Bake uncovered in 350 degree oven for 45 minutes. Drizzle with remaining butter. Bake about 20 minutes longer or until chicken is tender and brown.

12 chicken breast halves

2 cups sour cream

¼ cup lemon juice

3 teaspoons Worcestershire sauce

1 teaspoon celery salt

1 teaspoon paprika

2 cloves garlic, minced

½ teaspoon pepper

½ teaspoon salt

¾ cup dry bread crumbs

¾ cup butter or margarine

**Serves: 10 - 12**

2 extra large eggs

2 tablespoons milk or light cream

2 chicken breasts, skinned

2 chicken legs, skinned

2 chicken thighs, skinned

3 slices whole wheat bread

½ cup oatmeal

½ teaspoon dried thyme

½ teaspoon dried sage

½ teaspoon salt

½ teaspoon pepper

½ cup unsalted butter or margarine, melted

**Serves: 4**

# CRISPY OVEN FRIED CHICKEN

Whisk together eggs and milk in a large bowl. Add chicken pieces, turning to coat. Cover and refrigerate for 30 minutes. Preheat oven to 375 degrees.

Place bread in food processor; process into medium fine crumbs. Add oatmeal, thyme, sage, salt and pepper. Process just to mix. Transfer crumb mixture to shallow dish.

Pick up chicken pieces and let egg mixture drip off. Dip each egg-coated piece in melted butter, then into crumb mixture; turn to coat well.

Place crumb-coated chicken pieces in 13 x 9-inch baking dish sprayed with non-stick cooking spray. Bake for 45 minutes. Serve hot or at room temperature.

# HERBED CHICKEN BREAST

Place chicken pieces in a large shallow plate or tray.

Mix bread crumbs, salt, thyme, rosemary and pepper in a pie pan. Beat egg in pie plate. Dip each chicken piece in egg then into bread crumb mixture turning each piece to coat well.

Heat oil in a large heavy skillet. Sauté chicken until lightly brown on each side, about 5 minutes. Add wine to skillet and bring to a boil. Reduce heat and simmer covered for 15 minutes.

*Substitute other herbs as desired.*

4   boneless, skinless chicken breasts

2   cups soft bread crumbs

1   teaspoon salt

1   teaspoon crushed thyme leaves

¼   teaspoon crushed rosemary leaves

¼   teaspoon ground pepper

2   eggs

3   tablespoons salad oil

¾   cup white wine

**Serves: 4 - 8**

2 (1 ½-pound) Rock Cornish hens, split in half

⅓ cup soy sauce

¼ cup vegetable oil

3 garlic cloves, sliced

2 tablespoons sesame seeds, lightly toasted

2 teaspoons ground ginger

1 tablespoon brown sugar

3 tablespoons fresh lime juice

Toasted sesame seeds

Fresh lime wedges

**Serves: 4**

# LIME AND SESAME ROASTED CORNISH HENS

Place Cornish hens, skin side down in a glass dish just large enough to hold them in single layer. Prick each hen several times with a fork.

In an electric blender or food processor, blend soy sauce, oil, garlic, sesame seeds, ginger, sugar and lime juice about 1 minute or until smooth.

Pour marinade over hens; cover and refrigerate for at least 6 hours and up to 24 hours, turning occasionally.

When ready to cook, preheat oven to 400 degrees.

With a slotted spoon or tongs transfer Cornish hen pieces to a 13 x 9-inch baking dish, arranging in a single layer, skin side up. Reserve marinade.

Roast hens, uncovered, basting with marinade every 15 minutes until juices run clear when pierced with a fork and meat is no longer pink on the inside, about 40 to 60 minutes. Garnish with sesame seeds and lime wedges to serve.

*Roasted to a deep golden brown, these hens are delicious served hot or cold.*

*To toast sesame seeds simply place them in a skillet set over low heat for a few minutes until just golden.*

# TURKEY BREAST WITH ORANGE AND ROSEMARY

1   (1 ½ - 2-pound) boneless turkey breast half, skinned

½   cup fresh orange juice

3   tablespoons olive oil

2   teaspoons dried rosemary, crumbled

2   tablespoons balsamic vinegar

1   tablespoon honey

1   teaspoon salt

⅛   teaspoon dried red pepper flakes

**Serves 6**

Place turkey breast pieces between 2 sheets of plastic wrap. Flatten with meat pounder until uniformly 1-inch thick. Remove plastic wrap. Place turkey in zip-closure plastic bag or large shallow dish.

Combine orange juice, olive oil, rosemary, vinegar, honey, salt and red pepper flakes in a jar. Shake well to combine. Set aside.

Pour marinade over turkey in bag or dish; cover or seal tightly. Refrigerate several hours or overnight.

Prepare grill to medium heat. Remove turkey from bag; place on preheated grill. Brush occasionally with marinade. Grill 12 minutes on each side, turning once or twice, or until meat thermometer registers 155 degrees.

Carve turkey breast diagonally across grain into thin slices to serve.

*Basting more often will insure a juicier, moister meat.*

1   (3 - 5-pound) turkey breast, boned, skinned (reserve skin)

Butter, softened

Spinach Filling:

2   tablespoons butter

1   small onion, chopped

1   (10-ounce) package frozen spinach, thawed, moisture squeezed out

½   teaspoon rosemary

Cornbread Stuffing:

2   tablespoons butter

1   medium onion, chopped

2   cups cornbread stuffing mix

¼   teaspoon rosemary

¼   teaspoon thyme

1   tablespoon chopped fresh parsley

1   egg, slightly beaten

# TURKEY BREAST WITH TWO STUFFINGS

Preheat oven to 350 degrees.

Place turkey between plastic wrap and pound with a mallet to flatten slightly. Place turkey breast skin-side down on a large clean cutting board.

To make Spinach Filling, melt butter in skillet. Sauté onion until tender. Add spinach, toss and sauté 3 to 4 minutes. Remove from heat; add rosemary and stir to mix well. Set aside.

To make Cornbread Stuffing, melt butter in medium saucepan. Sauté onion until tender. Add dry stuffing mix, rosemary, thyme and parsley; mix well. Remove from heat. Stir in egg. Set aside.

*Recipe continued on next page*

*Gravy:*

> Drippings from roasting pan
>
> 1 cup vermouth or water
> 1 chicken bouillon cube

**Serves: 6 - 8**

Place spinach filling down center of turkey breast; spread evenly. Top spinach filling with cornbread stuffing mixture; spread evenly. Fold one side of turkey breast over stuffing mixture; repeat with second side of turkey breast, shaping into a roast and enclosing fillings. Tie tightly with string about every 2 inches to hold stuffings inside.

Rub reserved turkey skin with softened butter. Arrange loose skin over rolled turkey breast; place on rack in shallow roasting pan.

Roast, uncovered, in a 350 degree oven 25 minutes per pound of meat. Let stand about 10 minutes.

Scrape drippings loose from roasting pan; pour into saucepan. Add vermouth and chicken bouillon cube; bring to a boil. Reduce by about one-third.

Slice turkey breast and arrange on a serving platter. Spoon sauce over turkey or serve in separate bowl.

8 turkey breast cutlets (about 1-pound), pounded to ⅛-inch thickness

3 egg whites

½ teaspoon salt

Freshly ground black pepper, to taste

3 tablespoons virgin olive oil

2 - 3 tablespoons finely chopped shallots

⅓ cup white wine vinegar

½ cup water

10 whole peppercorns

3 bay leaves

3 tablespoons dried cherries

⅓ cup safflower oil

⅔ cup dry bread crumbs

½ cup finely chopped fresh parsley

2 garlic cloves, finely chopped

Grated rind of ½ orange

3 tablespoons pine nuts

**Serves: 4**

# Turkey Scallops with Pine Nuts and Dried Cherries

Beat the egg whites with the salt and pepper in a shallow bowl. Add the cutlets one at a time to the egg mixture, turning to coat well. Set aside.

Heat the olive oil in a small saucepan. Add the shallots and sauté over medium-high heat until translucent, about 5 minutes. Add the vinegar, water, peppercorns and bay leaves, and simmer for 20 minutes. Stir in the dried cherries and simmer for another 10 minutes, or until the liquid is reduced by half.

Heat the safflower oil in large skillet. Spread the bread crumbs in a plate. Dip the cutlets in the crumbs. Brown the cutlets in the skillet over medium-high heat for 2 minutes on each side. Put the cooked cutlets on a heated platter; cover and keep warm.

Combine the parsley, garlic and orange rind. Strain the reduced sauce, reserving the dried cherries, and pour it evenly over the turkey cutlets. Sprinkle with the dried cherries, parsley mixture and pine nuts.

# TURKEY MEDALLIONS WITH RED AND GREEN PEPPERS

Dredge the cutlets in flour, shake off the excess. Set aside.

Heat 1 tablespoon of oil in a large skillet over medium-high heat. Sauté 4 of the turkey cutlets for 45 seconds on each side, or until cooked. Transfer the cutlets to a heated platter. Add the remaining oil to the skillet and repeat with the remaining cutlets. Transfer the turkey to the heated serving platter. Cover loosely and keep warm.

Reduce the heat to medium-low. Heat the olive oil in the skillet; add the onion and garlic. Cook until the onion is translucent.

Add chicken broth, basil, vinegar, salt, ground pepper and pepper rings. Increase the heat to medium and cook just until the peppers are tender.

Spoon the pepper mixture over the warm cutlets. Serve immediately.

8  turkey cutlets (1-pound), pounded to ⅛-inch thickness

½  cup all-purpose flour

2  tablespoons vegetable oil, divided

1  teaspoon virgin olive oil

1  medium onion, thinly sliced

2  garlic cloves, minced

¾  cup chicken broth

2  tablespoons chopped fresh basil, or 2 teaspoons dried basil

1  tablespoon red wine vinegar

¼  teaspoon salt

   Freshly ground black pepper, to taste

1  large sweet green pepper, seeded, sliced in thin rings

1  large sweet red pepper, seeded, sliced in thin rings

**Serves: 4**

4 - 6  *whole duck breasts*

**Marinade:**

2   tablespoons soy sauce

½   teaspoon dry mustard

1   tablespoon Worcestershire sauce

1   garlic clove, crushed

¾   cup dry red wine


**Red Currant Sauce:**

4   tablespoons unsalted butter

1   (10-ounce) jar red currant jelly

¼   cup catsup

¼   cup light brown sugar, packed


**Serves:  4 - 6**

# GRILLED DUCK BREAST WITH RED CURRANT SAUCE

Remove meat in one piece from both sides of breast bone. Remove skin and trim tendons.  Place duck breast in zip-closure plastic bag or large shallow dish.

In a small bowl combine soy sauce, mustard, Worcestershire sauce, garlic and red wine.  Pour over duck, turning to coat all sides.  Cover and refrigerate at least 4 hours or overnight to marinate.

When ready to cook, heat barbecue grill to medium.  Arrange duck breasts on hot grill.  Grill for 5 minutes per side.  Meat should be rare to medium rare.  Let stand covered about 5 to 10 minutes.  Carve into 1/4-inch slices, cutting across grain. Serve with Red Currant Sauce.

To make Red Currant Sauce, melt butter in a small saucepan. Stir in jelly, catsup and brown sugar.  Heat until jelly melts and mixture boils.  Spoon over sliced duck.

*A gala way to serve wild duck.*

# ROSEMARY AND PORT MARINADE

1 cup port

3 tablespoons olive oil

Juice of 1/2 lemon

1 teaspoon brown sugar

2 tablespoons fresh chopped rosemary or 2 teaspoons dried

4 - 6 garlic cloves, crushed

Freshly ground black pepper

Combine all ingredients; stir well. Use to marinate lamb or beef before cooking. Brush over meat to baste during cooking.

*A sophisticated combination of flavors.*

**Yield: about 1 1/2 cups**


# TANGY BEEF MARINADE

1/4 cup soy sauce

2 tablespoons sesame oil

1 tablespoon Dijon mustard

1 tablespoon granulated sugar

2 teaspoons garlic, minced

1 teaspoon grated lemon peel

1/2 teaspoon dried red pepper flakes

Combine all marinade ingredients; stir until well blended. Pour mixture over beef and marinade 2 hours at room temperature or overnight in refrigerator. Use to baste during cooking.

*Perfect flavor enhancer for flank steak, sirloin steak or other cuts of beef.*

**Yield: about 1/2 cup**

1 cup cider vinegar

2 tablespoons dill pickle juice

3 - 4 tablespoons butter

2 tablespoons Worcestershire sauce

1 tablespoon lemon juice

1 tablespoon molasses

1 small onion, chopped

**Yield: about 1 ½ cups**

# NORTH CAROLINA VINEGAR MARINADE

Combine above ingredients. Heat over low heat until butter melts.

Pour mixture over meat rubbed with garlic salt. Marinate for several hours. Use to baste meat during cooking.

*A favorite choice for pork roast, chops or ribs.*

1 cup dry white wine

2 garlic cloves, minced

2 tablespoons parsley

2 teaspoons salt

¼ teaspoon fresh ground pepper

**Yield: about 1 cup**

# WHITE WINE MARINADE

Combine all marinade ingredients; mix well. Pour over meat; cover and refrigerate overnight. Use to baste meat during cooking.

*Adds a distinctive flavor to pork.*

# Honey-Lemon Marinade

Combine all ingredients, mix well. Use as a marinade for chicken, fish or other meats being grilled. Use to baste during cooking.

2 garlic cloves

½ cup safflower oil

⅓ cup honey

⅓ cup scotch or bourbon

⅓ cup soy sauce

¾ teaspoon salt

¾ teaspoon pepper

2 large lemons, squeezed, sliced

**Yield: about 1 ½ cups**

# Bayou Marinade

Combine all marinade ingredients. Use to marinate fish or chicken or to baste during cooking.

1 cup olive oil

1 tablespoon soy sauce

3 fresh limes or lemons, juiced

1 tablespoon lemon pepper

1 tablespoon chopped parsley

**Yield: about 1 ¼ cups**

2 cups half-and-half cream, divided

2 egg yolks, beaten

3 tablespoons dry mustard

1 cup sugar

½ teaspoon salt

2 tablespoons all-purpose flour

¾ cup white vinegar

**Yield: about 3 ½ cups**

# CREAMY MUSTARD SAUCE

Scald 3/4 cup half-and-half in double boiler. Add remaining cream to beaten egg yolks in a small bowl. Blend dry mustard, sugar, salt, and flour. Stir into egg mixture. Stir egg mixture into scalded cream; stirring constantly in double boiler until thickened. Heat vinegar and add to thickened mixture.

This sauce may be prepared and stored in the refrigerator for up to a week. To use; reheat on low heat.

*Wonderful for holiday baked ham or Herbed Chicken Nuggets.*

⅓ cup chunky peanut butter

⅓ cup teriyaki sauce

¼ cup fresh lemon juice

¼ cup vegetable oil

2 teaspoons ground ginger

2 teaspoons basil

2 teaspoons onion powder

2 teaspoons garlic powder

½ teaspoon red pepper flakes

**Yield: about 1 ½ cups**

# PEANUT SAUCE

Combine all ingredients; blending thoroughly.

Use as a baste for grilling poultry or pork.

*This unlikely combination of ingredients is delicious.*

# RASPBERRY BARBECUE SAUCE

1   (8-ounce) can tomato
    sauce
¼   cup minced purple onion
½   cup chili sauce
½   cup raspberry vinegar
1   tablespoon honey
1   teaspoon Worcestershire
    sauce
1   garlic clove, minced
½   teaspoon dry mustard
½   teaspoon ground
    cinnamon
¼   teaspoon ground cloves
⅛   teaspoon ground ginger

Combine tomato sauce, onion, chili sauce, raspberry vinegar, honey and Worcestershire sauce in a small saucepan. Add garlic, mustard, cinnamon, cloves and ginger. Bring to a boil, stirring frequently. Reduce heat and simmer for 8 minutes. Cool slightly. Use to marinate beef, chicken or pork before cooking or to baste during cooking.

*The raspberry vinegar adds a unique and unexpected flavor to this sauce.*

**Yield: about 2 ½ cups**

# RED PLUM CHUTNEY

1 cup cider vinegar

¼ cup fresh lemon juice

⅓ cup water

1 ¾ cups granulated sugar

2 teaspoons granular fresh fruit preserver

1 ½ teaspoons coarse salt

1 teaspoon yellow mustard seed

3 ¼ pounds ripe plums, halved, stoned, cubed

¼ cup golden raisins

3 small jalapeño peppers, stemmed, seeded, chopped

1 tablespoon chopped ginger, preserved in syrup

1 tablespoon syrup from ginger

1 tablespoon finely grated fresh ginger

**Yields: 3 pints**

Combine the vinegar, lemon juice, water, sugar, fruit preserves, salt and mustard seeds in a non-metallic 10-quart kettle. Cover and cook over low heat until sugar dissolves completely. Uncover pot, turn heat to high and boil for 2 minutes.

Add remaining ingredients to boiling syrup and simmer until plums are tender, about 5 minutes. Remove plums to a separate bowl with a slotted spoon; boil remaining mixture until lightly thickened - about 4 minutes. Pour hot syrup over plums and ladle into containers.

Mixture will keep in refrigerator for up to 3 months, or freezes nicely.

*This deliciously piquant chutney lends a perfect touch to simply grilled chicken or turkey, pork or almost any meat.*

# WINTER CHUTNEY

Combine all ingredients in a large stock pot. Stir and cook over medium heat until apples soften and flavors blend, about 45 minutes total cooking time.

Ladle into storage jars. Chill.

*Great served as a condiment for chicken or pheasant breast.*

2 (20-ounces each) bags frozen peaches, chopped

2 large Granny Smith apples, peeled, chopped

1 (18-ounce) jar apricot preserves

1 (12-ounce) jar peach preserves

3 tablespoons sherry vinegar

3 - 4 teaspoons chili puree with garlic or Szechwan sauce (or to taste)

2 teaspoons chopped fresh ginger

½ cup golden raisins

¼ cup tomato tapenade, chopped, sun-dried in oil

**Yields: 5 pints**

# CRANBERRY ALMOND CHUTNEY

In a medium saucepan, combine sugar and water. Bring to a boil over medium heat; simmer 5 minutes.

Add cranberries; simmer 5 minutes longer, or until berries begin to pop. Stir in preserves; grated rind and lemon juice. Remove from heat.

In a small skillet over medium heat, lightly toast almonds until golden. Shake pan often. Add almonds to cranberry mixture. Stir to mix well. Ladle into storage jars; chill. Keeps in refrigerator for up to 1 month.

*Serve as an accompaniment to poultry.*

2 cups sugar

1 cup water

4 cups fresh cranberries, washed

¼ cup pineapple preserves

Grated rind and juice of 2 lemons

1 cup almonds, slivered

**Yield: 1 quart**

# FRESH CATCH

*Fish*

*Shellfish*

*Fish Marinades*

◀ Herb-Marinated Salmon Steaks, 271

# FRESH CATCH

# HERB-MARINATED SALMON STEAKS

Arrange salmon steaks in shallow baking dish or zip-closure plastic bag. Combine marinade ingredients in a small bowl. Pour mixture over salmon steaks; cover and refrigerate to marinate for 2 to 4 hours.

Drain and reserve marinade. Place salmon steaks on an oiled broiler pan. Preheat broiler. Broil, basting frequently with marinade, 4 to 5 minutes on each side, or until fish flakes easily when tested with a fork. Garnish with lemon wedges, if desired.

*Try cooking this delicacy over a hot charcoal fire on an outdoor grill.*

4  salmon steaks, 1-inch thick

Marinade:

½  cup dry vermouth

½  cup vegetable oil

2  tablespoons fresh lemon juice

¼  teaspoon salt

¼  teaspoon pepper

½  teaspoon ground thyme

½  teaspoon oregano

¼  teaspoon chopped fresh basil leaves

1  tablespoon parsley, minced

Lemon wedges, optional

**Serves:  4**

4  baby Coho steaks or fillets

Marinade:

½  cup olive oil

¼  cup soy sauce

½  teaspoon chopped fresh
dill

⅛  cup lemon juice

Pinch of ground cloves

Fresh dill sprigs, optional

**Serves:  4**

# GRILLED BABY COHO

Place baby Coho steaks in a single layer in a baking dish or a zip-closure plastic bag.  Combine marinade ingredients in a small bowl.  Pour marinade over fish, turning to coat well.  Cover and refrigerate.  Marinate 1/2 to 1 hour.

Place steaks on oiled broiler pan.  Preheat broiler.  Broil, basting frequently, 4 to 5 minutes on each side, or until fish flakes easily when tested with a fork.  Garnish with fresh dill sprigs, if desired.

# Tuna Steaks with Mint Vegetable Vinaigrette

Season tuna with pepper; brush with 1 tablespoon of the oil. Cover and refrigerate 2 to 3 hours or overnight.

Peel garlic and blanch in boiling salted water 5 minutes. Mince garlic; combine with mint, parsley and shallots. Season with salt and pepper as desired. Allow to stand to develop flavor.

Preheat barbecue grill to medium-hot. Arrange tuna steaks on hot grill. Grill over moderate heat until medium-rare, about 4 minutes per side. To serve, top with vinaigrette; garnish with fresh mint sprigs, if desired.

6   fresh tuna steaks, 1 ¼ to 1 ½-inch thick

    Fresh ground white pepper

½   cup extra-virgin olive oil

2   cloves elephant garlic

2 - 3   tablespoons fresh chopped mint

1   tablespoon lime juice

1   tablespoon minced fresh parsley

6   shallots, minced

6   plum tomatoes, chopped

    Fresh mint sprigs

    Salt, optional

    Pepper

**Serves: 6**

4 tuna steaks, ¼-pound
   each

1 tablespoon honey

⅓ cup soy sauce

1 teaspoon fresh grated
   lemon peel

¼ cup fresh lemon juice

1 tablespoon Dijon mustard

½ cup salad oil

   Lemon wedges, optional

**Serves: 4**

# GRILLED FRESH TUNA

Place tuna in shallow dish or zip-closure plastic bag.

Combine honey, soy sauce, lemon peel, lemon juice, mustard, and salad oil in a small bowl. Whisk to blend. Pour marinade over fish and turn to coat well. Cover tightly. Marinate in refrigerator 1 to 3 hours or longer, if desired.

Preheat barbecue grill to medium-hot. Arrange tuna steaks on hot grill. Cook tuna over moderate heat about 4 to 6 minutes per side, basting occasionally until fish reaches desired doneness. Garnish with lemon wedges if desired.

# FRESH TUNA WITH PIQUANT SALSA

To make sauce, combine oil, parsley, pepper strips, onions, 2 tablespoons lemon juice, oregano, 1 tablespoon capers and salt in heavy medium saucepan over low heat. Cook 5 minutes to blend flavors, stirring occasionally. (May be prepared up to one week ahead, covered and refrigerated. Bring to room temperature before serving.)

When ready to cook place fish in single layer in shallow glass dish or zip-closure plastic bag. Drizzle with olive oil and lemon juice. Season with pepper. Turn fish to coat both sides. Sprinkle with oregano. Cover and let stand 30 minutes.

Preheat barbecue grill to high or preheat broiler. Arrange fish on hot grill. Cook to desired doneness, about 4 minutes per side for medium. Transfer fish to plates. Arrange tuna on serving plate. Top with Piquant Salsa to serve.

*Piquant Salsa:*

½ cup virgin olive oil

½ cup chopped fresh parsley

½ cup pickled red pepper strips, drained, diced

⅓ cup thinly sliced green onions

3 tablespoons fresh lemon juice

2 tablespoons fresh oregano or 2 teaspoons dried, crumbled

2 tablespoons capers, drained, rinsed

Salt, to taste

6 (¾-inch thick) tuna steaks, 8-ounces each

¼ cup olive oil

2 tablespoons fresh lemon juice

Freshly ground pepper, to taste

1 teaspoon oregano

**Serves: 6**

4 orange roughy fish fillets, rinsed and wiped dry

2 tablespoons butter

¼ cup green onions, finely chopped

1 clove garlic, crushed

1 (10-ounce) package frozen chopped spinach

½ cup fine dry bread crumbs

¼ cup crumbled feta cheese

½ cup dry white wine

Pepper, freshly ground

Lemon slices

Butter

**Serves: 4**

# ORANGE ROUGHY WITH SPINACH STUFFING

Preheat oven to 375 degrees. Lightly butter a 9-inch baking dish.

Melt butter in a large skillet. Add onions and garlic; cook over medium heat stirring often about 4 to 5 minutes or until onions are soft and translucent.

Thaw and drain spinach to remove excess moisture. Add to onion-garlic mixture. Add bread crumbs, feta cheese and wine to vegetable mixture; stir gently to combine.

Place about 3 tablespoons filling on each fish fillet; roll up. Spoon remaining stuffing into buttered dish. Arrange fish rolls over stuffing. Top with pepper, lemon slices and dots of butter.

Cover with foil; bake 15 to 20 minutes or until fish is flaky. Serve immediately.

# ORANGE ROUGHY AND TOMATO DIJONNAISE

To make sauce, melt butter in a medium saucepan; sauté onions 3 to 5 minutes. Add flour; cook 2 to 3 minutes. Add wine, water, salt, pepper and mustard. Stir and cook until thick. Add milk and cheese; stir to blend. Add tomato. Remove from heat, cover and keep warm.

When ready to cook fish, preheat broiler. Arrange fish on broiler pan turning under thin parts. Brush with melted butter. Sprinkle with lemon juice, salt and pepper. Broil 8 to 10 minutes until fish flakes.

Spoon sauce over fish to cover. Return to broiler; cook 2 to 3 minutes or until sauce browns.

*Sauce:*

- 2 *tablespoons butter*
- 1 *small onion, chopped*
- 2 *tablespoons flour*
- ⅓ *cup dry white wine*
- ¼ *cup water*
  *Salt and pepper, to taste*
- 1 *tablespoon Dijon mustard*
- ⅓ *cup milk*
- ⅓ *cup mozzarella cheese, grated*
- 1 *tomato, peeled, seeded, chopped*

- 2 *pounds orange roughy fillets*
- 2 *tablespoons butter, melted*
- 2 *tablespoons lemon juice*
  *Salt and pepper, to taste*

**Serves: 4**

4 (¾-inch) firm fish fillets (haddock or scrod), 5-ounces each

4 tablespoons butter or margarine, room temperature

2 tablespoons Dijon mustard

2 tablespoons chopped fresh basil leaves

1 (7-ounce) jar roasted red peppers, drained, cut

**Serves: 4**

# Fish Fillets with Sweet Red Peppers, Basil and Mustard

Preheat oven to 450 degrees.

Combine butter, mustard and basil in a small bowl; stir until well blended.  Set aside.

Tear off 4 (12-inch) squares of foil.  Brush each side of foil with oil to coat lightly.  Place one fillet  on each piece of foil.

Top with pepper strips; dot with mustard - butter mixture.  Fold and seal foil securely.  Arrange foil packets on ungreased baking sheet.  Bake at 450 degrees for 8 minutes.  Remove packets to plates and serve immediately.

*Parchment paper can be used to make packets.*

# HALIBUT OLYMPIA

6 - 8  *halibut fish fillets*

½  *cup fresh lemon juice*

Preheat oven to broil.  Lightly butter a broiler pan.

Place fillets on prepared pan.  Sprinkle with lemon juice. Place in oven about 4-inches from heat; broil 5 to 8 minutes or until fish is almost done.

Combine cheese, mayonnaise, butter, scallions, mustard and pepper sauce.  Set aside.

Remove fish from oven.  Spread topping evenly over fish fillets.  Broil an additional 2 to 3 minutes or until topping is golden brown and cooked to desired doneness.  Serve immediately.

*Salmon, trout or orange roughy also work well in this dish.*

*Topping:*

½  *cup grated Parmesan cheese*

3  *tablespoons mayonnaise*

¼  *cup soft butter*

3  *tablespoons chopped scallions*

½  *teaspoon hot mustard powder*

*Dash of hot pepper sauce*

**Serves:  6 - 8**

2 tablespoons butter

2 tablespoons olive oil

6 ounces haddock, cut into slices

6 ounces scallops, cut into halves

6 ounces raw shrimp, shelled, deveined, cut into round slices

1 clove garlic, peeled, crushed

2 teaspoons arrowroot

½ cup dry white wine, divided

2 teaspoons Dijon mustard

1 tablespoon fresh lemon juice

2 tablespoons parsley

2 tablespoons whipping cream

Salt, to taste

Pepper, to taste

Fresh dill

Red pepper

Hot cooked rice, optional

**Serves: 4 (small)**

# SEAFOOD IN WINE CREAM

Combine butter and oil in a large heavy skillet. When hot add fish, scallops, shrimp and garlic. Sauté quickly over low heat for 5 minutes.

Mix arrowroot with a little white wine and mustard. Set aside.

Add wine and lemon juice to seafood mixture. Stir in arrowroot mixture. Cook, stirring until sauce thickens. Stir in parsley, cream, salt and pepper. Sprinkle with dill and red pepper. Serve with hot cooked rice, if desired.

*Raw shrimp are essential for this dish. Cooked shrimp gets very tough in their second cooking.*

# BARBECUE BACON WRAPPED SHRIMP

Cut bacon slices in half. In a large heavy skillet, partially cook bacon over medium heat to render some of the fat without allowing pieces to crisp, about 4 to 6 minutes. Remove bacon pieces to paper towel; set aside to drain.

In a small bowl combine paprika, red pepper, curry, cumin, coriander, salt and pepper. Stir in olive oil, sugar and lemon juice.

Add shrimp and toss well to coat. Cover and let stand at room temperature 30 minutes to marinate. Refrigerate to marinate longer.

Preheat barbecue grill.

Remove shrimp from marinade, reserving marinade. Wrap a slice of bacon around each shrimp. Assemble 4 to 5 bacon wrapped shrimp on each skewer. Brush marinade over prepared skewers; turn and brush to coat well.

Place skewers on preheated grill. Brush with marinade. Cook over medium heat to desired doneness. Shrimp cook quickly. Do not overcook. Serve immediately.

*This will appeal to every shrimp lover.*

9  thin slices lean smoked bacon (about ½-pound)

2  teaspoons sweet paprika

½  teaspoon ground red pepper

½  teaspoon curry powder

½  teaspoon ground cumin

½  teaspoon ground coriander

½  teaspoon salt

½  teaspoon freshly ground black pepper

1  tablespoon olive oil

2  tablespoons sugar

2  tablespoons fresh lemon juice

18  jumbo shrimp, shelled, deveined (2-pounds)

**Serves: 3 (main course)**
**6 (appetizers)**

4 tablespoons vegetable oil

3 tablespoons butter

2 cloves garlic, minced

20 - 25 large shrimp, peeled, deveined

½ teaspoon crushed red pepper flakes

1 teaspoon oregano

½ teaspoon salt

2 tablespoons all-purpose flour

½ cup sherry

⅛ cup fresh lemon juice

¾ cup chicken broth

**Serves: 4 - 6**

# SHRIMP SCAMPI

Heat oil and butter in a large, heavy skillet.  Add garlic; sauté until lightly brown.

Add shrimp; cook until pink and firm.  Add red pepper, oregano, salt and flour.  Stir well; cook about 1 to 2 minutes. Blend in sherry, lemon juice and chicken broth.  Simmer on low heat for 5 to 10 minutes or until shrimp are cooked.

*Serve with fresh steamed vegetables and a nice chilled wine, this dish is sure to wow everyone.*

# Shrimp Stuffed Zucchini

Sauté shrimp in 2 tablespoons melted butter in a medium skillet until pink and firm; remove and set aside.

Cut zucchini in halves lengthwise; scoop out and reserve pulp. Put zucchini shells in boiling salted water; cook 3 to 5 minutes. Plunge into cold water to partially cool; drain well. Arrange zucchini shells in a baking dish. Set aside.

Melt remaining 2 tablespoons butter in skillet. Sauté onion until translucent; add reserved pulp, tomatoes, paprika, salt and pepper. Cook and stir over high heat to evaporate liquid. Stir in shrimp. Spoon shrimp mixture into zucchini shells.

Preheat oven to 425 degrees.

To make sauce, melt butter in small saucepan. Stir in flour; blend well. Cook over medium heat about 2 minutes. Slowly add half-and-half; stir until smooth. Add Parmesan cheese and mustard. Spoon sauce over stuffed zucchini. Sprinkle with Parmesan cheese. Bake, uncovered, for 10 to 15 minutes or until golden.

¾ pound small shrimp, shelled, deveined

4 tablespoons butter, divided

4 medium whole zucchini

1 green onion, minced

4 tomatoes, chopped

1 teaspoon paprika

1 teaspoon salt

1 teaspoon pepper

2 tablespoons Parmesan cheese

Sauce:

2 tablespoons butter

2 tablespoons all-purpose flour

1 ¼ cups half-and-half

¼ cup Parmesan cheese

½ teaspoon Dijon mustard

Parmesan cheese

**Serves: 6 - 8**

1 pound extra large raw shrimp, shelled, deveined

2 tablespoons dry sherry

2 tablespoons soy sauce

2 teaspoons granulated sugar

½ teaspoon salt

2 tablespoons catsup

2 tablespoons chili sauce

1 teaspoon red pepper flakes

2 tablespoons peanut oil

¼ cup minced green onions

2 tablespoons minced fresh ginger root

2 cloves garlic, minced

Steamed rice

**Serves: 6**

# SHRIMP SZECHWAN

Rinse shrimp; drain well. Spread on paper towel to dry well.

Combine sherry, soy sauce, sugar and salt; set aside. Combine catsup, chili sauce and red pepper flakes in a small bowl; set aside.

Heat oil in a wok or large heavy skillet. Add shrimp, green onions, ginger root and garlic. Stir-fry over medium-high heat until shrimp are pink.

Add soy sauce mixture; stir well. Add chili sauce to mixture; stir until well blended. Cook until shrimp is opaque. Serve with steamed rice.

# GRILLED SHRIMP AND VEGETABLES

Combine ingredients for shrimp marinade in a shallow dish or zip-closure plastic bag. Add shrimp; turn to coat shrimp with marinade. Cover tightly; refrigerate to marinate at least 1 hour or overnight.

Combine ingredients for vegetable marinade in medium bowl. Add mushrooms and tomatoes; toss to coat. Set aside at room temperature for at least 1 hour.

When ready to cook, skewer shrimp, mushrooms and tomatoes separately. Place mushrooms on medium heated grill first; cook for 4 to 6 minutes. Place shrimp and tomatoes on grill. Cook about 5 minutes on each side, or until browned.

Toss arugula with olive oil and balsamic vinegar in a medium bowl, while shrimp and vegetables are cooking. Place a small bed of arugula on each serving plate along with a lemon wedge.

Place shrimp and vegetables on top of arugula; season as desired with salt and pepper.

**Marinade for shrimp:**
- 1 cup olive oil
- 1 tablespoon minced garlic
- 1 lemon, thinly sliced
- ¼ cup brandy
- Salt, to taste
- Pepper, to taste

**Marinade for vegetables:**
- ½ cup olive oil
- ¼ cup lemon juice
- Salt, to taste
- Pepper, to taste

- 2 pounds large fresh shrimp, in shells
- 1 pound fresh mushrooms
- 1 pound cherry tomatoes
- 1 bunch fresh arugula, washed and drained
- 2 tablespoons extra-virgin olive oil
- 1 tablespoon balsamic vinegar
- 1 lemon, cut into 6 wedges
- Salt, optional
- Pepper, optional

**Serves: 6**

1 pound sea scallops

1 pound jumbo shrimp, peeled, deveined

2 cups orange juice

½ cup red wine vinegar

¼ cup molasses

3 tablespoons lime juice

Grated rind of 1 lime

½ teaspoon ground red pepper

1 teaspoon curry

2 tablespoons butter

Hot cooked rice

**Serves: 4**

# GRILLED SEAFOOD KABOBS WITH ORANGE CURRY GLAZE

Rinse shrimp and scallops under cold water; pat dry on paper towel. Thread shrimp and scallops alternately onto skewers. Set aside.

Combine orange juice, vinegar, molasses, lime juice, lime rind, red pepper and curry in a medium saucepan. Bring to a boil. Reduce heat slightly; boil about 10 to 15 minutes or until volume is reduced by half.

Cut 2 tablespoons butter into 4 pieces. Remove pan from heat. Whisk in butter one piece at a time until blended thoroughly into glaze.

Brush kabobs with glaze mixture; let set at room temperature for 30 minutes.

Preheat barbecue grill to medium-hot. Arrange kabobs on hot grill. Grill 2 to 3 minutes per side, basting frequently. When seafood is opaque and cooked, remove from grill. Serve immediately with hot cooked rice.

# BROILED SCALLOPS AND MUSHROOMS

1 ½ pounds large sea scallops

¾ cup butter, divided

½ cup herbed bread crumbs

¼ cup minced green onions, divided

¼ cup chopped fresh parsley

Juice of ½ lemon

¼ pound mushrooms, sliced

¼ cup dry white wine

**Serves: 4**

Drain scallops in a large strainer. Place on paper towel to drain and gently pat dry. Set aside.

Combine 1/2 cup butter, bread crumbs, 2 tablespoons green onions, parsley and lemon juice in a small bowl. Blend well. Shape into a 5 to 6-inch log. Refrigerate to chill well.

Lightly butter a shallow baking dish. Preheat broiler to 450 degrees.

Melt remaining butter in a large skillet. Add mushrooms and wine. Sauté about 4 to 5 minutes or until mushrooms are lightly cooked. Add scallops and wine; cook about 3 or 4 minutes more.

Pour mixture into buttered baking dish. Slice chilled butter mixture into thin pieces; arrange over scallop mushroom mixture.

Place about 5-inches from heat in preheated broiler. Broil until crumb mixture is a rich golden brown and scallop mushroom mixture is hot and bubbly.

Serve immediately.

2 (12-ounce) cans beer

3 cups water

1 pound smoked sausage, cut into 2-inch pieces

1 pound fresh green beans, washed, trimmed

6 ears of corn, cut in 3 inch pieces

1 pound shrimp, shells included

Butter, melted

Cocktail sauce

**Serves: 8**

# BACK COUNTRY COOKOUT

Bring beer and water to a boil in a large Dutch oven or pan. Add sausage; cover and simmer for 15 minutes. Add beans; cook 5 minutes. Add corn and shrimp. Cover and cook 3 to 5 minutes more, until shrimp turns pink and opaque. Do not overcook shrimp.

Remove all to a serving platter. Serve with ramekins of melted butter and cocktail sauce for dipping.

*Add an ice-cold beverage and this becomes a great leisurely summer meal.*

# Fresh Basil and Balsamic Marinade

Combine all ingredients; whisk until well-blended. Use as a marinade to enhance the flavor of any fish.

½ cup olive oil

2 tablespoons finely chopped fresh basil leaves

2 tablespoons balsamic vinegar

1 tablespoon chopped fresh parsley

1 tablespoon minced shallot or white part of green onion

¼ teaspoon salt

¼ teaspoon fresh ground pepper

**Yield: about ¾ cup**

# Greek Oregano Marinade for Fish

Combine oil, lemon juice, oregano and garlic. Stir to blend well. Add onion slices. Pour over fish and marinate about 30 minutes. Baste fish with the marinade while grilling.

½ cup olive oil

¼ cup fresh lemon juice

2 teaspoons chopped fresh oregano

1 teaspoon minced garlic

½ red onion, sliced very thin (½ cup)

**Yield: about 1 ¼ cups**

# GRANDE FINALE

*Cakes and Cheesecakes*

*Special Desserts and Sauces*

*Pies and Pastries*

*Cookies and Candies*

◀ Pears Poached in Cabernet, 327; Crème Fraiche, 322

# Grande Finale

# STRAWBERRY CREAM GATEAU

## Sponge Cake:

¾ cup granulated sugar

6 eggs, separated

¼ teaspoon vanilla

1 ½ cups cake flour, sifted

3 tablespoons orange-flavored liqueur

Preheat oven to 325 degrees. Butter and flour an 8-inch springform pan.

Combine sugar, egg yolks and vanilla in large mixing bowl. Place bowl over hot water; beat until light and lemon-colored.

Beat egg whites until stiff but not dry; gently fold into sugar mixture. Fold in flour. Pour into prepared pan. Bake 40 minutes or until a wooden pick inserted in center comes out clean. Cool. Cut cake horizontally into 3 equal layers. Sprinkle each layer with orange liqueur.

## Strawberry Cream Filling:

2 cups whipping cream, well chilled

2 - 4 tablespoons confectioners' sugar

1 quart (1 ½-pounds) strawberries, washed and hulled (3 to 4 cups)

In well chilled mixing bowl, beat cream until soft peaks form; beat in sugar until stiff.

Cut 1 cup strawberries into halves.

Place bottom cake layer on serving plate. Top with 1/2 cup cream mixture; spread evenly. Top with half of the sliced strawberries.

Repeat with second cake layer, 1/2 cup cream mixture and remaining strawberry halves. Top with remaining cake layer.

**Serves: 8 - 10**

Reserving 1 cup cream mixture, spread remainder over top and side of cake. Garnish with reserved cream and remaining whole berries. Refrigerate until serving time.

*A light and wonderful dessert!*

# APPLE-CARROT CAKE

3 cups all-purpose flour

2 teaspoons ground cinnamon

1 teaspoon baking powder

1 teaspoon baking soda

¾ teaspoon salt

¼ teaspoon ground nutmeg

¼ teaspoon ground cloves

1 ½ cups vegetable oil

1 cup firmly packed light brown sugar

¾ cup granulated sugar

3 eggs

2 teaspoons vanilla

2 cups peeled, coarsely grated apples, well drained

1 cup coarsely grated carrot

1 cup chopped pecans

Cream Cheese Frosting:

1 (8-ounce) package cream cheese, softened

½ cup (1 stick) butter or margarine

1 (1-pound) box confectioners' sugar

Finely grated rind of 1 orange

1 teaspoon vanilla

**Serves: 12**

Preheat oven to 350 degrees. Grease a 13 x 9-inch baking pan.

In a medium bowl, sift together flour, cinnamon, baking powder, baking soda, salt, nutmeg and cloves. Set aside.

In large mixing bowl, combine oil, brown sugar, granulated sugar, eggs and vanilla. Beat until smooth. Add flour mixture; beat until smooth.

Stir in grated apples, carrots and pecans. Spoon into prepared pan.

Bake 50 minutes or until wooden pick inserted in center comes out clean. Cool completely on rack.

To prepare frosting, in medium bowl, beat cream cheese, butter, confectioners' sugar, orange rind and vanilla until smooth. Spread on cooled cake. Cut in squares to serve.

# Fruited Carrot Cake with Cream Cheese Frosting

Preheat oven to 350 degrees. Line bottom of two 9-inch round layer cake pans with parchment paper or wax paper. Cover raisins with hot water; set aside to "plump." Drain well.

Sift together flour, baking soda, salt and cinnamon; set aside.

Beat eggs in large bowl. Add sugar; continue beating until light and frothy. Add flour mixture alternately with oil; mixing until blended. The mixture will be very thick and stiff.

Stir in raisins, carrots, coconut, walnuts and pineapple; mix well. Pour into prepared pans. Bake 35 to 45 minutes until sides pull away from pans and top springs back when lightly touched.

Cool completely; remove from pans.

To prepare frosting, in medium bowl, beat butter, cream cheese, confectioners' sugar and vanilla until smooth. Fill and frost cake layers; garnish with walnuts if desired.

*This is a moist cake which will stay fresh for several days. It also freezes well, either frosted or unfrosted.*

*A traditional favorite.*

### Cake:

½ cup golden raisins

2 cups all-purpose flour

2 teaspoons baking soda

1 teaspoon salt

2 teaspoons ground cinnamon

3 eggs

2 cups granulated sugar

1 ½ cups vegetable oil

3 cups grated carrots

1 cup shredded coconut

1 cup walnuts, coarsely chopped

1 (8-ounce) can crushed pineapple, undrained

### Frosting:

½ cup (1 stick) butter or margarine, softened

1 (8-ounce) package cream cheese, softened

1 (1-pound) box confectioners' sugar

1 teaspoon vanilla

Chopped walnuts, optional

**Serves: 12**

## Cake:

- 2 ¼ cups all-purpose flour
- ¾ cup sugar
- 2 teaspoons ground cinnamon
- 1 teaspoon baking powder
- 1 teaspoon ground ginger
- ½ teaspoon baking soda
- ½ teaspoon salt
- ½ teaspoon ground nutmeg
- ¼ teaspoon ground cloves
- ¾ cup water
- ¾ cup vegetable oil
- ¾ cup dark molasses
- 2 eggs

## Sauce:

- 1 cup granulated sugar
- ½ cup butter or margarine
- ¼ cup lemon juice
- Confectioners' sugar

**Serves: 12**

# GINGERBREAD WITH LEMON BUTTER SAUCE

Preheat oven to 350 degrees. Grease a 13 x 9-inch or 10-inch fluted tube pan.

Combine flour, sugar, cinnamon, baking powder, ginger, baking soda, salt, nutmeg and cloves in a large mixing bowl. Stir in water, oil, molasses and eggs; beat with mixer for 3 minutes. Pour in prepared pan. Bake 35 to 40 minutes in 13 x 9-inch; 50 to 60 minutes in 10-inch fluted tube pan or until wooden pick inserted near center comes out clean.

To prepare sauce, mix sugar, butter or margarine and lemon juice in a small saucepan. Cook and stir over medium heat until sugar dissolves. Pour boiling sauce over hot cake, immediately after removing from oven. Cool. Just before serving, dust with confectioners' sugar. Cut in squares or wedges.

*This gorgeously glazed gingerbread does justice to any occasion.*

# DOUBLED CHOCOLATE GLAZED FUDGE CAKE

Preheat oven to 300 degrees.  Grease and flour a 10-inch fluted tube pan; set aside.

Beat butter in large mixing bowl until fluffy; gradually add sugar beating until smooth.  Add eggs, one at a time, beating well after each addition.

Combine buttermilk and baking soda, stir well.  Add to sugar mixture alternately with flour.  Add melted chocolate, chocolate-flavored syrup and vanilla.  Mix well.  Stir in 1 cup mini chips.

Pour batter into prepared tube pan.  Bake 1 hour and 20 minutes or until wooden pick comes out clean when inserted in center.  Immediately invert cake onto serving plate; cool completely.

Melt white chocolate and 1 tablespoon shortening in top of a double boiler, stirring constantly until smooth.  Remove from heat; drizzle over cooled cake.

Melt remaining 1/2 cup mini chips and 2 teaspoons shortening in a small saucepan over low heat, stirring until smooth.  Remove from heat; cool 10 minutes.  Drizzle over the white chocolate.

*An outrageous cake!*

1 cup butter or margarine, softened

1 ½ cups sugar

4 eggs

1 cup buttermilk

½ teaspoon baking soda

2 ½ cups all-purpose flour

2 (4-ounce) bars sweet baking chocolate, melted and cooled

1 cup chocolate-flavored syrup

2 teaspoons vanilla

1 ½ cups mini semi-sweet chocolate chips, divided

2 ounces white chocolate, chopped

1 tablespoon plus 2 teaspoons shortening, divided

**Serves:  10 - 12**

5 ounces semi-sweet chocolate, chopped

3 tablespoons butter or margarine

4 eggs, room temperature, separated

4 tablespoons sugar, divided

1 - 2 tablespoons orange-flavored liqueur

¼ teaspoon cream of tartar

Whipped cream

Fresh strawberries

**Serves: 6 - 8**

# RICH FLOURLESS CHOCOLATE CAKE

Preheat oven to 275 degrees. Line one 9-inch round layer cake pan with parchment or waxed paper. Butter paper; set aside.

Melt chocolate and butter in top of double boiler. Stir until smooth. Remove from heat.

With electric mixer, beat egg yolks and 2 tablespoons sugar until doubled in volume and consistency of whipped cream, 5 to 8 minutes. Blend in liqueur. Fold in melted chocolate mixture.

Using clean beaters and bowl, beat whites with cream of tartar until soft peaks form. Gradually add remaining sugar; beat until stiff but not dry. Fold into chocolate mixture. Pour into prepared pan.

Bake 35 minutes or until top springs back when lightly touched. Cool completely in pan. Turn onto serving plate. Cut into wedges. Serve with whipped cream and fresh berries.

*A scrumptious chocolate dessert!*

# DARK CHOCOLATE FILLED CAKE

Preheat oven to 350 degrees. Butter and flour a 10-inch fluted tube pan.

In small bowl, beat cream cheese, 1/2 cup granulated sugar, egg and vanilla until smooth; set aside.

In large mixing bowl, beat sugar, oil and eggs until well blended; beat 1 minute on high speed. Sift together flour, cocoa, baking soda, baking powder and salt; add alternately with buttermilk, water and vanilla to sugar mixture. Beat on medium speed 3 minutes.

Pour half of the cake batter into prepared pan. Spoon cream cheese mixture over batter; top with remaining batter.

Bake 50 to 60 minutes or until wooden pick inserted near center comes out clean. Cool in pan on rack 15 minutes. Remove cake from pan; cool completely.

For glaze, in small bowl, combine ingredients; beat until smooth (mixture will be syrupy). Drizzle over cooled cake. Refrigerate.

*This cake must be refrigerated but preferably served at room temperature.*

## Filling:
- 1 (8-ounce) package cream cheese, softened
- ½ cup granulated sugar
- 1 egg
- 1 teaspoon vanilla
- 1 cup mini semi-sweet chocolate chips

## Dark Chocolate Cake:
- 2 cups granulated sugar
- 1 cup vegetable oil
- 2 eggs
- 3 cups all-purpose flour
- ¾ cup unsweetened cocoa
- 2 teaspoons baking soda
- 2 teaspoons baking powder
- ½ teaspoon salt
- 1 cup buttermilk
- 1 cup hot water
- 2 teaspoons vanilla

## Glaze:
- ½ cup sifted confectioners' sugar
- 2 tablespoons unsweetened cocoa
- 3 tablespoons butter or margarine, softened
- 2 teaspoons vanilla
- 1 - 3 tablespoons hot water

**Serves: 12 - 16**

## Cake:

- 1 cup (2 sticks) butter or margarine
- 3 cups granulated sugar
- ½ cup vegetable oil
- 5 eggs
- 3 cups all-purpose flour
- ½ teaspoon baking powder
- ¼ teaspoon salt
- 1 cup milk
- 1 teaspoon vanilla
- 1 teaspoon lemon extract
- 1 teaspoon orange extract

## Glaze:

- ½ cup confectioners' sugar
- 3 tablespoons butter or margarine
- 1 teaspoon lemon juice
- ¼ teaspoon grated lemon rind
- 1 - 3 tablespoons hot water

**Serves:  12 - 16**

# THREE FLAVORS POUND CAKE

Preheat oven to 325 degrees.  Grease a 10-inch fluted tube pan.

In large mixing bowl, beat butter and sugar until light and fluffy; beat in oil.  Add eggs, one at a time; beat well.

Sift together flour, baking powder and salt.  Add alternately with milk to batter.  Add vanilla, lemon and orange extracts.  Blend well.

Pour into prepared pan.  Bake 1 hour and 15 minutes or until wooden pick inserted near center comes out clean.  Cool on rack 10 minutes; remove from pan.  Cool completely.

For glaze, combine confectioners' sugar, butter, lemon juice and rind and water.  Blend well.  Drizzle over cooled cake.

*Variation:  Add 3/4 cup unsweetened cocoa with flour to make chocolate pound cake.  Bake in loaf pans for another variation.*

*A marvelous blend of flavors!*

# EXCEPTIONAL POUND CAKE

Preheat oven to 325 degrees. Butter and flour 9 x 5-inch loaf pan.

In large mixing bowl, beat butter and sugar until light and fluffy. Add eggs, one at a time, beating well after each addition. Add remaining ingredients; beat on low speed to combine.

Pour batter into prepared pan. Bake 1 hour 10 minutes or until wooden pick inserted in center comes out clean. Cool on rack 10 minutes; remove from pan. Cool completely.

*This exceptional pound cake can be served with fresh fruit and a dollop of Crème Fraiche, Raspberry Chocolate Sauce or any of our dessert sauces.*

*Wonderful, even by itself.*

1 cup (2 sticks) butter or margarine

2 cups granulated sugar

5 eggs

2 cups all-purpose flour

¼ teaspoon salt

¼ teaspoon baking powder

½ teaspoon mace

1 teaspoon ground nutmeg

1 teaspoon vanilla

1 tablespoon brandy, amaretto, or orange-flavored liqueur

**Serves: 6 - 8**

1 tablespoon finely
  chopped, toasted pecans

4 ounces premium white
  chocolate, coarsely
  chopped

3 cups all-purpose flour

½ teaspoon salt

¼ teaspoon baking soda

1 cup (2 sticks) unsalted
  butter, softened

2 cups granulated sugar

1 cup whipping cream

2 teaspoons vanilla

6 eggs, room temperature

  Confectioners' sugar


**Serves:  10 - 12**

# WHITE CHOCOLATE
# POUND CAKE

Preheat oven to 300 degrees.  Place rack in center of oven.
Lightly grease and flour a 10-inch fluted tube pan.  Sprinkle
pecans evenly on the bottom.

Melt white chocolate in top of a double boiler, stirring constantly
until smooth.  Remove the top pan of chocolate; set aside to cool
slightly.

Sift together flour, salt and baking soda in large bowl.

In separate large mixing bowl, beat butter until fluffy.  Add
sugar, 1 cup at a time; beat well.  Beat in cream, melted white
chocolate and vanilla.  Add eggs, one at a time, mixing well after
each addition.  Reduce mixer speed to low and slowly add flour,
mixing until blended.

Pour batter into prepared pan.  Bake 1 hour and 15 minutes,
or until wooden pick inserted near center comes out clean.  Cool
in pan on rack 10 minutes.  Invert cake onto wire rack; cooling completely.

Dust cooled cake with confectioners' sugar.  Serve with whipped
cream and fresh blueberries or strawberries if desired.

*The very best white chocolate available is preferred for this
moist and rich cake.  It is destined to become one of your new
favorites.*

# Praline Cheesecake

Preheat oven to 350 degrees.

Combine crumbs, granulated sugar and butter. Press on bottom of 9-inch springform pan. Bake 10 minutes. Cool.

Combine cream cheese, sugar and flour in large mixing bowl; mix well. Add eggs, one at a time, beating well after each addition. Blend in vanilla and chopped pecans. Pour into prepared pan.

Bake 50 to 55 minutes or until top springs back when lightly touched. Cool completely before removing from pan. Garnish with pecan halves. Refrigerate.

*Praline flavor at its finest.*

**Crust:**

| | |
|---|---|
| 1 | cup graham cracker crumbs |
| 3 | tablespoons granulated sugar |
| 3 | tablespoons butter or margarine, melted |

**Filling:**

| | |
|---|---|
| 3 | (8-ounce) packages cream cheese, softened |
| 1 ¼ | cups firmly packed dark brown sugar |
| 2 | tablespoons all-purpose flour |
| 3 | eggs |
| 1 ½ | teaspoons vanilla |
| ½ | cup finely chopped pecans |
| | Pecan halves |

**Serves: 10 - 12**

**Crust:**

- ½ cup (1 stick) butter or margarine, softened
- 1 cup confectioners' sugar
- 1 egg yolk
- 1 cup all-purpose flour
- 2 tablespoons unsweetened cocoa
- ½ teaspoon baking powder
- 1 cup chopped and lightly toasted walnuts or pecans

**Filling:**

- 3 (8 ounce) packages cream cheese, softened
- 1 cup granulated sugar
- 1 egg white
- 1 ½ teaspoons vanilla
- 4 eggs

  Fresh raspberries, optional

  Grated chocolate, optional

**Serves: 48 bite-size portions**

**12 - 20 dessert portions**

# CLASSIC CHEESECAKE WITH CHOCOLATE NUT CRUST

Preheat oven to 350 degrees. Grease and flour a 13 x 9-inch baking pan.

For crust, beat butter, confectioners' sugar and egg yolk in large mixing bowl. Add flour, cocoa and baking powder; mix well. Stir in nuts. Press on bottom of prepared pan; set aside.

To prepare filling, combine cream cheese, sugar and vanilla in large mixing bowl; beat until fluffy. Add eggs, one at a time, beating well after each addition. Pour mixture over prepared crust; spread evenly.

Bake 40 to 45 minutes, or until filling is set and lightly browned around edges. Cool completely.

Chill thoroughly. Cut into squares. Store covered in refrigerator. Garnish with fresh raspberries and grated chocolate if desired.

*This can also be cut into 1-inch pieces to fit into a dessert buffet or holiday dessert tray where you need smaller portions.*

# Mandarin Orange Cheesecake

Preheat oven at 375 degrees. Butter 10-inch springform pan.

For crust, combine crumbs, sugar and butter; press evenly on bottom and up side of prepared pan. Bake 8 minutes; cool to room temperature.

To prepare filling, combine mandarin oranges, orange juice and liqueur; set aside.

Combine cream cheese, orange rind and flavorings in large mixing bowl; beat at high speed until fluffy. Gradually add sugar, beating well. Add eggs, one at a time, beating well after each addition.

Pour filling into prepared crust. Bake 50 minutes or until filling is almost set. Turn oven off and partially open door. Leave cake in oven 30 minutes. Remove from oven. Cool to room temperature on wire rack.

Drain mandarin orange mixture reserving liquid. Arrange mandarin oranges on top of cooled cheesecake.

In small saucepan, combine reserved mandarin orange liquid, reserved orange juice-liqueur mixture and cornstarch. Stir well and cook over medium heat 5 minutes or until thickened; cool slightly. Spoon glaze over top of cheesecake. Chill thoroughly.

Garnish with fresh mint leaves if desired.

*A fresh taste.*

## Crust:

- 1 ½ cups graham cracker crumbs
- 2 tablespoons sugar
- ⅓ cup butter or margarine, melted

## Filling:

- 1 (11-ounce) can Mandarin oranges, drained, reserving ½ cup liquid
- ½ cup orange juice
- ¼ cup orange-flavored liqueur
- 4 (8-ounce) packages cream cheese, softened
- 2 tablespoons finely grated orange rind
- 2 teaspoons orange extract
- 1 teaspoon vanilla
- 1 ⅓ cups sugar
- 4 eggs
- 1 tablespoon plus 1 teaspoon cornstarch

  Fresh mint leaves, optional

**Serves: 10 - 12**

## Crust:

- 1 (8 ½-ounce) package chocolate wafer cookies, finely crushed (about 2 cups)
- ¼ cup granulated sugar
- ⅓ cup butter or margarine, melted

## Filling:

- 2 (8-ounce) plus 2 (3-ounce) packages cream cheese, softened
- ½ cup granulated sugar, divided
- 3 eggs
- 1 ½ teaspoons vanilla extract, divided
- 2 (1-ounce) squares semi-sweet chocolate , melted
- 1 ⅓ cups sour cream, divided
- ⅓ cup firmly packed dark brown sugar
- 1 tablespoon all-purpose flour
- ½ cup chopped, toasted pecans
- 2 tablespoons amaretto liqueur

# TRIPLE LAYER CHEESECAKE WITH CHOCOLATE-GLAZE

Preheat oven at 325 degrees.

For crust, combine crumbs, sugar and butter. Press on bottom and 2 inches up sides of 9-inch springform pan; set aside.

For chocolate filling layer, in mixing bowl, beat 1 (8-ounce) package cream cheese and 1/4 cup granulated sugar until fluffy. Beat in 1 egg and 1/4 teaspoon vanilla until smooth. Stir in melted chocolate and 1/3 cup sour cream. Spoon into prepared pan.

For second filling layer, in mixing bowl, combine 1 (8-ounce) package cream cheese, brown sugar and flour; beat until fluffy. Beat in 1 egg and 1 teaspoon vanilla. Stir in pecans. Gently spoon over chocolate layer.

For third filling layer, in mixing bowl, beat 2 (3-ounce) packages cream cheese and 1/4 cup sugar until fluffy. Beat in 1 egg. Stir in remaining 1 cup sour cream, 1/4 teaspoon vanilla and the amaretto. Gently spoon over layer.

*Recipe continued on next page*

6   (1-ounce) squares semi-
    sweet chocolate

¼   cup butter

¾   cup confectioners' sugar,
    sifted

2   tablespoons water

1   teaspoon vanilla

    Toasted pecan halves


**Serves:  12 - 16**

Bake 1 hour or until center is just set.  Turn off oven; leave
cheesecake in oven 30 minutes.  Open oven door; cool in oven
additional 30 minutes.  Remove from oven; cool completely.
Chill 8 hours.  Remove side of pan.

For glaze, melt chocolate and butter over low heat.  Stir in confectioners' sugar, water and vanilla until smooth.  Spread
over cheesecake while warm.  Garnish with pecan halves.
Store covered in refrigerator.

*A dramatic attraction when you want to serve something very
special.*

8 ounces semi-sweet chocolate

⅓ cup water

1 teaspoon peppermint extract or 1 tablespoon white creme de menthe

5 eggs, separated*

Pinch of salt

Whipped cream flavored with a dash of peppermint extract

Fresh mint leaves

**Serves: 6**

# MINT CHOCOLATE MOUSSE

Melt the chocolate and water in a heavy saucepan over low heat; cool.

In small mixing bowl, beat egg yolks on high speed until light yellow in color. Gradually add cooled chocolate mixture, beating only until smooth; add peppermint extract.

In large mixing bowl, beat egg whites until foamy. Add salt; continue beating until stiff but not dry. Stir about a fourth of the egg whites into the chocolate mixture; blend until smooth. Gently fold the chocolate mixture into the egg whites until well blended.

Spoon mousse into individual serving dishes or small wine glasses. Garnish with flavored whipped cream and mint. Chill.

*Raw egg is used in this recipe - see special notes.

Always an elegant dessert.

# CHILLED RASPBERRY SOUFFLÉ

Tape or tie a 3-inch parchment or wax paper "collar" securely around rim of 5 or 6-cup soufflé dish.

In blender or food processor, puree raspberries. Pour into a saucepan.

Soften gelatine in water; add to puréed raspberries. Heat until gelatine is dissolved. Stir in liqueur and vanilla; chill until partially set.

Meanwhile in large mixing bowl, beat egg whites with salt until foamy; gradually add sugar, beating until stiff but not dry.

Gently fold egg whites and whipped cream into chilled raspberry mixture. Spoon into prepared soufflé dish. Chill several hours or until set. Garnish with fresh raspberries and mint leaves.

*Raw egg is used in this recipe - see special notes.

A cool heavenly experience!

2 (10-ounce) packages frozen red raspberries, thawed

3 envelopes unflavored gelatine

1 cup cold water

1/3 cup orange-flavored liqueur

1 teaspoon vanilla

6 egg whites*

1/8 teaspoon salt

1/2 cup sugar

1 1/2 cups whipping cream, whipped

Fresh raspberries and mint leaves, optional

**Serves: 6**

Granulated sugar

4 ounces semi-sweet chocolate

¼ cup (½ stick) butter or margarine

4 eggs, separated

2 tablespoons orange-flavored liqueur

¼ teaspoon cream of tartar

**Serves: 4**

# SENSATIONAL CHOCOLATE SOUFFLÉ

Preheat oven to 475 degrees. Butter a 1-quart soufflé dish and coat with sugar.

In a saucepan, melt chocolate and butter over low heat. Remove from heat; beat in egg yolks, 1 at a time, until smooth. Stir in liqueur. Set aside.

In large bowl, beat egg whites until foamy. Add cream of tartar; beat until stiff but not dry. Whisk one-third of the egg whites into chocolate mixture. Gently fold chocolate mixture into egg whites.

Pour mixture into prepared dish. Bake 5 minutes. Reduce oven temperature to 425 degrees; continue baking 5 to 7 minutes or until top is puffed and dry.

Serve soufflé with Crème Anglaise for a spectacular dessert.

*A match made in heaven!*

# Mocha Cream Torte

1 large, prepared angel food cake

Slice cake horizontally into 5 slices. Set aside.

For filling, in large mixing bowl, beat butter until fluffy; gradually beat in confectioners' sugar until smooth. Beat salt, vanilla, and 2 egg yolks until smooth. Add chocolate and coffee; mix well.

In small bowl, beat egg whites until stiff peaks form; fold into chocolate mixture.

On a serving platter, place bottom cake layer; top with one-fourth of the mocha mixture. Repeat, using all cake layers and fillings. Cover tightly with plastic wrap; refrigerate overnight.

Just before serving, prepare topping by beating whip cream, confectioners' sugar and vanilla until stiff peaks form. Generously frost top and side of cake with the whipped cream. Serve immediately.

*Raw egg is used in this recipe - see special notes.*

*Beautiful on a holiday table, garnished with holly, fresh edible flowers, chocolate shavings or seasonal fruits.*

Filling:

1 cup (2 sticks) butter or margarine, softened

1 ½ cups confectioners' sugar

Pinch of salt

1 teaspoon vanilla

2 eggs, separated *

2 squares semi-sweet chocolate, melted, cooled

¼ cup very strong coffee

Topping:

2 cups whipping cream

2 tablespoons confectioners' sugar

1 teaspoon vanilla

**Serves: 10 - 12**

**Crepes:**

- ¾ cup all-purpose flour
- 3 tablespoons unsweetened cocoa
- 3 tablespoons granulated sugar
- Pinch of salt
- 1 ¼ cups milk, divided
- 1 egg
- 2 tablespoons unsalted butter, melted, cooled
- ½ teaspoon vanilla
- 3 tablespoons clarified butter or vegetable oil

**Orange Crème Anglaise:**

- 6 egg yolks
- ½ cup granulated sugar
- 1 ½ cups half-and-half
- 2 tablespoons orange-flavored liqueur

# ORANGE AND CHOCOLATE FILLED CREPES

To make crepes, sift together flour, cocoa, sugar, and salt. Make a well in center of mixture; pour in 1 cup milk, egg, melted butter and vanilla. Whisk until smooth. Cover and chill 1 hour or overnight. The batter will thicken after setting. Whisk in 1/4 cup milk if needed until batter is the consistency of heavy cream. Strain batter if desired.

In a 6-inch skillet over medium-high heat, brush pan with clarified butter or oil. Pour 2 tablespoons batter into skillet, tilting to coat pan. Cook 45 seconds or until edges are firm and lightly browned; remove to plate. Repeat until all batter is used. (Crepes can be prepared up to 2 days ahead, wrapped with wax paper between each crepe. Refrigerate or freeze up to 1 month.)

To prepare Orange Creme, in medium bowl, whisk together egg yolks and sugar. In medium saucepan, bring the half-and-half to a gentle boil over medium heat. Gradually whisk egg yolk mixture into half-and-half. Continue to cook over medium-low heat, stirring constantly until thickened enough to coat the back of a wooden spoon. (Do not boil.) Pour into a small bowl; stir in liqueur. Cool. Cover; chill at least 2 hours. (Can be prepared up to 1 day ahead.)

*Recipe continued on next page*

## Chocolate Fudge Filling:

- 1/2 cup sweetened condensed milk
- 1/2 cup whipping cream
- 4 ounces semi-sweet chocolate, finely chopped
- 2 tablespoons Cognac or other brandy

## Garnish:

- 1/2 cup whipping cream
- 2 tablespoons confectioners' sugar
- 1 pint fresh raspberries, optional
- 3 blood oranges, cut into segments, optional

    Fresh mint, optional

**Yield:  18 - 20 crepes**

**Serves:  6**

For Chocolate Filling, in medium saucepan over low heat, combine sweetened condensed milk, cream and chocolate.  Cook and stir until chocolate is melted and mixture has thickened. Remove from heat; stir in the Cognac.  Cool to room temperature.

To assemble crepes, in a small chilled bowl, beat cream and confectioners' sugar until soft peaks form.

Spread about 1 tablespoon of the Chocolate Filling over one half crepe.  Fold the crepe into quarters.  Repeat with remaining filling and crepes.  (Filled crepes can be prepared up to 4 hours ahead, covered and refrigerated.)

Position oven rack in center of oven and preheat to 450 degrees.  Arrange crepes on a large baking sheet; cover with aluminum foil.  Bake 3 minutes or until hot.

On each serving plate, arrange 3 crepes.  Spoon Orange Crème Anglaise around the crepes.  Top with whipped cream.  Garnish with raspberries, orange and mint if desired.

*A showpiece and an impressive presentation makes this worth the time and effort.*

## Custard:

2 ⅔ cups half-and-half

4 eggs, well beaten

¾ cup firmly packed dark brown sugar

3 tablespoons all-purpose flour

1 ¼ teaspoons vanilla

1 cup whipping cream

1 ¼ teaspoons instant coffee

3 tablespoons Scotch whisky

## Trifle:

1 (16-ounce) frozen pound cake, thawed, cut into ¾-inch cubes

6 tablespoons Scotch whisky

1 (10-ounce) jar raspberry jam, heated

1 (12-ounce) bag frozen whole unsweetened red raspberries, thawed or 1 pint (2 cups) fresh red raspberries

2 cups whipping cream

3 tablespoons confectioners' sugar

3 tablespoons Scotch whisky

½ pint fresh red raspberries

Semi-sweet chocolate, curled or grated

**Serves:  12 - 15**

# CARAMEL SCOTCH BERRY TRIFLE

To make custard, heat half-and-half in 1-quart glass measure in microwave on 100% power (high) 2 to 3 minutes.  In large microwave safe bowl or 2-quart measure, whisk together eggs, sugar, and flour.  Gradually whisk in half-and-half.  In microwave, cook on 100% power (high) 5 to 6 minutes or until custard mixture is very thick.  (Custard can also be made in a double boiler or heavy saucepan on low heat.)

Cover and chill, whisking occasionally.  Stir in vanilla.  (To chill custard quickly, place bowl in sink filled with ice.)

Combine whipping cream and coffee in a large mixing bowl, stirring to dissolve coffee.  Beat until stiff peaks form; fold into custard in 2 additions.  Cover; chill.  (Custard can be made a day ahead.)

To prepare the trifle, place cake cubes in large bowl and sprinkle with Scotch; stir gently.  Add milk as needed to custard to thin to pouring consistency.

In large glass serving bowl, layer one-fourth each of the cake, jam, custard and raspberries.  Repeat 3 times.  Cover and refrigerate until set.  (This can be made a day in advance.)

Whip cream and sugar in large bowl until stiff peaks form.  Beat in 3 tablespoons Scotch.  Top trifle with whipped cream and garnish with fresh raspberries and chocolate.

# ORANGE CRÈME SOUFFLÉ

Preheat oven to 375 degrees.

In a medium saucepan, melt butter, stir in flour and cook for 1 minute. Add milk slowly and stir constantly until thickened over medium heat. Remove from heat. Cool.

In a small bowl, beat egg yolks with 1/4 cup sugar until lemony in color and thick. Beat in liqueur. Stir the egg yolk mixture into cooled milk mixture. This portion of the recipe can be prepared and refrigerated up to 2 hours before serving.

In a large bowl, beat egg whites with 1 tablespoon of sugar until stiff but not dry. Whisk 1/4 of egg whites into yolk mixture until well blended. Gently fold the remaining egg whites into egg yolk mixture.

Pour mixture into a buttered and sugared two quart soufflé dish.

Bake in 375 degree oven for 30 to 35 minutes. The soufflé should appear puffed and golden in color when done. Serve immediately on a plate of Crème Anglaise.

To make Crème Anglaise, in a saucepan, heat cream but do not boil.

In a small bowl, beat egg yolks and sugar until lemony in color and thick.

Add egg yolk mixture into cream and stir with a wire whisk until blended. Cook over medium heat until sauce thickens. Cool. Stir in orange-flavored liqueur before serving.

3 tablespoons butter or margarine

3 tablespoons all-purpose flour

1 cup milk

4 egg yolks

¼ cup granulated sugar

¼ cup orange-flavored liqueur

6 egg whites, room temperature

1 tablespoon granulated sugar

Crème Anglaise:

¾ cup whipping cream

2 egg yolks

¼ cup granulated sugar

1 ½ tablespoons orange-flavored liqueur

**Serves: 4 - 6**

2　(8-ounce) packages cream cheese or mascarpone cheese

¼　teaspoon salt

½　cup plus 2 tablespoons confectioners' sugar, divided

⅓　cup plus 3 tablespoons coffee-flavored liqueur, divided

1 ½　teaspoons vanilla, divided

4　(1-ounce) squares semi-sweet chocolate, grated, divided

1 ½　cups whipping cream, divided

2　teaspoons instant espresso powder

2　tablespoons water

2　(3 to 4 ½-ounce) packages ladyfingers

1　teaspoon coffee-flavored liqueur, optional

**Serves:  10 - 12**

# TIRAMISU

In large bowl beat cream cheese, salt, 1/2 cup confectioners' sugar, 3 tablespoons liqueur, 1 teaspoon vanilla and 2 ounces chocolate until well blended.  Reserve remaining grated chocolate for garnish.

In small mixing bowl, beat 1 cup whipping cream until stiff peaks form; fold into cheese mixture.

In a small bowl, combine espresso powder, remaining 1/3 cup coffee-flavored liqueur, remaining 1/2 teaspoon vanilla and 2 tablespoons water; mix well.

Separate ladyfingers into halves.  Line 13 x 9-inch or 2 1/2-quart glass bowl with about a fourth of the ladyfinger halves; brush with 2 tablespoons espresso mixture.  Spoon one-third of cheese mixture over ladyfingers.  Repeat layering twice.  Top with remaining ladyfingers, gently pressing into cheese mixture.  Brush ladyfingers with remaining espresso mixture.  Sprinkle with half the reserved chocolate.

In small mixing bowl, beat remaining 1/2 cup whipping cream, 2 tablespoons confectioners' sugar and 1 teaspoon coffee-flavored liqueur if desired until stiff peaks form.

Pipe or dollop whipped cream on top of dessert.  Sprinkle with remaining reserved chocolate.  Chill at least 2 hours.

*This dessert is best when prepared one day in advance. May be frozen.*

*This is an elegant, light but rich dessert.*

# AMARETTO BREAD PUDDING

Break bread into small pieces. Place in medium bowl; add half-and-half. Cover; let stand 1 hour.

Preheat oven to 325 degrees. Butter a 13 x 9-inch baking dish.

Combine eggs, granulated sugar and amaretto in small bowl. Stir into bread mixture. Gently fold in raisins and almonds.

Spread bread mixture evenly in prepared dish. Bake on the middle rack of oven 50 minutes or until golden. Cool.

To make amaretto sauce, combine butter and confectioners' sugar in a heavy saucepan or double boiler; cook and stir constantly until sugar is dissolved and mixture is very hot. Remove from heat.

Add a small amount of sugar mixture to the egg. Whisk egg into the sugar mixture, beating until sauce has come to room temperature. Add amaretto.

To serve, preheat broiler. Cut pudding into 8 to 10 squares; arrange on oven proof serving dish. Spoon sauce over pudding squares; broil until sauce bubbles. Serve immediately.

1 loaf French bread

1 quart half-and-half

2 tablespoons butter or margarine, at room temperature

3 eggs

1 ½ cups granulated sugar

2 tablespoons amaretto liqueur

¾ cup golden raisins

¾ cup sliced almonds

### Amaretto Sauce:

½ cup (1 stick) butter or margarine, at room temperature

1 cup confectioners' sugar, sifted

1 egg, well beaten

¼ cup amaretto liqueur

**Serves: 8 - 10**

- 1 tablespoon unflavored gelatine
- ⅓ cup cold water
- 1 ½ cups milk
- ¾ cup sugar
- 1 tablespoon all-purpose flour
- 3 egg yolks
- Pinch salt
- 1 teaspoon vanilla
- 1 pint whipping cream
- 1 large angel food cake, preferably freshly baked
- Seasonal fresh fruit (strawberries, peaches, blueberries)

# ANGEL CUSTARD CHARLOTTE

Combine gelatine and water; set aside to soften. In saucepan, combine milk, sugar, flour, egg yolks, salt and vanilla. Cook over low heat until mixture thickens. Remove from heat; add gelatine mixture. Cool. Whip cream; fold into custard.

Slice cake in thirds horizontally. Fill and frost layers with cream mixture. Chill completely.

Garnish with seasonal fresh fruit.

*Texture is very light; cake is sure to become a requested favorite.*

# FROZEN COFFEE CRUNCH CAKE

1 (3 to 4 ½-ounce) package lady fingers

3 pints coffee ice cream, softened

¼ cup coffee-flavored liqueur

1 tablespoon instant coffee, divided

6 (1 ³⁄₁₆-ounce) milk chocolate-covered English toffee candy bars, cut into bite-size pieces

Line a 9-inch springform pan with ladyfingers. Mix ice cream, liqueur, 1 teaspoon instant coffee and candy.

Pour into pan; smooth mixture evenly. Cover tightly and freeze.

To serve, spoon into dessert dishes; top with purchased hot fudge sauce or Dark Chocolate Sauce.

*Deliciously crunchy!*

***Serves: 12***

3 eggs

1 cup sugar

2 quarts half-and-half

1 (16-ounce) can chocolate-flavored syrup

½ teaspoon ground cinnamon

1 tablespoon vanilla

¼ teaspoon almond extract

**Yield: about 1 gallon**

# MEXICAN CHOCOLATE ICE CREAM

In mixing bowl, beat eggs until frothy. Gradually add sugar, beating until thick.

Heat half-and-half in a 3-quart saucepan over low heat until hot. Gradually stir about one cup of half-and-half into eggs; add to remaining half-and-half, stirring constantly. Cook over low heat, stirring constantly until mixture thickens and reaches 165 degrees.

Remove from heat; stir in chocolate syrup, cinnamon, vanilla and almond extract. Cool in refrigerator. Pour into 1-gallon ice cream freezer container.

Freeze according to manufacturer's instructions. Let set at least 1 hour before serving.

*This dessert will be the finale to any Mexican dinner.*

# RASPBERRY SORBET

3 cups sugar

1 cup water

1 (20-ounce) package frozen whole unsweetened red raspberries, thawed

2 tablespoons fresh lemon juice

2 egg whites*

Fresh mint leaves

Fresh raspberries

**Serves: 6 - 8**

In a saucepan, dissolve sugar in water over low heat. When dissolved, increase heat and boil rapidly for 5 minutes. Cool completely.

Puree raspberries; strain to remove seeds. Add lemon juice and cooled syrup.

Pour raspberry mixture into ice cream freezer container. Follow manufacturer's instructions and freeze 15 minutes. Remove mixture to large bowl.

Beat egg whites until stiff peaks form; fold into raspberry mixture. Return mixture to freezer container; continue freezing.

To serve, spoon into parfait glasses; garnish with fresh mint and raspberries.

*Raw egg used in this recipe - see special notes.

1 ½ cups sugar

4 cups boiling water

¾ cup fresh lemon juice

2 teaspoons grated lemon rind

**Yield: about 3 pints**

# LUSCIOUS LEMON SORBET

Combine sugar and water. Stir to dissolve; cool. Stir in juice and lemon rind. Pour mixture into ice cream freezer container. Freeze according to manufacturer's directions.

*Refreshing to the palate!*

1 cup sour cream

2 cups whipping cream

**Yield: about 2 cups**

# CRÈME FRAICHE

Combine sour cream and whipping cream in a saucepan. Over low heat, warm gently.

Pour into a clean jar or bowl. Cover; let stand at room temperature overnight or longer until mixture has thickened.

This will keep in the refrigerator for 1 week.

*A very versatile sauce to keep on hand.*

# Bourbonnaise Sauce

2 cups sugar

¼ cup (½ stick) butter or margarine

½ cup whipping cream

½ cup bourbon

**Yield: 2 cups**

Heat a heavy skillet over medium heat; add sugar. Stir with wooden spoon until melted and golden in color. Remove from heat; stir in butter.

Gradually add cream; mix well . Stir in bourbon. Cool completely. Pour into a clean glass jar; cover and store in refrigerator.

*Great on fresh fruits, ice cream, and cakes.*

# Raspberry Chocolate Sauce

1 (10-ounce) package frozen red raspberries in syrup, thawed

¾ cup unsweetened cocoa, preferably Dutch process

1 ½ cups sugar

¼ cup (½ stick) butter or margarine, softened

⅓ cup light corn syrup

¾ cup whipping cream

**Yield: 2 ½ cups**

Puree raspberries and syrup in a blender or food processor, then press through a fine strainer to remove seeds. Set aside.

In large saucepan, combine cocoa and sugar; add butter, corn syrup and pureed raspberries. Stir in cream.

Over medium heat, bring mixture to a boil, stirring often. Reduce heat; continue to boil, but do not stir, for 8 minutes. Remove from heat; cool.

Serve warm. Sauce will keep for 1 month refrigerated. Heat slowly if refrigerated.

1 ¼ cups whipping cream

4 egg yolks

½ cup sugar

1 tablespoon vanilla

**Yield: about 2 cups**

# CRÈME ANGLAISE

Heat cream in a small saucepan, but do not boil.

In a small bowl, beat egg yolks and sugar until light yellow in color. Whisk into cream until blended.

Cook over medium heat until sauce thickens. Add vanilla.

Cool and serve. Store covered in refrigerator.

*Variation: 1 to 2 tablespoons orange-flavored liqueur can be used instead of vanilla.*

*A rich and luscious sauce.*

1 cup whipping cream

3 tablespoons honey

1 teaspoon grated lime rind

1 egg white, at room temperature*

**Yield: 2 cups**

# HONEY-LIME SAUCE

In large bowl, whip cream until stiff peaks form; fold in honey and lime.

In small, clean bowl with clean beaters, beat egg white until soft peaks forms. Fold into whipped cream mixture. Cover and refrigerate 2 hours for flavors to blend.

*\*Raw egg is used in this recipe - see special notes.*

# Dark Chocolate Sauce

8 ounces semi-sweet chocolate

1 cup milk

5 tablespoons whipping cream

¼ cup sugar

2 tablespoons butter or margarine

Melt chocolate in a double boiler or heavy saucepan.

In another saucepan, heat milk to boiling; add cream and bring to a boil again. Remove from heat; blend in sugar, chocolate and butter.

Return saucepan to heat; boil 1 minute. Remove from heat; pour into container to cool. Store covered in refrigerator.

*Variations: Add 1 tablespoon amaretto, bourbon, coffee-flavored, orange-flavored or raspberry-flavored liqueur.*

*A chocolate lover's delight!*

**Yield: 2 cups**

1 ½ cups fresh or frozen
cranberries

1 cup cranberry juice
cocktail

1 cup firmly packed brown
sugar

¼ cup cranberry, rum or
applejack (liqueur),
optional

¼ cup (½ stick) unsalted
butter

3 cinnamon sticks

6 large baking apples (Rome
Beauty or Granny Smith)

2 tablespoons granulated
sugar

Whipped cream, optional

**Serves: 6**

# CRANBERRY BAKED APPLES

Preheat oven at 375 degrees.

Combine cranberries, juice, brown sugar, liqueur, butter and cinnamon sticks in a medium saucepan. Bring to a boil, stirring often. Remove from heat. Let stand 10 minutes, then remove cinnamon sticks.

Core apples, leaving bottoms intact. Arrange apples in a large baking dish. Stuff apple centers half full with cranberry mixture; sprinkle with sugar. Fill apple centers with cranberry mixture.

Pour remaining mixture around apples. Bake 45 minutes or until tender, basting several times. Cool slightly.

Spoon cranberry sauce over apples. Serve warm with whipped cream if desired.

*A warm and inviting dessert.*

# Fresh Melon with Raspberry Puree

1 pint (2 cups) fresh raspberries, reserve few for garnish if desired

Sugar, to taste

2 medium cantaloupes

1 medium honey dew melon

Mint leaves, optional

**Serves: 4**

Puree raspberries in blender or food processor; strain to remove seeds. Add sugar; mix well. Chill.

Cut cantaloupes and honey dew in half. Remove and discard seeds; peel melons. Cut into thin slices. Cover and refrigerate.

When ready to serve, arrange cantaloupe and honeydew alternately on a chilled serving platter. Drizzle with raspberry puree. Garnish with reserved raspberries and mint leaves if desired.

*Colorfully appealing and simple enough to serve anytime.*

# Pears Poached in Cabernet

6 - 8 small firm pears, peeled, stems remain

2 teaspoons vanilla

½ cup sugar

1 (750 ml) bottle Cabernet, Zinfandel or other red wine

½ cup creme de cassis

2 tablespoons lemon juice

½ teaspoon dried or 3 tablespoons fresh rosemary leaves

4 whole cloves

4 whole black peppercorns

**Serves: 6 - 8**

Place the pears in a large, deep saucepan. Combine remaining ingredients in medium bowl; mix well. Pour over pears; cover. Bring to a boil. Reduce heat; simmer covered 30 minutes or until tender, turning pears occasionally.

Refrigerate at least 24 hours in juice; remove cloves and peppercorns before serving. Drain and serve.

Serve with Crème Fraiche.

*Simplicity in its most elegant form.*

¾ cup sugar

1 cup water

1 cup dry red wine

2 whole cloves

1 stick cinnamon

1 inch vanilla bean

4 lemon slices

6 large seedless oranges,
  peeled and, thinly sliced


**Serves: 6**

# SPIRITED ORANGES

Combine sugar and water in a saucepan; cook, stirring until sugar dissolves.

Add wine, cloves, cinnamon, vanilla bean and lemon slices. Bring to a boil; reduce heat. Simmer 15 minutes, stirring occasionally; strain.

Pour hot syrup over the orange slices. Chill at least 4 hours.

Arrange orange slices, overlapping, on serving plates. Generously drizzle with the syrup.

2 cups water

3 thin slices lemon

8 - 10 large whole cling peaches,
       unpeeled

1 cinnamon stick or
  ¼ teaspoon ground
  cinnamon

¼ - ½ cup sugar

⅓ cup amaretto liqueur

Whipped cream


**Serves: 8 - 10**

# AMARETTO POACHED PEACHES

In a large pan, bring water and lemon slices to a boil. Place peaches in a single layer in the pan; add cinnamon. Cover; simmer until peaches are tender, about 20 minutes. Add sugar and amaretto; cook 3 to 5 minutes longer. Remove from heat.

While peaches are still hot, carefully remove skins and pits; slice. Pour syrup over peaches. Chill 1 to 2 hours before serving.

Garnish with a dollop of whipped cream. A perfect complement to our Exceptional Pound Cake.

*Peach skins will add to the color of the peaches. The longer you leave the cooked skins, the more color will appear on your peeled peach.*

# Chilled Peaches in Chablis

Place peaches into a saucepan with sugar, water, orange rind and cinnamon stick. Simmer covered 15 minutes.

Add Chablis; cook uncovered 15 minutes longer or until peaches are tender. Remove peaches from pan; continue cooking liquid to reduce to a light syrup consistency.

While peaches are still hot, carefully remove skins and pits; slice into a large bowl.

Pour syrup over the peaches; cover and chill. Serve in stemmed glasses topped with whipped cream, if desired, or spoon over angel food cake slices.

6 small whole ripe peaches, unpeeled

1 cup sugar

1 cup water

1 tablespoon grated orange rind

1 cinnamon stick, broken

1 cup Chablis or other dry white wine

Whipped cream, optional

*Serves: 8*

## Crust:

1   recipe Pâté Brisée

2   tablespoons red currant jelly, heated

## Pastry Cream:

1   cup milk

3   egg yolks

⅓   cup sugar

½   teaspoon vanilla

¼   cup all-purpose flour

## Fruit Topping:

Choose one or more of the following to fit your flavor and preference:

½   cup red currant jelly, heated

1   pint fresh strawberries, hulled and sliced

1   pint fresh raspberries

2 - 3   ripe fresh peaches, peeled and sliced

2   cups fresh blueberries, washed and drained

2   kiwifruits, peeled and sliced

2   cups white and red seedless grapes, cut in half

**Serves:  8 - 10**

# SIMPLE FRESH FRUIT TART

To make crust, press Pâté Brisée into a 10-inch tart pan; trim edges.  Chill at least 30 minutes.

Preheat oven to 375 degrees.  Place aluminum foil over crust; fill center with dried beans.  Bake in middle rack of oven 25 to 30 minutes or until pastry is golden brown.  Remove foil and beans from crust.  Return crust to oven; continue baking 5 to 10 minutes or until golden brown.  Cool.  Brush the crust with heated jelly.

To make Pastry Cream, in a heavy saucepan, heat milk to a boil; set aside.

Beat egg yolks, sugar and vanilla in small mixing bowl until light and fluffy; beat in flour.  On medium speed, slowly add hot milk to egg mixture, beating for 1 minute.

Return mixture to saucepan used for milk; cook over medium heat whisking gently until mixture boils.  Reduce heat; cook stirring constantly 2 minutes.  Pour into clean bowl; press a sheet of plastic wrap directly onto custard to prevent a skin from forming.  Cover and refrigerate until completely cool.

Spread cooled pastry cream into baked Pâté Brisée; cover and refrigerate while preparing fruit topping for tart.

For fruit topping, arrange selected fruits over cooled pastry cream filling in circles to completely cover filling.

In saucepan, heat currant jelly until it melts to a liquid; cool to the consistency of egg whites.  Use a small pastry brush; brush each piece of fruit to coat with the currant jelly glaze.

# CRANBERRY CHOCOLATE TART

Preheat oven to 450 degrees.

Cut shortening into flour until mixture resembles coarse crumbs. Sprinkle flour mixture with vinegar; add water, 1 tablespoon at a time, while tossing and mixing with a fork. Add water just until moist enough to hold together.

Press dough evenly into a 10-inch tart pan with removable bottom or 9-inch pie pan. Prick bottom and sides of pastry with a fork. Bake at 450 degrees for 8 to 12 minutes or until lightly browned.

In a small saucepan, melt chocolate chips. Add half and half stirring until smooth. Spread chocolate filling on the bottom of baked pastry shell. Cool and refrigerate until chocolate is firm.

In a small saucepan, combine cranberries, sugar, water and orange liqueur. Bring to a boil, stirring until the sugar is dissolved. Boil gently 3 to 4 minutes or until most of the cranberries pop. Cool 30 minutes.

In a small bowl, combine sour cream, milk, orange liqueur and pie filling mix. Beat at low speed 1 minute; let stand 5 minutes. Pour over chocolate layer, spreading to cover evenly. Spoon cooled cranberries evenly over filling to cover completely. Refrigerate at least 1 hour. Let stand at room temperature for 10 minutes before cutting into wedges to serve.

*Pastry:*

- 1/3 cup shortening
- 1 1/4 cups all-purpose flour
- 1 teaspoon vinegar
- 2 - 4 tablespoons cold water
- 1/2 cup semi-sweet chocolate chips
- 1/4 cup half-and-half cream

*Topping:*

- 2 cups fresh or frozen cranberries
- 1 cup granulated sugar
- 1/2 cup water
- 1 teaspoon orange-flavored liqueur

*Filling:*

- 1 cup dairy sour cream
- 3/4 cup milk
- 2 tablespoons orange-flavored liqueur
- 1 (3 1/2-ounce) package instant vanilla pudding and pie filling mix

**Serves:  10**

1 ½  cups unbleached all-
     purpose flour

½  cup (1 stick) cold butter,
   cut into small pieces

¼  cup ice water

**Yield: 1 (9 or 10-inch)
pie shell or 5 or 6 small
tart shells.**

# PÂTÉ BRISÉE

In a food processor, combine flour and butter; process with repeated pulses until the mixture resembles coarse meal.

With machine running, add ice water through the feed tube and process until the dough leaves the side of the bowl.

Turn the dough on a lightly floured surface. Shape into a thick round circle and wrap in plastic wrap. Refrigerate at least 30 minutes before using.

# Two Chocolate Raspberry Tart

Preheat oven to 450 degrees.

Place crust into a 10-inch tart pan; press into bottom and up sides one inch. Trim uneven edges. Prick crust with fork. Bake 9 to 11 minutes, or until lightly browned. Cool.

In food processor, puree thawed raspberries; strain to remove seeds.

Combine cornstarch and 1 tablespoon sugar in a small saucepan. Gradually whisk in raspberry puree. Cook over low heat until thickened. Remove from heat and cool. Spoon cooled raspberry mixture into crust. Arrange fresh raspberries over puree and refrigerate.

In small bowl, beat 1/2 cup butter with sugar until light and fluffy. Gradually beat in melted white chocolate. Add eggs, one at a time, blending well with mixer after each. Pour mixture over fresh raspberries in prepared crust. Refrigerate until set.

Melt semi-sweet chocolate and 2 tablespoons of butter over low heat until smooth. Carefully spoon over white chocolate layer and gently spread to cover. Refrigerate to set, 2 hours.

To serve, let stand at room temperature for 30 minutes. Garnish with fresh mint leaves, raspberries and white chocolate leaves.

*This is an exquisite dessert!*

---

*Pastry for one 10-inch pie crust*

**Filling:**

- 1  (10-ounce) package frozen red raspberries in syrup, thawed
- 1  tablespoon cornstarch
- 1/3  cup plus 1 tablespoon sugar
- 1  cup fresh raspberries
- 1/2  cup (1 stick) butter or margarine, softened
- 4  ounces white chocolate, melted
- 2  eggs
- 2  (1-ounce) squares semi-sweet chocolate, cut into pieces
- 2  tablespoons butter or margarine

**Serves: 10**

## Pastry:

1 cup all-purpose flour

2 tablespoons sugar

⅛ teaspoon salt

½ cup (1 stick) butter or margarine, cold

2 - 3 tablespoons cold water

## Filling:

¼ teaspoon ground cinnamon

⅔ cup sugar

¼ cup all-purpose flour

6 cups fresh raspberries, divided

Whipping cream

**Serves: 10**

# Indiana Raspberry Tart

Preheat oven to 400 degrees.

To prepare pastry, in a medium bowl combine flour, sugar and salt. Cut in butter until crumbly. Sprinkle water, 1 tablespoon at a time, until pastry mixture is just moist and holds together. Press pastry into the bottom and 1-inch up the side of a 9-inch springform pan. Set aside.

Combine cinnamon, sugar and flour in small bowl. Sprinkle half the flour mixture over the bottom of pastry. Top with 4 cups raspberries. Sprinkle remaining flour mixture over raspberries.

Bake tart on lowest oven rack, 50 to 60 minutes, or until golden and bubbly. Remove from oven; cool on wire rack.

Remove side of springform pan carefully after tart has completely cooled. Top with remaining 2 cups raspberries. Cut into wedges.

To serve, pour 2 tablespoons cream on individual plate; arrange a tart wedge on cream.

*A unique recipe combining cooked and uncooked berries with exceptional results.*

# Rhubarb Raspberry Pie

Preheat oven to 375 degrees.

Line 9-inch pie plate with crust; set aside.

In large bowl, combine sugar, flour and nutmeg. Add eggs, 1 at a time, beating well after each addition.

In large bowl, gently stir together rhubarb and raspberries; spoon into crust. Gently pour egg mixture over fruit. Loosely cover top of pie with aluminum foil, tent shaped.

Bake 20 minutes. Remove foil and continue baking another 20 minutes.

To make topping, combine flour, sugar, almonds, cinnamon and nutmeg. Cut in butter until crumbly. Sprinkle on pie.

Bake 15 minutes longer. Cool completely, then chill 2 hours before serving.

*A perennial pie favorite teamed in a taste tempting duet.*

Pastry for one 10-inch pie crust

Filling:
- 1 ¼ cups sugar
- 1 tablespoon all-purpose flour
- ¼ teaspoon ground nutmeg
- 4 eggs
- 3 cups frozen cut-up rhubarb, thawed
- 1 cup frozen whole unsweetened raspberries, thawed

Topping:
- ¼ cup all-purpose flour
- ¼ cup sugar
- ¼ cup slivered almonds, chopped
- ½ teaspoon ground cinnamon
- ¼ teaspoon ground nutmeg
- 2 tablespoons cold butter or margarine

**Serves: 8**

Pastry for one 9-inch
pie crust

1 ½ cups whipping cream

½ cup sugar

3 egg yolks

1 teaspoon vanilla

1 tablespoon orange-
flavored liqueur

1 ½ - 2 cups whole fresh
strawberries

1 kiwifruit, peeled and sliced

¼ cup apricot jam, heated

**Serves: 10 - 12**

# STRAWBERRY KIWI TART

Preheat oven to 425 degrees.

Roll out pastry on a floured surface to 1/8-inch thickness; line a 9-inch tart pan, pressing into bottom and 1-inch up sides. Trim edges. Place aluminum foil over pastry; fill center with dried beans. Bake 9 minutes or until lightly browned. Remove foil and beans from crust; set aside to cool. Reduce oven temperature to 325 degrees.

Beat together cream, sugar, egg yolks, vanilla and liqueur in a medium bowl. Pour into prepared crust.

Bake 35 minutes or until firm. Cool completely.

Arrange fresh strawberries around edge of tart. In center, arrange kiwifruit.

Brush jam on fruit to glaze. Chill completely. Cut in wedges to serve.

*A beautiful fresh fruit dessert.*

# A Peach of a Strawberry Pie

Preheat oven to 350 degrees.

Unfold pie crust; line 9-inch pie plate (pastry will extend over edge of pan). Set aside.

In large bowl, combine peaches, strawberries, lemon juice and almond extract.

In separate bowl, combine brown sugar, flour, ginger, cinnamon and nutmeg; stir until blended. Gently stir into the fruit. Stir in 1/4 cup cream, butter or margarine and egg; blend well.

Spoon filling into prepared pastry shell. Unfold remaining crust; cut into 3/4-inch strips. Arrange on top of fruit in a lattice pattern. Trim pastry overhang to 1-inch; fold over edge of pie and flute.

Brush pastry with cream or egg mixture. Bake 45 minutes or until pastry is golden brown and fruit is tender.

A decorative flair can be added by cutting out a peach and strawberry fruit shape from the extra flattened dough. This can be attractively placed in the center of the pie.

Cool slightly before serving.

*This will become a summer favorite.*

1 (15-ounce) package refrigerated pie crusts (2 crusts)

3 cups sliced fresh peaches

2 cups fresh strawberries, sliced

1 tablespoon lemon juice

¼ teaspoon almond extract

⅔ cup firmly packed light brown sugar

2 tablespoons all-purpose flour

¼ teaspoon ground ginger

¼ teaspoon ground cinnamon

¼ teaspoon ground nutmeg

¼ cup whipping cream

2 tablespoons butter or margarine, melted

1 egg, slightly beaten

2 tablespoons whipping cream

OR

1 egg yolk beaten with 1 teaspoon water

**Serves: 8**

## Pastry:

1 ½ cups all-purpose flour

½ teaspoon salt

¾ cup shredded Cheddar cheese

½ cup (1 stick) cold butter or margarine

3 - 4 tablespoons cold water

## Filling:

2 cups fresh or frozen cranberries

½ cup water

1 ½ cups sugar

⅓ cup all-purpose flour

1 teaspoon ground nutmeg

⅛ teaspoon salt

2 tablespoons butter or margarine

3 cups thinly sliced tart cooking apples

**Serves: 8 - 10**

# CRANBERRY APPLE PIE WITH CHEDDAR CHEESE CRUST

Preheat oven to 375 degrees.

For pastry, sift together flour and salt in a medium bowl. Add cheese; toss with a fork to combine. Cut in butter until dough mixture is crumbly. Gradually add water, 1-tablespoon at a time, until dough forms a ball. Wrap and chill until ready to use.

Divide dough into 2/3 and 1/3. Roll two-thirds piece of dough, on a floured surface, to fit a 9-inch pie pan. Line in pie pan. Set prepared crust aside.

To prepare filling, bring cranberries and water to a boil in a saucepan over medium heat. Stir constantly until skin begins to pop, approximately 5 minutes.

In small bowl combine sugar, flour, cinnamon, nutmeg and salt. Add to cranberries and cook until thickened, stirring often. Cook an additional 2 minutes.

Blend apples and butter into cranberry mixture. Bring to a boil, then remove from heat and cool slightly. Pour filling into prepared crust.

Roll out top dough; gently place over filling. Flute and trim edges. Bake 40 to 45 minutes. Serve either warm or cooled with a scoop of vanilla ice cream.

*A cozy ingredient combination with a wonderful aroma.*

# PLUMP APPLE RAISIN PIE

### Crust:

- 2 cups all-purpose flour
- 1 teaspoon salt
- ⅔ cup shortening
- 1 tablespoon white vinegar
- 5 - 6 tablespoons cold water

### Filling:

- 6 large Granny Smith apples, peeled, cored, sliced
- ¾ cup granulated sugar
- 2 tablespoons all-purpose flour
- ¼ teaspoon cinnamon
- ¾ cup golden raisins

**Serves: 8**

Preheat oven to 350 degrees.

Blend flour, salt and shortening in a medium bowl; cut with pastry blender or two forks until mixture is crumbly. Add vinegar and gradually add water, one tablespoon at a time, until smooth dough forms.

Divide dough into 2/3 and 1/3. On a floured surface, roll out larger dough to fit a 10-inch pie pan, allowing a half inch overhang. Ease pastry into pie pan. Wrap and chill remaining dough until needed.

To prepare filling, in a large bowl toss together apples, sugar, flour, cinnamon and raisins. Spoon mixture into pastry crust.

Roll out remaining dough and place on top of apple mixture. Pinch together outside edges; flute edges and trim excess pastry. Make several pricks with a fork on top crust.

Bake in 350 degree oven for 1 hour to 1 hour 15 minutes, or until richly browned.

Place on wire rack; cool 1 hour before cutting to serve.

## Pastry:

- 2 ½ cups all-purpose flour
- ¼ cup sugar
- 1 teaspoon salt
- ½ cup (1 stick) butter or margarine
- ¼ cup vegetable oil
- ¼ cup water
- 1 egg

## Apple Filling:

- 6 medium apples, peeled and sliced (about 6 cups)
- 1 cup sugar
- ⅓ cup all-purpose flour
- 2 teaspoons grated lemon rind
- 2 teaspoons fresh lemon juice
- 1 ½ teaspoons ground cinnamon

## Caramel Sauce:

- 8 ounces (about 28) caramels, unwrapped
- ½ cup half-and-half or evaporated milk

## Topping:

- 1 (8-ounce) package cream cheese, softened
- ⅓ cup sugar
- 1 egg
- ⅓ cup chopped walnuts

**Serves: 8**

# CARAMEL APPLE PIE

Preheat oven to 375 degrees.

For pastry, combine flour, sugar and salt in large bowl. Cut in butter or margarine until mixture is crumbly. In small bowl, combine oil, water and egg; beat until smooth and creamy. Blend flour and oil mixtures until dough is smooth.

Press dough into bottom and up side of a 10-inch pie pan or 10-inch springform pan.

To prepare filling, combine apples, sugar, flour, lemon rind and juice, and cinnamon in large bowl; toss lightly. Spoon mixture into the prepared pie crust.

To make caramel sauce, combine caramels and half-and-half in small saucepan; melt over low heat, stirring occasionally until smooth. Drizzle over apples mixture in crust.

Combine topping ingredients, except nuts in a medium saucepan; cook over low heat until melted and smooth. Spoon topping over apple mixture. Sprinkle with nuts.

Bake 35 to 40 minutes, or until golden. Cool to room temperature; cut in wedges to serve. Refrigerate any leftover pie.

*This pie always receives rave reviews.*

# CREAMY APPLE CRISP

Preheat oven to 350 degrees.

Place prepared apples in a 2-quart buttered casserole. Beat cream cheese, sour cream, sugar, flour, egg and vanilla until light. Stir cream mixture into apples.

Cut butter into oatmeal, flour, sugars and cinnamon. Sprinkle on top of apples. Bake in 350 degree oven for 35 to 40 minutes or until apples are tender.

*Refrigerate any leftovers.*

3 cups peeled, sliced, tart baking apples

1 (3-ounce) package cream cheese

¾ cup sour cream

¾ cup granulated sugar

2 tablespoons all-purpose flour

1 egg

½ teaspoon vanilla

Crisp Crumb Topping:

¼ cup butter, room temperature

¼ cup quick-cooking oatmeal

¼ cup all-purpose flour

¼ cup granulated sugar

¼ cup brown sugar

1 teaspoon cinnamon

**Serves: 4 - 6**

## Crust:

½ cup (1 stick) butter or margarine

⅓ cup sugar

¼ teaspoon vanilla

1 cup all-purpose flour

## Cheese Layer:

1 (8-ounce) package cream cheese

¼ cup sugar

1 egg

½ teaspoon vanilla

## Topping:

⅓ cup sugar

½ teaspoon ground cinnamon

4 cups cooking apples, peeled, cored, sliced

¼ cup slivered almonds

**Serves: 8 - 10**

# BAVARIAN APPLE TORTE

Preheat oven to 450 degrees.

For crust, beat butter, sugar, and vanilla in medium bowl. Add flour; mix well. Press dough into bottom and 1 to 1 1/2-inches up side of a 9-inch springform pan.

To make filling, combine cream cheese, sugar, egg, vanilla in medium bowl; beat to blend well. Spread filling over dough in pan.

Combine sugar and cinnamon for topping in medium bowl. Toss with apples. Arrange over cheese filling layer. Sprinkle with almonds.

Bake at 450 degrees for 10 minutes. Reduce heat to 400 and bake 25 minutes or until bubbly and golden brown. Cool completely; remove pan side if using a springform pan. Cut in wedges and top with whipped cream to serve.

*Toasted coconut makes a wonderful substitute for slivered almonds.*

*This looks as good as it tastes!*

# RUM RAISIN APPLE PIE WITH LEMON

Preheat oven to 350 degrees.

To prepare pastry, combine flour and sugar; cut in cold butter with pastry blender until mixture resembles coarse meal. Knead crumb mixture until dough forms a ball. Measure 1/4 cup dough and set aside.

Press remaining dough in bottom and 1 1/2 inches up side of an ungreased 9-inch springform pan. Set aside.

For filling, grate rind from lemons; squeeze to remove juice. Set aside. Combine raisins and rum in medium saucepan; simmer 8 to 10 minutes or until raisins are soft. Blend in butter, sugar, cinnamon, lemon juice and grated lemon rind. Continue to simmer 5 to 10 minutes until slightly thickened.

Place apples, water and sugar in a Dutch oven; cover and steam over medium-low heat or until apples are soft. Stir occasionally. Drain excess liquid from apples; pour rum and raisin mixture over cooked apples; stir to coat apple slices.

Place apples in prepared crust. Crumble reserved dough over apples. Set pie on baking sheet.

Bake 40 minutes. Remove from oven; sprinkle 2 tablespoons of sugar evenly over pie. Cool on wire rack for 20 minutes; place on a serving platter. Release rim around springform pan and continue cooling completely before cutting to serve.

*A delightful variation of an old theme!*

## Pastry:

- 2 cups all-purpose flour
- 1 cup sugar
- ¾ cup (1 ½ sticks) cold unsalted butter

## Filling:

- 2 lemons
- 1 cup golden raisins
- ¼ cup light rum
- ¼ cup (½ stick) butter or margarine
- ½ cup sugar
- 1 tablespoon ground cinnamon
- 9 medium Granny Smith apples, peeled, cored and thinly sliced
- 3 tablespoons water
- 2 tablespoons sugar

**Serves: 8 - 10**

1 cup all-purpose flour

1 cup sugar

¼ teaspoon salt

2 teaspoons baking powder

¾ cup milk

½ cup (1 stick) butter or
margarine, melted

2 ½ cups blackberries

1 - 2 drops almond extract


**Serves: 6 - 8**

# BLACKBERRY COBBLER

Preheat oven to 350 degrees.

Mix flour, sugar, salt and baking powder in an 8 x 8-inch baking dish. Stir in milk; blend. Pour melted butter over dough.

Toss blackberries with almond extract. Spoon on top of dough.

Bake 45 to 60 minutes or until dough rises to top and is brown.

*Other fruits may be substituted.*

*Just like grandma's, only better!*

# PEACHES IN CRUST

## Crust:

- 5 tablespoons butter, frozen and cut into pieces
- 4 tablespoons shortening, frozen and cut into pieces
- 1 ½ cups all-purpose flour
- 4 tablespoons cold water

## Filling:

- 6 large ripe peaches, peeled, pitted and sliced
- ¼ cup firmly packed brown sugar
- ¾ cup granulated sugar
- ¼ cup (½ stick) butter or margarine

**Serves: 6 - 8**

Preheat oven to 450 degrees. Butter a 2-quart baking dish.

In a food processor, place butter, shortening and flour. Process until mixture is crumbly. Slowly add water, one tablespoon at a time until it just holds together. Form into a ball; wrap and refrigerate until needed.

Flour a smooth surface liberally. Roll dough into a large circle. Carefully roll up pastry on rolling pin and gently ease into prepared baking dish. Let excess hang over sides.

Spoon peaches into pastry. Add brown sugar and granulated sugar. Dot with butter.

Fold excess dough in toward center; loosely overlap and arrange to cover peaches.

Bake at 450 degrees 5 minutes. Reduce heat to 375 degrees; bake an additional 40 to 50 minutes, or until crust is golden. Remove and cool completely before serving.

*Serve at room temperature or chilled. Great with vanilla ice cream or whipped cream.*

*Another way of enjoying the fresh bounty of summer!*

1 (6-ounce) package semi-
  sweet chocolate chips
  (1 cup)

1 tablespoon instant
  expresso powder

1 cup unsalted butter,
  softened

1 cup sugar

8 egg, separated*

  Sweetened whipped cream

  Raspberry Sauce


Raspberry Sauce:

2 (10-ounce) packages
  frozen red raspberries in
  syrup, thawed

¼ cup sugar

2 - 3 tablespoons orange-
  flavored liqueur


**Serves: 10 - 12**

# SIMPLY ROYALE CHOCOLATE TORTE

Preheat oven to 325 degrees. Butter and flour a 9-inch spring-form pan.

In double boiler or heavy saucepan over low heat, melt chocolate; add expresso powder.

In large bowl, combine chocolate mixture, butter and sugar; beat well. Cool. Add egg yolks, 2 at a time, beating well after each addition.

In a separate clean, dry mixing bowl with clean beaters, beat egg whites until stiff but not dry; gently fold into chocolate mixture.

Pour two-thirds of chocolate mixture into prepared pan. Cover and refrigerate remaining chocolate mixture. Bake torte 35 to 40 minutes or until wooden pick inserted in center comes out clean.

Cool to room temperature (center will fall). Spread remaining chocolate mixture on top. Refrigerate at least 8 hours or overnight. Use a hot knife to cut into wedges. Serve with whipped cream and Raspberry Sauce.

Drain raspberries, reserving half the syrup. Puree fruit, reserved syrup, sugar and liqueur in a food processor or blender; strain to remove seeds. Chill until ready to use.

*Raw eggs use in this recipe - see special notes.*

# PANTRY PECAN PIE

Preheat oven to 400 degrees.

For crust, mix flour, salt, sugar, shortening and butter in a food processor bowl; process until mixture resembles corn meal. Add ice water, a little at a time, until a dough forms. Cover and refrigerate until ready to use. Flatten on a floured surface and roll out to 1/8-inch thickness to fit in a 9-inch pie pan.

To make filling, in a large bowl, beat eggs. Add sugar, corn syrups, butter and vanilla. Mix well.

Place nuts in the bottom of pie shell; pour filling over nuts. Nuts will float to the top.

Bake in 400 degree oven for 10 minutes. Reduce heat to 350 degrees; bake an additional 40 minutes. May use whipping cream, whipped as topping. Serve warm or cool.

### Crust:

1 ½ cups unbleached all-purpose flour

1 teaspoon salt

½ teaspoon sugar

¼ cup solid shortening, frozen

¼ cup (½ stick) butter, frozen

3 - 4 tablespoons ice water

### Filling:

3 eggs, slightly beaten

½ cup sugar

½ cup light corn syrup

½ cup dark corn syrup

4 tablespoons butter, melted

1 teaspoon vanilla

1 ¼ cups pecan halves

Whipped cream, optional

**Serves: 8**

## Crust:

½ cup all-purpose flour

½ cup confectioners' sugar

¼ cup unsweetened cocoa

½ cup (1 stick) butter or margarine, melted

¾ cup slivered almonds, chopped, lightly toasted

## Filling:

⅓ cup water

⅓ cup granulated sugar

1 ½ cups chocolate chip mini-morsels

4 egg yolks*

2 - 3 tablespoons coffee-flavored or amaretto liqueur

2 ¼ cups whipping cream

½ cup sliced almonds, toasted

**Serves: 10**

# CHOCOLATE ALMOND TRUFFLE PIE

Preheat oven to 350 degrees.

For crust, combine flour, sugar and cocoa in small bowl. Stir in melted butter and almonds. Press mixture onto bottom of 9-inch springform pan.

Place springform pan on baking sheet; bake 15 minutes. Set aside to cool.

For filling, combine water and sugar in small saucepan. Bring to a boil over medium heat; cook 3 minutes. Add chocolate chips, stir to melt and blend.

In separate clean, dry bowl, beat egg yolks until light in color and well blended. Add small amount of hot chocolate mixture to yolks, whisking constantly. Continue adding small amounts until yolks are warm; stir egg mixture into chocolate mixture. Blend well. Stir in liqueur. Cover; chill.

Whip cream until soft stiff peaks form. Fold chocolate mixture into whipped cream and blend. Spread onto cooled crust. Chill at least 2 hours before serving.

Garnish with toasted almonds.

*Raw eggs used in this recipe - see special notes.*

*A perfect marriage of chocolate and almonds.*

# Rum Walnut Fudge Pie

Preheat oven to 375 degrees. Roll out pie crust; place in 9-inch pie plate.

In large mixing bowl, beat butter and sugar until fluffy; add eggs, 1 at a time, beating well after each addition. Add chocolate, instant coffee and rum. Combine flour and broken walnuts; stir into chocolate mixture.

Pour mixture into prepared crust; top with walnut halves. Bake 25 minutes or until firm and cooked. Remove from oven; place on wire rack to cool completely.

Top with whipped cream to serve.

*Easy and divinely rich!*

Pastry for one 9-inch pie crust

1 (12-ounce) package semi-sweet chocolate chips, melted

¼ cup (½ stick) butter or margarine, melted

¾ cup firmly packed brown sugar

3 eggs

2 teaspoons instant coffee

1 tablespoon rum

¼ cup all-purpose flour

1 cup coarsely broken walnuts

½ cup walnut halves

Whipped cream, optional

**Serves: 8**

**Pastry:**

- 1 cup all-purpose flour
- ⅛ teaspoon salt
- 1 tablespoon sugar
- 7 tablespoons cold butter, cut in pieces
- 3 - 4 tablespoons cold water

**Filling:**

- 3 ounces semi-sweet chocolate, melted
- ¼ cup (½ stick) butter or margarine
- ⅓ cup sugar
- ½ cup whipping cream
- 1 tablespoon honey
- 1 ¾ cups hazelnuts, lightly toasted, skinned, coarsely chopped

**Serves: 10 - 12**

# HAZELNUT TART

To prepare pastry, in a food processor, combine flour, salt and sugar; process to blend. Add cold butter; process until mixture resembles coarse meal. Add 3 tablespoons water just until dough holds together and looks moist (add more water if needed). Do not over process. Wrap pastry; chill at least 1 hour.

Roll out pastry on a floured board to fit a 9 1/2-inch tart pan with removable bottom. Trim excess pastry. Freeze 20 minutes. Cover pastry with aluminum foil; fill with dried beans. Bake in a preheated 425 degree oven 15 minutes.

Remove foil and beans; prick shell thoroughly with fork. Reduce oven temperature to 350 degrees; bake 15 minutes longer or until golden. Remove from oven; place on a rack to cool.

Brush bottom of tart shell with a thin layer of melted chocolate; set aside. Reserve remaining chocolate.

In small saucepan, melt butter; add sugar, cream and honey. Bring to a boil, stir to dissolve sugar. Boil 2 to 3 minutes; add hazelnuts. Remove from heat and pour mixture into tart shell.

Bake 30 minutes or until golden brown. Remove from oven; place on wire rack to cool.

Reheat reserved chocolate; drizzle on top of tart.

*This is richly elegant.*

# Pumpkin Torte

Preheat oven to 350 degrees.

For crust, combine crumbs, sugar and butter; press into a 9-inch springform pan.

To prepare filling, beat cream cheese in a large bowl until fluffy; add sugar and beaten eggs. Beat until smooth. Pour into prepared pan. Bake 20 minutes.

In saucepan over low heat, combine pumpkin, egg yolks, 1/2 cup sugar, milk, cinnamon and salt; stir until mixture thickens. Remove from heat.

Dissolve gelatine in water; blend into pumpkin mixture. Cool.

In small mixing bowl, beat egg whites and remaining 1/4 cup sugar to form soft peaks; fold into pumpkin mixture. Pour over cooled baked mixture in crust. Refrigerate to set for approximately 2 hours before serving.

Garnish top with toasted walnuts and serve with whipped cream if desired.

*Raw egg used in recipe - see special notes.*

*A different version of the traditional pumpkin pie.*

## Crust:

| | |
|---|---|
| 1 ¾ | cups (12-2 x 5-inch) graham cracker crumbs |
| ⅓ | cup sugar |
| ½ | cup (1 stick) butter or margarine, melted |

## Filling:

| | |
|---|---|
| 1 ½ | cups sugar, divided |
| 1 | (8-ounce) package cream cheese, softened |
| 2 | eggs, beaten |
| 2 | cups canned pumpkin |
| 3 | eggs, separated |
| ½ | cup milk |
| 1 | tablespoon ground cinnamon |
| ½ | teaspoon salt |
| 1 | envelope unflavored gelatine |
| ¼ | cup cold water |
| | Toasted walnuts, optional |
| | Whipped cream, optional |

**Serves: 12 - 16**

½ cup (1 stick) unsalted butter

½ cup firmly packed brown sugar

½ cup granulated sugar

1 teaspoon vanilla

1 egg

½ teaspoon salt

⅓ cup Dutch process cocoa

½ teaspoon baking soda

1 cup all-purpose flour

1 (10-ounce) package white chocolate chips (good quality, not confectioners' coating)

**Yield: 2 - 2 ½ dozen**

# CHOCOLATE-WHITE CHOCOLATE CHIP COOKIES

In large mixing bowl, beat butter and sugars. Beat in vanilla and egg. Combine salt, cocoa, baking soda and flour; stir into butter mixture.

Stir in white chocolate chips. Cover and chill dough at least 2 hours or until firm.

When ready to bake, preheat oven to 350 degrees. Drop dough by rounded tablespoons placed 2-inches apart on a lightly greased baking sheet. Bake 7 to 8 minutes or until light brown around edge.

Place baking sheet on wire rack to cool about 5 minutes. Remove cookies to wire rack to cool completely.

*A chocolate sensation!*

# Colorful Thick 'N' Chewy Cookies

Preheat oven to 350 degrees.

In large mixing bowl, beat butter and sugars until mixture is light and fluffy. Add eggs, vanilla and peanut butter; beat until well blended.

Combine oats and baking soda; add to dough and stir to mix. Stir in candies, raisins and chocolate chips.

Form balls of 1/2 cup dough each. On lightly greased baking sheets, place 3-inch balls of dough; flatten to 5-inches in diameter (cookies spread about 1-inch more during baking).

Bake 10 to 12 minutes until edges are lightly browned. Place baking sheets on racks; cool 5 minutes. Remove cookies from pans; place on flat surface to cool completely.

*Children love this colorful chewy cookie.*

½ cup (1 stick) butter or margarine, softened

1 cup firmly packed brown sugar

1 cup granulated sugar

3 eggs

1 teaspoon vanilla

2 cups (1 pound) peanut butter

4 ½ cups quick-cooking oats

2 teaspoons baking soda

1 cup multicolored candy coated chocolate candies

1 cup raisins

1 cup semi-sweet chocolate chips

**Yield: 10 large cookies**

- 1 cup (2 sticks) butter or margarine
- ¾ cup firmly packed light brown sugar
- ½ cup granulated sugar
- 1 egg
- 1 teaspoon vanilla
- ½ teaspoon almond extract
- 1 ¾ cups all-purpose flour
- 1 teaspoon baking soda
- ¼ teaspoon salt
- 1 (10-ounce) package fine quality white chocolate chips, (not confectioners' coating)
- 1 cup sliced or slivered almonds, toasted

**Yield: 3 dozen**

# WHITE CHOCOLATE ALMOND COOKIES

Preheat oven to 375 degrees.

In large mixing bowl, beat butter and sugars together. Add egg and flavorings. Continue beating until light and fluffy.

Combine flour, soda and salt. Blend into creamed mixture.

Add white chocolate chips and almonds to dough. Mix well. Drop by teaspoons onto an ungreased baking sheet. Bake 8 to 10 minutes or until lightly brown.

Allow to stand 2 minutes before removing from baking sheet; place on wire rack or flat surface to cool.

*A sophisticated combination!*

# ALMOND LACE COOKIES

In medium bowl, mix almonds, sugar, flour and baking powder; set aside.

In a small bowl, beat egg white until soft peaks form. Stir in vanilla.

Fold egg white into dry ingredients and pour into a small tray lined with wax paper. Spread mixture 1/2-inch thick and place tray in freezer until mixture hardens (approximately 2 hours).

When ready to bake, preheat oven to 375 degrees. Line a baking sheet with parchment paper. Unmold mixture; cut into 1-inch squares. Place batter squares 1-inch apart on prepared baking sheets; press lightly to flatten.

Bake 12 - 15 minutes. Remove to a flat surface covered with brown paper to cool completely.

*Delicate!*

2 cups sliced almonds, lightly toasted

¾ cup sugar

5 tablespoons all-purpose flour

½ teaspoon baking powder

1 egg white

1 ½ teaspoons vanilla or almond extract

**Yield: 4 dozen**

# THREE-GINGER COOKIES

¾ cup (1 ½ sticks) unsalted butter, softened

1 cup firmly packed dark brown sugar

¼ cup molasses

1 egg

2 ¼ cups all-purpose flour

2 teaspoons ground ginger

2 teaspoons baking soda

½ teaspoon salt

1 ½ tablespoons finely chopped fresh ginger root

½ cup crystallized ginger, finely chopped

½ cup chopped almonds

**Yield:  3 - 4 dozen**

Beat butter and brown sugar in large bowl until light and fluffy. Add molasses and egg; beat until well blended.

Sift together flour, ground ginger, baking soda and salt; stir into butter mixture with a wooden spoon until blended.

Add fresh ginger root and crystallized ginger; stir in almonds; mix well.  Cover dough and refrigerate at least 2 hours or overnight.

When ready to bake preheat oven to 350 degrees.  Lightly grease baking sheets.  Shape the dough into 1-inch balls; place 2-inches apart on prepared baking sheets.

Bake until lightly browned, approximately 10 minutes.  Remove to a wire rack to cool.

# Warm and Wonderful Spice Cookies

2 ½ cups all-purpose flour

2 teaspoons baking soda

½ teaspoon ground cloves

½ teaspoon ground allspice

½ teaspoon ground cinnamon

¼ teaspoon ground ginger

¾ cup (1 ½ sticks) butter or margarine

1 cup granulated sugar

1 egg

¼ cup light molasses

Confectioners' sugar

**Yield:  5 - 6 dozen**

Combine flour, baking soda, cloves, allspice, cinnamon and ginger; set aside.

In large mixing bowl, beat butter, sugar and egg until light and fluffy.

Alternately add flour mixture and molasses to sugar mixture. Cover and refrigerate dough at least 1 hour or overnight.

When ready to bake, preheat oven to 350 degrees.  Grease baking sheets.

Shape dough into 1/2-inch balls; roll in confectioners' sugar. Place 1-inch apart on prepared baking sheets.

Bake 8 to 10 minutes or until lightly browned.  Remove to a wire rack to cool; sprinkle with confectioners' sugar while still warm.

*This cookie says, "Home again!"*

¾ cup (1 ½ sticks) unsalted butter or margarine

¼ cup vegetable shortening

1 ¼ cups sugar

2 eggs

2 ½ teaspoons vanilla

4 ounces semi-sweet chocolate, melted, cooled

2 ¼ cups all-purpose flour

1 teaspoon baking soda

¼ teaspoon ground cinnamon

¼ teaspoon salt

12 ounces semi-sweet chocolate, chopped into ½-inch chunks

1 cup chopped pecans, toasted, optional


**Yield: 4 dozen**

# CHOCOLATE BITTERSWEET COOKIES

Preheat oven to 375 degrees. Grease large baking sheets.

In large bowl, beat together butter, shortening and sugar. Beat in eggs one at a time. Stir in the vanilla and melted chocolate.

Mix together flour, baking soda, cinnamon and salt in small bowl. Add flour mixture to chocolate mixture one third at a time until just blended. Stir in the chocolate chunks and pecans.

Drop dough by rounded tablespoons 2-inches apart on prepared baking sheet. Bake 10 to 12 minutes or until lightly browned.

Place baking sheet on wire rack to cool slightly; remove cookies to wire rack or flat surface; cool completely.

*A sinful cookie that's hard to resist.*

# Double Chocolate Peanut Butter Chunks

6 (1-ounce) squares semi-sweet chocolate

1 cup crunchy peanut butter

¾ cup brown sugar, packed

½ cup (1 stick) butter

1 egg

1 teaspoon vanilla

1 ½ cups all-purpose flour

¾ teaspoon baking soda

1 ½ cups semi-sweet chocolate chips

**Yield: 4 - 5 dozen**

Preheat oven to 300 degrees.

In heavy saucepan or double broiler melt chocolate. Stir until smooth; set aside.

In large mixing bowl, beat peanut butter, brown sugar and butter until mixture is creamy. Add the egg; beat on high to mix thoroughly, about 1 minute. Add vanilla and cooled melted chocolate; beat to mix well.

Combine flour and baking soda in medium bowl; stir in chocolate chips. Add to peanut butter mixture, stirring until well mixed.

Roll 1 rounded tablespoon of dough for each cookie into a ball; place on an ungreased baking sheet. Press with tines of fork to flatten slightly.

Bake 12 to 15 minutes or until fingerprint does not remain when top of cookie is touched. Do not overbake. Cookies will not be firm.

*Not just another peanut butter cookie... we've added chocolate!*

- 2 cups (4 sticks) butter or margarine
- 2 cups granulated sugar
- 2 cups firmly packed brown sugar
- 4 eggs, lightly beaten
- 6 cups all-purpose flour
- 4 teaspoons baking soda
- 1 teaspoon salt
- 5 cups unpeeled, grated apples
- 2 teaspoons vanilla

# HARVEST APPLE DROP COOKIES

Preheat oven to 375 degrees. Lightly grease baking sheets.

In large mixing bowl, beat butter and sugars until light and fluffy. Add eggs; beat well.

Sift together flour, baking soda and salt; add to creamed mixture. Add grated apples and vanilla. Stir until mixed.

Drop batter by teaspoonfuls on prepared baking sheets. May need to flatten with a fork.

Bake 10 to 15 minutes or until golden brown. Remove to a wire rack to cool completely before frosting with Cream Cheese Icing.

Cream Cheese Icing:

- 1 (8-ounce) package cream cheese
- 6 tablespoons butter or margarine
- 3 cups sifted confectioners' sugar
- 1 teaspoon vanilla

**Yield: 8 - 10 dozen**

In large mixing bowl, beat cream cheese and butter until light and creamy. Slowly sift in sugar; beat until fluffy. Add vanilla and beat to combine. Spread over cooled baked cookies.

*This recipe is great for a large family gathering; the uncooked batter also freezes well.*

# PINEAPPLE NUT COOKIES

Preheat oven to 400 degrees.

In large mixing bowl, beat butter and sugar until light and fluffy. Add egg and beat well. Stir in pineapple with juice. Add flour, soda, salt, nutmeg, golden raisins and nuts. Blend well.

Drop dough by teaspoonfuls on ungreased baking sheets. Bake 8 to 10 minutes or until golden brown and no imprint remains when lightly touched with finger. Remove to wire rack to cool.

1 cup (2 sticks) butter or margarine

1 ½ cups sugar

1 egg

1 (8 ½-ounce) can juice-packed crushed pineapple

3 ½ cups all-purpose flour

1 teaspoon baking soda

½ teaspoon salt

¼ teaspoon ground nutmeg

1 cup golden raisins

½ cup chopped nuts, optional

**Yield: 5 dozen**

# Tea Time Almond Shortbread

**Crust:**

- 2 ⅔ cups all-purpose flour
- 1 ⅓ cups sugar
- ½ teaspoon salt
- 1 ⅓ cups unsalted butter or margarine
- 1 egg

**Filling:**

- 1 cup almonds, finely chopped
- 1 teaspoon grated lemon rind
- ½ cup sugar
- 1 egg, slightly beaten

**Yield:  36 (1-inch) squares**

Preheat oven to 325 degrees.  Grease 8 x 8-inch glass pan.

For crust, in large mixing bowl, mix flour, sugar, salt, butter and egg.  Beat until a soft dough forms.  Divide dough in half; spread half in bottom of prepared pan.

For filling, combine almonds, lemon rind, sugar and egg in a mixing bowl.  Beat to mix well.  Spread over dough layer in pan to within 1/2-inch of sides.

Spread remaining dough on top of filling to form another layer.

Bake 45 to 55 minutes or until light golden brown.  Cool and cut into 1-inch squares.

*Use food processor for mixing both shortbread crust and filling.  Process almonds first; remove and set aside.*

*A must for your afternoon tea.*

# CHOCOLATE PECAN BARS

Preheat oven to 375 degrees.

In large mixing bowl beat butter and sugar until light and fluffy. On low speed, blend in flour only until mixed. Pat dough on bottom of ungreased 9-inch square dish. Bake 10 minutes.

For filling, place preserves in a small bowl; mix to break up pieces of fruit. Set aside.

Grind pecans until a fine powder in a food processor; set aside.

In small mixing bowl, beat eggs at high speed 2 to 3 minutes until lemon colored and slightly thickened. Add salt and vanilla, on low speed add sugar and cocoa. Increase speed and beat 2 to 3 minutes. Reduce speed; add ground pecans.

Spread preserves over warm crust leaving 1/2-inch border. It will be very thin. Pour pecan filling over preserves and tilt to spread and level. Bake at 375 degrees for 25 minutes. Let cool completely.

For icing, melt chocolate chips. Add corn syrup, rum and water. Stir until smooth. Spread icing on cooled batter. Sprinkle with nuts. Let stand until icing firms. Cut into small bars and serve.

*The preserves add to this unique tasting bar cookie!*

*Crust:*

- ½ cup (1 stick) butter
- ¼ cup dark brown sugar
- 1 ¼ cups all-purpose flour, sifted

*Chocolate Pecan Filling:*

- ¼ cup apricot preserves
- 1 ½ cups pecans pieces
- 2 eggs
- ¼ teaspoon salt
- ½ teaspoon vanilla
- ¾ cup dark brown sugar
- 2 tablespoons unsweetened cocoa

*Chocolate Icing:*

- 1 (6-ounce) package semisweet chocolate chips
- 2 tablespoons light corn syrup
- 1 teaspoon rum
- 2 teaspoons very hot water
- ½ cup pecans, toasted, chopped

**Yield: 32 pieces**

2 ¼ cups unbleached all-
purpose flour

¾ cup sugar

1 ½ teaspoons baking powder

¼ teaspoon salt

2 eggs

1 egg yolk

⅔ cup unblanched slivered
almonds

1 egg yolk

1 tablespoon milk

Chocolate Glaze:

¼ cup whipping cream

1 cup (6 ounces) semi-sweet
chocolate chips

2 teaspoons light corn syrup

**Yield: 16 - 18 cookies**

# ALMOND BISCOTTI WITH CHOCOLATE GLAZE

Preheat oven to 400 degrees. Lightly flour baking sheets.

In large mixing bowl, combine flour, sugar, baking powder, salt, whole eggs and egg yolk; blend to form a smooth dough. Knead in almonds by hand if dough is too heavy for mixer.

Divide dough into 4 parts; form each into an 8-inch long flat loaf. For glaze, mix together 1 egg yolk and 1 tablespoon milk; brush over each log. Place dough logs on prepared baking sheets. Bake approximately 20 minutes or until golden brown.

While loaves are still warm, cut into 1-inch thick slices. Separate slices. Place on baking sheets and bake again for another 5 minutes at 450 degrees.

Place on wire racks to cool completely. Store in airtight container. Serve either plain or decorated with Chocolate Glaze.

Heat cream in heavy saucepan until bubbles appear around edge. Remove from heat. Stir in chocolate chips and corn syrup; cover and let stand for 15 minutes.

Mix with spoon or wire whisk gently so as not to create bubbles in the chocolate mixture.

Dip half of cooled cookie into chocolate glaze; arrange on a baking sheet covered with wax paper. Chill cookies in refrigerator for 10 minutes.

*Deliciously crunchy and so perfect with a cup of coffee or tea.*

# CHOCOLATE MINT BARS

Preheat oven to 350 degrees.

In a large mixer bowl, cream butter and sugar until light and fluffy. Beat in eggs and vanilla. Blend in melted chocolate. Add flour; stir to blend. Add nuts and stir well.

Pour batter into a greased 9 x 9-inch pan. Bake 25 minutes. Cool completely.

For frosting, beat ingredients well and spread over cooled crust. Chill slightly.

To make glaze, melt both chocolate and butter. Stir; spread or paint on top of frosted bars with a pastry brush.

Chill bars 10 minutes before cutting.

*Crust:*

- ½ cup (1 stick) butter or margarine
- 1 cup granulated sugar
- 2 eggs
- 1 teaspoon vanilla
- 2 (1-ounce) squares unsweetened chocolate, melted
- ½ cup all-purpose flour
- ½ cup pecans

*Frosting:*

- 1 ¼ cups confectioners' sugar
- ¼ cup (½ stick) butter or margarine
- ¼ teaspoon peppermint extract
- 1 tablespoon milk
- 1 drop green food coloring, optional

*Glaze:*

- 1 (1-ounce) square unsweetened chocolate
- 1 tablespoon butter or margarine

**Yield: 16 bars**

¾ cup (1 ½ sticks) unsalted butter

6 (1-ounce) squares unsweetened chocolate, chopped

2 ½ cups sugar

4 eggs

1 egg yolk

1 ½ teaspoons vanilla

1 teaspoon amaretto liqueur or almond extract

1 cup plus 2 tablespoons all-purpose flour

1 teaspoon ground cinnamon

1 cup dried cherries

1 cup semi-sweet chocolate chips

Confectioners' sugar, optional

**Yield: 16 - 32**

# DRIED CHERRY CHOCOLATE BROWNIES

Preheat oven to 350 degrees. Butter one 13 x 9-inch glass baking dish.

In a heavy large saucepan, melt butter and chocolate over low heat stirring until smooth. Remove from heat. Mix in sugar, eggs one at a time, then yolk. Add vanilla , liqueur or extract, flour, cinnamon; stir until blended. Stir in cherries and chocolate chips.

Spread batter in prepared baking dish. Bake 30 to 35 minutes or until brownies are firm around the edges and wooden pick comes out with a few crumbs when inserted in center. Sprinkle with confectioners' sugar while still warm, if desired.

*The dried cherries and chocolate chips make this brownie very distinctive.*

# CARAMEL APPLE BARS

Preheat oven to 400 degrees.

In large bowl combine and beat butter, shortening and brown sugar. Stir in 1 3/4 cups flour, oats, salt and baking soda. Reserve 2 cups of mixture. Press remaining mixture into a 13 x 9-inch baking pan.

Toss apples with 3 tablespoons flour; spread over mixture in pan.

In small saucepan, heat caramels and milk over low heat. Pour melted caramel mixture over apples. Top with reserved batter; press lightly.

Bake 25 to 30 minutes until golden brown and apples are tender. Cut into bars, 2 x 2-inches, while warm. Refrigerate.

Reheat and serve warm on a plate with a scoop of vanilla ice cream.

*A great fall dessert!*

½ cup (1 stick) butter or margarine

¼ cup vegetable shortening

1 cup brown sugar

1 ¾ cups all-purpose flour

1 ½ cups oats

½ teaspoon salt

½ teaspoon baking soda

4 ½ cups chopped apples, peeled, cored

3 tablespoons all-purpose flour

1 (14-ounce) package caramels, unwrapped

2 teaspoons milk

**Yield: 32 bars**

1 ¾ cups all-purpose flour

1 ½ cups confectioners' sugar

½ cup unsweetened cocoa

1 cup (2 sticks) cold butter or margarine

1 (8-ounce) package cream cheese

1 (14-ounce) can sweetened condensed milk

1 egg

2 teaspoons vanilla

½ cup chopped pecan, (toasted, optional)

**Yield: 24 - 36 bars**

# CHOCOLATE CHEESECAKE BARS

Preheat oven to 350 degrees. Lightly butter a 13 x 9-inch baking pan.

In large bowl, combine flour, sugar and cocoa. Cut in butter until mixture is crumbly. This step can also be done in a food processor.

Reserve 2 cups of crumb mixture; press the remainder firmly on bottom of prepared baking pan. Bake 15 minutes.

In a large mixing bowl, beat cream cheese until fluffy. Gradually beat in sweetened condensed milk until smooth. Add egg and vanilla; mix well. Pour over crust.

Combine nuts with reserved crumb mixture. Spread over cream cheese batter.

Bake 25 to 30 minutes or until bubbly. Place on wire rack to cool completely. Chill; cut into bars. Store covered in refrigerator.

*A yummy bar that everyone will love!*

# Rum Glazed Raisin Bars

Preheat oven to 350 degrees.

In a small bowl, combine raisins and rum. Stir well to coat; set aside.

In a small bowl, combine flour and baking powder; set aside.

In a large mixer bowl, combine butter and sugar. Beat at medium speed to cream lightly. Add egg; continue beating until mixture is light and fluffy.

Add flour mixture alternately with milk to egg mixture; stir just until blended. Stir in rum and raisins.

Spread batter evenly in a well-buttered 9-inch baking pan. Bake 20 to 25 minutes or until toothpick inserted in center comes out clean. Place on a rack and cool until barely warm.

For glaze, beat together butter and sugar until well mixed. Add rum; stir well. Add more sugar if mixture is too thin.

Spread glaze evenly over top of warm cookie dough. Cool completely before cutting into 32 bars.

½ cup raisins

2 tablespoons rum

1 cup all-purpose flour

½ teaspoon baking powder

½ cup (1 stick) butter or margarine

½ cup sugar

1 egg

¼ cup milk

Rum Glaze:

2 tablespoons butter or margarine

¾ cup sifted confectioners' sugar

1 tablespoon rum

**Yields: 32 bars**

1 ⅔ cups whipping cream

7 tablespoons unsalted butter

1 pound semi-sweet chocolate, cut or broken into pieces.

2 tablespoons orange-flavored liqueur

Unsweetened cocoa

**Yield: 50**

# DARK CHOCOLATE TRUFFLES

In a heavy saucepan, heat whipping cream and butter over medium heat. Stir until cream and butter begins to boil. Remove from heat. Stir in chocolate pieces until melted.

Stir liqueur into chocolate mixture; cover and refrigerate. Let mixture thicken for at least 2 hours. Stir 3 to 4 times while cooling.

Scoop up a portion of chocolate with a spoon. Dust your hands with plenty of cocoa and roll between your palms to form balls. Store in container with wax paper separating layers. Refrigerate.

*For a different taste, replace the orange-flavored liqueur with amaretto, bourbon or white creme de menthe.*

*Sensuous!*

# Amaretto Kisses

Melt chocolate in a heavy saucepan or double boiler over low heat. Remove from heat; stir in sugar and corn syrup. Add liqueur and blend.

Combine vanilla wafer crumbs and nuts in bowl; stir in chocolate mixture. Mix well.

Form mixture into 1-inch balls; roll in granulated sugar. Store in an air tight container several days before serving.

1 (6-ounce) package semi-sweet chocolate chips

½ cup granulated sugar

3 tablespoons light corn syrup

½ cup chocolate amaretto or regular amaretto liqueur

2 ½ cups finely crushed vanilla wafer crumbs

1 cup finely chopped pecans

Granulated sugar for rolling candy

**Yield: 5 dozen**

# Perfect Fudge

In a sauce pan, mix sugar, evaporated milk and salt; bring to a boil over medium heat. Stir for 10 minutes on a low boil.

Remove from heat; add corn syrup, chocolate chips and bourbon. Stir until melted. Pour mixture into an 8-inch square greased pan. Refrigerate 2 hours or until firm. Cut into small pieces.

*Variation: For a different taste, replace 1 tablespoon bourbon for amaretto or orange-flavor liqueur.*

*An old-fashioned favorite with a flair!*

2 ¼ cups sugar

¾ cup evaporated milk

½ teaspoon salt

⅓ cup light corn syrup

1 (12-ounce) package semi-sweet chocolate chips (2 cups)

1 tablespoon bourbon, amaretto or orange-flavored liqueur

**Yield: 64 (1-inch) pieces**

# GATHERINGS

◀ Apple Asiago Salad with Dijon Vinaigrette, 183; Turkey Scallops with Pine Nuts and
Dried Cherries, 258; Oven Roasted Winter Vegetables, 211

# GATHERINGS

# WINTER ESCAPES

## WINTER DINNER PARTY FOR 8 – 10

Though Indiana weather in January can be frosty, competition is heated throughout the state as high school, college, university, and professional teams focus Hoosiers' attention on the time-honored tradition of Indiana basketball. The season moves into full swing in the first month of the year, and fans follow their teams devotedly. A welcome respite from the rush and hubbub of the games is a winter dinner party where guests can enjoy the warmth of a crackling fire, elegant food and spirited conversation about — what else? — basketball.

FRESH BASIL CREAM CHEESE
27

---

APPLE ASIAGO SALAD WITH
DIJON VINAIGRETTE
183

---

TURKEY SCALLOPS WITH PINE
NUTS AND DRIED CHERRIES
258

---

OVEN ROASTED WINTER
VEGETABLES
211

---

SIMPLY ROYALE
CHOCOLATE TORTE WITH
RASPBERRY SAUCE
346

---

WINE

# MAGIC MOMENTS

## INTIMATE DINNER FOR 2 – 4

W hen the snow is falling softly and Valentine's Day is near, what could be more appropriate than a romantic dinner? Candlelight and music set the mood for enchantment. Strains of "Stardust" or "Night and Day" — written by Indiana natives Hoagie Carmichael and Cole Porter respectively — are perfect accompaniments to an evening of romance.

# COFFEE AND CONVERSATION

## NEIGHBORHOOD COFFEE

The winds of March gust through Indianapolis bringing with them the promise of softer breezes of spring. Hostesses in the capital city enjoy gathering neighbors together for coffee and conversation. Whether they are in Lockerbie Square, a revitalized area of Victorian houses and cottages downtown, in stately homes of the Meridian-Kessler neighborhood, on the tree-lined streets of the Butler-Tarkington district, or any other section of the city, Hoosier neighbors care about one another and welcome the opportunity to be together.

# GARDEN SPRING LUNCHEON

## LADIES LUNCH

In April, Indianapolis is at its loveliest. Forsythia, daffodils, tulips, dogwood, and redbud burst into bloom, their beauty softening the stark winter landscape. The gardens at the Indianapolis Art Museum and the Eiteljorg Museum of Southwestern Art are popular springtime attractions. Residential gardens provide a perfect backdrop for outdoor luncheons where guests can enjoy the welcome of friendship and the warmth of spring.

# MAY DAZE

## DESSERT BUFFET

May in Indianapolis is Race Month. Attention turns to the Indianapolis Motor Speedway where race car owners, drivers, crews, and spectators converge to prepare for the Indy 500. Checkered banners fly from lamp posts all over town. Black and white are the colors of choice for everything from clothing to dinnerware, and even race humbugs get caught up in the carnival atmosphere. Luncheons, dinners, balls, and parties enhance the festivities as Indianapolis welcomes visitors from around the world, and hostesses know that an elegant dessert buffet will be a sure winner.

# GREAT EXPECTATIONS

## SHOWER OR GRADUATION PARTY

June is a month of celebrations. Graduations, showers, weddings, all bring families and friends together to share in the joy of milestone moments and the anticipation of futures filled with promise. The comfortable ease of a buffet dinner is an ideal way to bring well-wishers together and welcome them back home again.

# Stars and Stripes

### GRILL-OUT

The Fourth of July starts the month with a bang and sets the stage for the outdoor activities so much a part of this time of year. A tradition for many Hoosiers is celebrating the Fourth at Conner Prairie, a re-constructed pioneer village. And, of course, gathering friends and family together at back yard cookouts is a favorite way to entertain on warm summer evenings.

FRESH BASIL CREAM CHEESE
27

DRAGON'S BREATH DIP
WITH CHIPS
40

SUMMER CORN SALAD
155

CRUNCHY GREEN BEANS
190

PERFECT PICNIC
POTATO SALAD
166

SUMMER BEEF AND
CHICKEN KABOBS
219

EASY CHEESY BREAD
90

DRIED CHERRY
CHOCOLATE BROWNIES
366

BLACKBERRY COBBLER
344

VANILLA ICE CREAM

# PICNIC 'N' PLAY

## CHILDREN'S PICNIC

As summer draws on and children become as lazy as the long, hot days, special activities perk them up and help make the last month of summer memorable. Indianapolis moms and dads plan trips to the world-renowned Children's Museum and visits to the fair grounds during the fun-filled days of the Indiana State Fair. A picnic, whether in one of the city's lovely parks or in the back yard, is a special gathering all children enjoy.

# INDIAN SUMMER FEAST

## HARVEST DINNER

The beginning of the school year brings with it a flurry of activities. Practices, lessons, organization and committee work all resume in September. So does a new season of performances at Clowes Memorial Hall at Butler University where a rendition of Annie, which is based on "Little Orphan Annie" by Indianapolis poet James Whitcomb Riley, might be on the program. Despite the active time of year, Indianapolis hostesses find time to gather friends and neighbors for an early fall dinner party.

# AUTUMN HARVEST

BREAKFAST FOR WEEKEND GUESTS

When the days become crisp and the trees are aflame with the brilliant reds and golds of October, attention turns to football — and to welcoming visitors who come back for college homecomings or to see Indianapolis' NFL team, the Colts, play at the Hoosier Dome. A hearty pre-game breakfast is the perfect start to an exciting day of gridiron action.

# COMPANY'S COMING

## HOMECOMING DINNER PARTY

Thanksgiving brings families back home to Indianapolis from all over the country. Returning Hoosiers look forward to visiting familiar sites and attending a performance of one of the city's many theatre or ballet groups. Most heartwarming, though, is gathering around the table with loved ones to enjoy a traditional holiday feast that creates the most compelling reason to come home for the holidays.

SAVORY GRUYERE
CHEESECAKE
9

---

ALMOND BAKED BRIE WITH
CRANBERRY CHUTNEY
30

---

GRILLED BEEF TENDERLOIN
PARTY SANDWICHES
25

---

PROVOLONE, SUN-DRIED
TOMATOES AND BASIL BREAD
20

---

TORTELLINI AND VEGETABLES
IN GARLIC VINAIGRETTE
180

---

FRESH FRUIT WITH
GOLDEN SALAD DRESSING
184

---

ALMOND LACE COOKIES
355

---

DOUBLE CHOCOLATE GLAZED
FUDGE CAKE
297

---

CARAMEL SCOTCH
BERRY TRIFLE
314

---

CLARET CUP
47

---

# DECEMBER DAZZLE

## HOLIDAY OPEN HOUSE

The sparkle of the holidays puts everyone in a festive mood. The lighting of the Christmas tree on Monument Circle and the special holiday performances of the Indianapolis Symphony Orchestra enhance the spirit of the season. Hoosier hospitality and the holidays go hand in hand as Indianapolis hostesses welcome guests and visitors to their homes for gala open houses.

The Junior League of Indianapolis, Inc. reaches out to women of all races, religions and national origins who demonstrate an interest in and a commitment to voluntarism.

Proceeds from the sale of Back Home Again will be returned to the community through the League's support of these and other volunteer projects:

## JLI
## VOLUNTEER PROJECTS
## PRESENT AND PAST

*Child Advocates*

*Dyslexia*

*Indianapolis Campaign for Healthy Babies*

*Riley Hospital Child Life Services*

*Indiana Youth Institute*

*Homeless*

*Oasis (Older Adult Service and Information System)*

*Komen Race for the Cure*

*The Nature Conservancy*

*Youth as Resources*

*Training, Inc.*

*DO-IN-A-DAY*

*Fairbanks Hospital*

*Now for the Future*

*The Ryan White Foundation*

*Women's Appointment Collaboration*

*Family Support Center*

*Schnull-Rauch House*

*Ronald McDonald House*

*Conner Prairie Pioneer Settlement*

*Garfield Park Conservatory*

*Heritage Place of Indianapolis, Inc.*

*Early Prevention of School Failure with IPS*

*US National Figure Skating*

*Pan American Games*

*NCAA Basketball Championship*

*PBS Channel 20*

*Circle Theatre*

# ACKNOWLEDGMENTS

The Junior League of Indianapolis, Inc. gratefully acknowledges the following businesses and individuals for sharing their valuable services, talents and commitment to quality throughout the production of Back Home Again.

**MacCollum Paper Company Inc.,** *paper supplier;* **Nicholstone,** *bindery;* **Joe O'Malia's Food Markets,** *food for photography;* **Lisa DeVille,** *Culinary Stylist;* **Woodie Howgill,** *Copywriter;* **Annie Watts, Lila Chiappetta,** *Recipe Editors;* **Charles R. Reeves,** *Patent and Trademark Attorney;* **Holy Beaumont, Lisa Tyner,** *Photographic Support;* **Joan Griffits,** *Indexer;* **Jay Koenig,** *Art Director, Image Concepts, Inc.;* **LMB Microcomputers,** *computer support;* **Leanne Scott,** *typist;* **Mary Durlacher,** *Mostly Linens;* **Dow Brands Home Economist Advisory Panel, Sue Brames, Gail L. Heeb,** *title and cover design review;* **Printsly Creations, Inc.,** *promotional material;* **UN Printing,** *promotional material;* **Pat Quinn,** *computer consultant;* **Details,** *photography props;* **Theobolds** *for the following photography props: Lenox, Symphony; Noritake, Fitzgerald; Royal Worchester, Gold Feather; Arthur Court, Acorn Tray; Gallo Design, Intarsia; Val St. Lambert, Balmoral.*

The Junior League of Indianapolis, Inc. is indebted to our many members and friends who have shared their special recipes and suggestions. We sincerely appreciate your generosity and hope we have not inadvertently omitted anyone's name.

Anne Adams, Lisa Brenner Allen, Amy Alley, Courtney Amodeo, Richard Amodeo, Barbara Anderson, Nancy Aquino, Ann Arthur, Christine Arthur, Theresa Arness, Helen Aschenbrener, Margaret Avevill.

Cyndy Bailey, Adele Baker, Nell Baker, Lisa Baldwin, Nancy Barnes, Rosie Barnhard, Alrita Barton, Nancie Baxter, Pamela Baxter, Kathy Beasley, Anne Becker, Juanita Becker, Betty Beckers, Beth Bedwell, Cathy Beeblam, Marni Beerbower, Sheryl Beerbower, Pam Bell, Debbie Bennett, Ann Bernstein, Denise Berry, Bobbie Blachly, Karen Black, Joan Blackwell, Kristie Blankenhorn, Betsy Block, Linda Blue, Marina Boguslavsky, Julie Bohannon, Jill Borst, Dr. Paul W. Borth, Linda Borth, Megan Boschini, Betty Breidenbach, Gina Bremner, Janice Brennan, Donna M. Brooks, Tonya Brown, Jane Browne, Laura Brueckmann, Mary Ann Burkes, Gay Burkhart, Tanya Bush, Catherine Butz, Ellen Butz, Rose Marie Butz, Kristen Byers.

Mary Caito, Barbara Campbell, Harriet Campbell, Mary Martha Cannady, Paula Cardoza, Jeanne Carmody, Bonnie Carter, Susan Casper, Debbie Catton, Ann Chaney, Sandra Chenoweth, Ellen Chrapla, Gretchen Christensen, Lisa Clarke, Celeste Cohen, Bethanne Collins, Lisa Conaway, Diane Confer, Lynda Cook, Susie Cooper, Margo Cory, Lisa Cotter, Sarah Cover, Kay Crawford, Jane Creveling, Sandra Crosley, Linda Curts.

Kimberly Danforth, Judy Danges, Barbara Danquist, Kathy Dansker, Kim Dant, Betsy Davidson, Julie Davis, Mrs. Robert Dean, Sally DeMars, Carolyn DeTarnowsky, Jackie Devich, Karen DeVries, Keene Donnellan, Lisa Drake, Karen Drook, Mary Durlacher, Jennifer Dwyer, Christopher Earle, Elaine Eckhart, Jayme Edwards, Sara Ellerhorst, Evelyn Eschenhoff, Barbara Ettl.

Dr. and Mrs. James Fadely, Alyson Faircloth, Patricia Fansler, Saleme Farah, Karen Farrar, Pat Fausler, Marni Fechtman, Mary Feeney, Mary Ellen Fellegon, Lisa Fennig, Mary Ellen Fennig, Judy Fertig, Lynn Fink, Joan Finney, Cindee Fisher, Cynthia Fleming, Jo Ellen Flynn, Janyce Foster, Susan Fountain, Cheryl Fowler, Julie Fox, Nancy Frick.

Jan Gaines, Betsy Gallagher, Anne Terese Garber, Clodagh Garry, Mary Geaub, Anne Gerus, Ken Gerus, June Giesler, Karen Glaser, Linda Goad, Rosalie Gollner, Karen Goodwell, Sandra Gordner, Mary Graub, Gwen Groves, Dana Guild, Maeve Guzek.

# CONTRIBUTORS

Colleen Haboush, Tricia Hackett, Sally Hamer, Barbara Hamilton, Marcie Hammel, Katherine Harbour, Mark Harbour, Deana Harmon, Priscilla Harrington, Elizabeth Harris, Amy Hart-Ramey, Mary Hauck, Jane Hawks, Joe Hayes, Brenda Hedback, Patty Hefner, Bonnie Heim, Mrs. Richard Henkel, Florence Hermayer, Julie Herrick, Bev Hill, Bonnie Hinkle, Penny Holcomb, Deborah Holtsclaw, Jane Horen, Liz Hourigan, Jane Hoven, Becky Huber, Susie Hulett, Paige Hunkin, Tammy Hurm, Kathy Hursh, Rosalie Hurst, Patty Huse, Estelle Huston.

Marcia Inselberg, Suzanne Irwin, Ivan Ivancevich.

Sarah Jackson, Jody Jacobs, Nancy Jeffrey, Jennifer Johnson, Amy Johnston, Mary Anne Jones, Jane Jones, Kendra Jordan, Lane Jordan, Jennifer Joyce.

George Kalbouss, Paula Kalbouss, Robert Kalbouss, Kenwyn Kealing, Cathleen Keim, Julie Keller, Anne Kennedy, Susan Kiley, Sandee Kleymeyer, Betsy Kranz, Caroline Kroot, Sally Kubinski, Donna Kuhn, Kathleen Kunkel.

Lynda Lacy-Higgins, Holly W. Lambert, Martha Lamkin, Beth Lammers, Julia Landis, Diana Lanman, Kathy Lauck, Rosalind Laurien, Ruth Lawrence, Kristi Lawson, Cathy Lawson, Linda Leiden, Anne Lennon, Phyllis Lentz, Mary Leuders, Lisa Liles, Mary Liles, Julia Litzsinger, Raney Litzsinger, Jean Locke, Linda Long, Kathryn Long, Anne Loomis, Sara Lootens, Linda Lugar, Linda Lukens, Ann Lunsford.

Marilyn MacCollum, Alice MacPhail, Cheri Mahoney, Sue Maine, Tricia Mandelbaum, Mary Mandeville, Dorothy Lane Market, Liz Markey, Joyce Marshall, Diane Marshall, Patty Martin, Evelyn Masloob, Mrs. William Matthews, Stacy Maurer, Marnie Maxwell, Barbara Mayer, Shelli McDonald, Christina McGarvey, David McGarvey, Barbara McGowan, Jayne McGivney, Lisa McKibban, Kimberly McKinley, Jane McLain, Barbara McLaughlin, Karen McMahan, Lynne McMahan, Lyn McMillin, Sarah McNaught, Ruth Medernach, Jean Merkle, Kelley Merritt, Gayle Meyer, Sally Meyers, Sally Michaud, Barb Miller, Lindsay Miller, Libby Miller, Mary Miller, Peggy Miner, Marty Morris, Mary Morris, Noel Morris, Ann Moss, Becky Moss, Kelcy Mullins-Whitman, Kathy Mulvaney, Hooley Murray, Marilyn Murray, DeeDee Mutschler.

Cindy Newcomer, Doris Newton, Carolyn Nierman, Debra Norman, Alberta Norton.

Courtney O'Connor, Becky O'Hara, Cami O'Herren, Adrian Oleck, Lori Olivier, Lisa Olsson, Sandy Ossip, Jennie Oukada.

Elisabeth Palmer, Jessie Palmer, Kris Payne, Marilyn Peachin, Amy Pearce, Faye Philippsen, Father Leo Piquet, Stephanie Piratzky, Christine Plews, Kim Pohlman, Eileen Potenza, Priscilla Price-Johnson, Kim Purucker, Doris Purucker.

Lori Queisser, Lydia Quilhot, Pat Quinn.

Susan Rathman, Barbara Reahard, Ann Reel, Scott Reeves, Carole Reeves, Jane Reeves, Sarah Rehberg, Sherri Reider, Lindy Reith, Shannon Rezek, Liz Richards, Susan Richardson, Teresa Rieth, Betty Ritenour, Denise Rogers, Cathy Rooney, Patty Rosiello, Carol Roth, Elizabeth Ruddell, Richard Ruddell, Susan Ryan.

Debbie Saeger, Marianne Salaymett, Karen Santarossa, Meredith Savadove, Ann Scott, Janet Sebald, Eve Seligson, Marge Sexton, Nicole Sexton, Candes Melanie Shelton, Eve Shirley, Barbara Shortle, Lois Shytle, Peg Sidebottom, Cathy Simmons, Stacy Singer, Cheryl Sinkovic-Pethe, Melissa Sinkus, Mark Slorer, Diane Smith, Dorothy Smith, Virginia Smith, Jane Spahn, Karen Speer, Barbara Stackhouse, Sally Standley, Barbara Starwilder, Barbara Stayton, Audrey Stehle, Cindy Stevens, Lisa Stewart, Jane Stone, Ann Strong, Sharon Stuart, Shirley Stucki, Patty Sweeney, Anne Swengel, Theresa Swenson.

Lori Tanberg, Carolyn Tarnowsky, Vickie Theis, Suzanne Thomas, Lynn Thompson, Kate Tilden, Megan Tipton, Sherrie Tollefson, Debbie Tolley, Susan Tonnemacher, Ann Margaret Toon, Sue Trainer, Lori Tranberg, Jerilyn Tucker, Angie Forbis Tuckerman, Janet Tuckerman, Bonnie Turner.

Susan VanHuss, Rebecca VanWinkle, Ann Vest, Laura Villanyi, Terilyn Voegtle.

Heather Wachholz, Ann Wade, Ruth Ann Wade, Brenda Walker, Cynthia Walker, Cheryl Walters, Malorie Walters, Heather Warkhoe, Cheryl Warrens, Melissa Warriner, Cheryl Warriner, Marie Warshauer, Evelyn Waters, Lore Weas, Wendy Weidberg, Susan Weber, Barbara Weiss, Annie Wells, Barb Werling, Janet White, Joy White, Maureen Whiting, Maureen Whitman-Mullins, Kelcy Wickliff, Wendy Wickliff, Kay Wicks, Barbara Wilder, Peggy Buroker Williams, Lauri Williams, Joyce Wilson, Susan Winckelbach, Kelly Wiseman-Hammond, Susan Woodworth, Terry Worsley, Audrey Wright.

Rosemarie Yaros, Patricia Yeager, Marty Young, Bee Young.

Pamela Zarvas, Amy Ziegert.

# SPECIAL
# COOK'S NOTES

**To make Bouquet Garni,** place sprigs of parsley, thyme and a bay leaf (1 clove garlic optional) on a square of cheesecloth. Tie cloth with a thin string leaving a long end free. Tie string to saucepan handle. Immerse in soups or dishes that are being stewed. Remove at the end of the cooking process before serving.

**Crush herbs** in the palm of your hand to bring out the full flavor.

**Parsley will stay fresh and crisp** for several weeks if stored in a covered glass jar in the refrigerator.

**Tarragon** gets bitter and tough when boiled.

**Garlic roasted,** tends to be sweeter and milder than raw or sautéed garlic and even delicious as a vegetable. Make a lot of it and preserve in olive oil for later use in salads and dips.

**Garlic can be kept** indefinitely in the freezer. Peel and chop before thawing.

**Ginger comes in several forms** - as fresh ginger root, in crystallized chunks, dried and ground. Ground ginger is the best for baking; crystallized is delicious in chutneys and desserts or with after dinner coffee. Ginger root is wonderful when you want intense flavor. The root is fibrous and should be peeled and then either cut into rounds, grated, or finely minced. Store fresh ginger root in a cool, dark place or in the refrigerator.

**To store ginger,** cover it with dry sherry in a small glass jar. This can be stored in the refrigerator for 1 year.

**If fresh wild mushrooms are unavailable,** use dried ones instead, allowing 1 1/2 ounces dried for 8 ounces fresh. Rinse the dried mushrooms quickly under cold water to remove any dirt, place them in a small bowl, and pour warm water over them to cover. Let them soak for 30 minutes, or until plumped, then drain them through a fine-meshed sieve set over another small bowl. Gently squeeze excess liquid from the mushrooms before adding them to the dish.

**Asparagus will stay fresh and crisp** if stored right side up in an inch of water in the refrigerator.

**To make croutons,** cut up an old baguette of bread and toss with butter and garlic. Place in a shallow baking dish at 325 degrees for 30 minutes, stirring occasionally.

**Rolls and breads brushed with olive oil** before baking will have a tender crust. Rolls and breads brushed with milk or a combination of an egg and one tablespoon of milk will have a crisp crust.

**If buttermilk is unavailable,** 3/4 cup thin yogurt mixed with 1/4 cup milk may be used instead.

**If honey has hardened in the cupboard or refrigerator;** stand the jar, uncovered, in a saucepan of barely simmering water for 15 to 20 minutes, or until the honey softens.

**When measuring molasses,** lightly butter or oil the measuring cup; the molasses then slides from the cup without sticking to the sides. This also increases the accuracy of the measuring.

# Special Cook's Notes

**To avoid lumpy glazes and frostings,** sift confectioners' sugar before blending it in.

**To make chocolate shavings,** use a vegetable peeler; for fine shavings, use a hand grater.

**Pastry shells will hold their shape** better if thoroughly chilled or frozen before baking.

**To reheat leftover coffeecake on microwave plates,** microwave on high(100% power) for 10 to 15 seconds or until warm.

**Substitute quick-rising yeast** to cut rising time in half when using yeast.

**A pastry bag can be substituted** by using a zip-closure bag and cutting one corner from the bottom to pipe the filling. You can also use pastry tips for a more uniform design. (Fillings, icings, cheeses, chocolate, whipped cream.)

**To peel peaches,** bring a medium saucepan of water to a boil. Drop 1 peach at a time gently into the boiling water, leave it for 5 seconds, and retrieve it by piercing the flesh with a fork. With a paring knife, slit the skin, which will then slip off easily.

**Frosted fruit** such as grapes (red, green) or cranberries make a pretty garnish. Beat egg white with a small amount of water. Dip clusters or individual fruits (on wooden picks) in egg white, then in granulate sugar. Let dry on wire racks.

**For ease in cutting dried or candied fruits** such as apricots, dates and cherries; dip scissors into a cup of warm water frequently. This technique is also useful for cutting marshmallows or gumdrops.

**After you have squeezed a lemon for its juice,** wrap and freeze the rind. Citrus peels can be grated and frozen for later use.

**Juice lemons** at room temperature. Heat in microwave for 30 seconds on high. Store juice in glass jar; good for weeks and easy to use when needed.

**To toast pecans or almonds,** spread in a single layer on baking sheet. Toast in 350 degree oven for 5 to 7 minutes or until lightly brown and fragrant. Cool completely. Toasting nuts enhances the flavor, especially if used in baked goods.

**Nut meats** shelled should be refrigerated up to 6 months and can be frozen up to one year.

**To plump raisins,** cover with water, liqueur, brandy or rum. Place in a microwave bowl and cook on high for 45 seconds or until raisins are soft. Let stand covered for 1 minute; drain and use.

**Toss raisins, dates or candied fruit** with flour before adding to breads or cakes to prevent them from sinking to the bottom.

**To skin a tomato simply and quickly,** spear the stem end with a fork and dip it into a saucepan of boiling water for several seconds.

**If you forget to soak the beans overnight,** you can prepare them by boiling the well rinsed beans in water in a covered pan for 5 minutes.

**A leaf of cabbage** dropped in a pot of soup absorbs fat from the top.

**To save a soup that is too salty,** simmer a slice of potato for a few minutes. Repeat with fresh slices of potato until desired seasoning has been achieved.

**For quicker preparation of crumbled bacon,** chop before cooking.

# Special Cook's Notes

**To make hard boil eggs,** place eggs in a pan, cover with cold water and pour in some white vinegar or salt. Bring to a boil, cover pan and remove from heat for 15 minutes. Drain off hot water. Now shake the pan back and forth, causing the eggs to crack against the sides of pan. Cool with cold water and peel.

**To sterilize Egg Yolks use,**
> 1 egg yolk
> 1 tablespoon water
> 1 teaspoon lemon juice

Microwave on high 6 to 10 seconds until the egg begins to move. Repeat one time; repeat a second time. Let stand 1 minute.

**To ensure that the eggs will not crack while boiling,** add 2 tablespoons vinegar or salt to the water. Peeling the eggs as soon as they cool enough to handle makes the whites come away from the shells more easily.

**To keep ice cubes from diluting drinks,** freeze tea, coffee, and fruit juices in ice cube trays and use these flavored cubes to cool the appropriate beverages.

**When planning a floral centerpiece,** slip in a few herbs appropriate for the occasion, such as rosemary for friendship, lavender for luck and marjoram for happiness.

**The flowers of kitchen herbs and other edible blooms** make delicate decorations for dishes throughout the meal. Bright nasturtium or soft chive blossoms on green salads, meats, or fish; white basil flowers on sliced tomatoes; and tiny sprigs of rosemary with their mauve flowers on lemon soufflés - all hint at the possibilities of striking combinations.

**Flowers for garnish include** Apple blossom, Borage, Chamomile, Chive blossoms, Dandelion flowers, Honeysuckle, Johnny Jump-ups, Lavender, Lemon blossom, Marigold, Mustard flowers, Nasturtiums, Rose Petals, Squash blossoms and Violets.

**To make homemade Christmas Scent,** in a 1-quart saucepan combine the peeling (chopped) from half of an orange and half of a lemon, 1 large cinnamon stick, 8 cloves and 2 bay leaves. Add 2 cups water and bring to a boil. Simmer whenever you would like the lovely scent. Add additional water as liquid evaporates.

# SUBSTITUTIONS

Dash .................................................less than ⅛ teaspoon

3 teaspoons.......................................1 tablespoon

4 tablespoons ..................................¼ cup

5 ⅓ tablespoons ...............................⅓ cup

8 tablespoons ..................................½ cup

2 tablespoons ..................................1 ounce

8 ounces ..........................................1 cup (dry) or ½ pint (liquid)

16 ounces ........................................1 pound (dry) or 1 pint (liquid)

2 pints..............................................4 cups or 1 quart

4 quarts ...........................................1 gallon


1 teaspoon baking powder ..................¼ teaspoon baking soda plus ½ teaspoon
 cream of tartar

1 cup cake flour.................................1 cup minus 2 tablespoons all purpose flour

1 ounce unsweetened chocolate ..........3 tablespoons cocoa plus 1 tablespoon fat

1 tablespoon cornstarch .....................2 tablespoons flour or 4 teaspoon quick cooking tapioca

1 cup heavy cream..............................¾ cup milk plus ⅓ cup margarine or butter

1 clove garlic....................................⅛ teaspoon garlic powder or 1 teaspoon dried  herbs

1 tablespoon fresh herbs....................1 teaspoon dried herbs

1 cup honey .....................................1 ¼ cup sugar plus ¼ cup liquid

1 cup sour milk or buttermilk ..............1 tablespoon lemon juice or vinegar plus milk
 to make 1 cup (let stand 5 minutes)

1 teaspoon dried mustard...................1 tablespoon prepared mustard

¼ cup chopped fresh onion ................1 tablespoon instant minced onion rehydrated

| Ingredient | Amount | Yields |
|---|---|---|
| Bread, dry | 3 to 4 slices | 1 cup dry crumbs |
| Bread, fresh, soft | 1 ½ slices | 1 cup crumbs |
| Graham cracker | 13 squares | 1 cup crumbs finely crushed |
| Regular long grain rice | 1 cup | 3 to 4 cups cooked |
| Macaroni, uncooked | 1 cup | 2 cups cooked |
| Noodles, uncooked | 1 cup | 1 ¾ cups cooked |
| Spaghetti, uncooked | ½ pound | 4 cups cooked |
| Potatoes, white | 3 medium | 2 cups cubed/mashed |
| Corn on the cob | 2 medium | 1 cup kernels |
| Onions | 1 medium | ½ cup chopped |
| Apples | 3 medium | 3 cups sliced |
| Berries | 1 quart | 3 to 4 cups |
| Lemon | 1 medium | ¼ cup juice, 2 teaspoons grated rind |
| Lime | 1 medium | 1 to 2 tablespoons juice |
| Orange | 1 medium | ⅓ cup juice, 2 tablespoons grated rind |
| Peaches, Pears | 2 medium | 1 cup sliced |
| Nuts, chopped (peanuts, pecans, walnuts) | 4 ½ ounces | 1 cup |
| Bacon, cooked | 8 slices | ½ cup crumbled |
| Chicken, breasts | 2 whole | 2 cups diced cooked |
| Shrimp, raw in shell | 1 ½ pounds | 2 cups (¾ pound) cleaned and cooked |
| Chocolate | 1 square | 4 tablespoons grated |
| Whipping Cream | 1 cup | 2 cups whipped |
| Sugar: | | |
| Brown | 1 pound | 2 ¼ cups packed |
| Confectioners | 1 pound | 4 ½ cups sifted |
| Granulated | 1 pound | 2 ¼ cups |
| Cheese, natural chunk or process | 4 ounces | 1 cup shredded or cubed |

# Cooking Terms

**AL DENTE:** Slightly under done with a chewy consistency, from the Italian phrase "to the tooth". Usually applied to the cooking of pasta, but can also apply to vegetables that are blanched, not fully cooked.

**AU GRATIN:** To cover top of scalloped or sauced dishes with a light but thorough coating of cheese, bread crumbs or other types of crumbs.

**BAKE:** To cook by means of dry heat, usually in an oven. Do not crowd things in the oven; free circulation of air is important. Always preheat the oven for 10 to 15 minutes unless otherwise indicated.

**BALSAMIC VINEGAR:** An aged vinegar made in the Modena, Italy area from unfermented juice of the Trebbiano grape. Delicious used as part of a salad vinaigrette or with fresh fruit.

**BARBECUE:** To cook on a grill over intense heat or over open fire made with wood or charcoal. True barbecuing requires basting with a spicy sauce while the meat cooks.

**BASTE:** To moisten food with liquid or fat while cooking by means of a spoon, bulb baster or brush.

**BATTER:** A mixture containing flour and liquid, usually thin enough to pour. Batter is used for dipping, coating or for pancakes, cake, etc.

**BEAT:** To mix rapidly in order to make a mixture smooth and light by incorporating as much air as possible. By hand use a whisk, a fork or wooden spoon in a rhythmic, circular motion, lifting mixture up and over. Tip the bowl while beating. If using a rotary egg beater or electric mixer, use a rounded bowl for proper beating.

**BLANCH:** To plunge food into rapidly boiling water, a little at a time, so as not to disturb the boiling. Cook for the amount of time indicated in the recipe. Plunge food into cold water to arrest the cooking. Drain immediately.

**BLEND:** To combine two or more ingredients thoroughly; to mix by hand or with an electric mixer until smooth.

**BOIL:** To heat a liquid until bubbles break continually on the surface. Boiling temperature at sea level is 212 degrees Fahrenheit. For a rolling boil, bubbles do not break on the surface.

**BONE:** To remove the bones from meat, fish, poultry or game, often with a thin boning knife.

**BRAISE:** To brown meat in fat over high heat, then cover and cook slowly in the oven in a small amount of liquid.

**BREAD:** To dredge or coat with bread crumbs. For example, fish or chicken is dipped in buttermilk, coated with crumbs and pan-fried or baked.

**BROCHETTE:** Meat, fish, and vegetables threaded on a skewer and then baked, broiled, or grilled.

**BROIL:** To cook over or under direct heat, close to the fire or other source of heat. Pan broiling is like frying but with little or no fat.

**BROWN:** To sear or seal the juices into meat and to give it a good color. When browning meat, make sure it is absolutely dry, and turn so all sides are seared. Do not crowd pan or meat will steam in the pan rather than brown. Browning may be done under a broiler, in fat in a skillet or in a hot oven.

**CHILL:** To place in refrigerator until cold.

**CHOP:** To cut solids into pieces with a sharp knife or other chopping device.

# COOKING TERMS

**CHUTNEY:** A mixture of fruit and/or vegetables cooked with vinegar, sugar, and spices, used as a condiment - most often with meat and poultry.

**COAT:** To roll or shake in flour or sugar until lightly covered.

**COOL:** To let stand at room temperature until no longer warm to the touch.

**CREAM:** To blend together softened shortening or butter with any other ingredient by rubbing with the backside of a wooden spoon or using an electric mixer.

**CRÈME FRAICHE:** A dairy product that is similar in taste to sour cream but a bit more tart. Widely available in specialty grocery stores or easily made at home.

**CUBE:** To cut into small (about 1/2-inch) chunks.

**DASH:** A small quantity. Often used when measuring worchestershire, one or two quick shakes yields a dash.

**DEGLAZE:** To remove and preserve the brown bits and dried juices that accumulate in a cooking pan. Add liquid to the pan in which meat, fish or poultry has been cooked, scraping up any remaining bits. Deglazing makes a small amount of natural sauce that can be poured over meat or used as a base for a more elaborate sauce.

**DEVEIN:** To remove the intestinal tract of a shrimp. After a shrimp has been shelled, make a slit lengthwise on the outermost curve with a knife and remove the intestinal tract. Rinse under cold water.

**DICE:** To cut into very small (about 1/4-inch) cubes.

**DISSOLVE:** To mix a dry substance with liquid until a solution forms.

**DOT:** To scatter small bits, as of butter or cheese, over surface of food to be cooked or baked.

**DREDGE:** To coat a solid food with sugar, flour, crumbs or dry mixture. Dredging can be done by dragging the solid food through the powdery substance, by shaking the food in a bag with the dry ingredient or by sifting dry ingredients over the food.

**DRIPPINGS:** The juices, fats and browned bits that collect in the pan after meat or poultry has been roasted. Unless burned or very greasy, the drippings are valuable for a sauce. (See DEGLAZE)

**DRIZZLE:** To slowly pour liquid in a fine stream over food.

**DUST:** To sprinkle food with dry ingredients. Use a strainer or jar with a perforated cover.

**FILLETING:** To remove the bones from meat or fish. The resulting pieces are called fillets.

**FOLD:** To incorporate an aerated substance like whipped cream or beaten egg whites into a heavier substance. Using a spatula, gently cut through mixture, lift, and turn over. Repeat process, rotating bowl until ingredients are combined. The purpose of folding is to retain volume and lightness by taking care not to deflate the pockets of air.

**FRY:** To cook foods in hot oil or other fat. Pan-frying is done in a skillet. Deep-frying requires a deep heavy pan with 3 to 4 cups of hot fat into which the food is lowered until covered by the oil. Vegetable or solid shortening is recommended for deep frying. Do not use butter or olive oil.

**GARNISH:** Anything added to a dish after preparing. To decorate a dish, both to enhance its appearance and to provide a flavorful foil. Parsley, lemon slices, raw vegetables, chopped chives and other herbs are all forms of garnishes.

**GLAZE:** To apply a thickish liquid over the surface to give a final sheen. Vegetables cooked in butter combined with their own juices form a glaze. Sauce can be glazed by running it under a broiler until brown.

**GRATE:** To break up a solid into small particles, usually by rubbing against a metal object with sharp-edged holes. Small, medium or large particles may be grated. When grating a lemon rind, use only the colored part of the rind to avoid a bitter taste.

**GREASE:** To lightly coat a pan with some fat to prevent foods from sticking.

**GRILL:** To cook over open intense heat.

**FLUTE:** To make a decorative, scalloped or undulating edge on a pie crust or other pastry.

**FRITTER:** Small pieces of meat, vegetable, or fruit dipped in or mixed with a batter and then fried.

**JULIENNE:** To cut into thin strips. A julienne of vegetables would be a mixture of vegetables that have been so cut. To julienne, make a stack of 1/8-inch thick slices about 2 inches long. Cut downward at 1/8-inch intervals to make match-stick pieces.

**KNEAD:** To work dough with hands or dough hook appliance until the gluten in the flour develops and the dough becomes smooth and elastic.

**MARINADE:** Liquid, usually containing vinegar or wine, spices, herbs and oil used for pickling, seasoning or tenderizing.

**MARINATE:** To cover foods in a seasoned liquid, always containing some acid, such as lemon juice, vinegar or wine, to tenderize and infuse the flavor.

**MINCE:** To chop very fine. If using a French blade, rock the blade back and forth from one end of roughly chopped pieces to the other, then repeat crosswise.

**MIX:** To combine two or more ingredients.

**PARE:** To use a thin knife to remove skin or rind from fruits and vegetables.

**PEEL:** To remove the peels from vegetables and fruits.

**PLUMP:** To soak dried fruits in liquid until they swell.

**POACH:** To cook in a liquid just below the boiling point; to simmer gently.

**POUND:** To flatten or tenderize meat, often between sheets of waxed paper, with a heavy mallet. Boneless chicken breasts and veal for scallopine are often prepared this way.

**PROOF:** To test yeast to see if it is active. Dissolve the yeast in warm water with a little sugar. Let it stand in a warm place for 5 to 10 minutes. If the yeast is active, it will bubble and foam.

**PUREÉ:** To mash to a smooth blend, or press through a fine sieve or food mill. The result is also referred to as a pureé.

**REDUCE:** To boil down in order to reduce the volume.

**SAUTÉ:** To cook food quickly over a high heat in a small amount of oil. Sauté has come to mean in American terminology, cooking or browning food in small amount of fat over low or medium heat until food is tender, as in sautéing mushrooms and onions.

**SHRED:** To cut or tear into narrow strips.

**SIFT:** To separate coarse pieces from fine by shaking through a sieve or sifter, thus removing lumps.

# COOKING TERMS

**SIMMER:** To boil gently so that bubbles come to the surface and just barely break.

**SKEWER:** To fasten with a wood or metal pin in order to hold something in place while cooking.

**SKIM:** To spoon off fat or scum that rises to the surface of a cooked liquid.

**SLIVER:** To cut or split into long, thin pieces.

**SOUFFLÉ:** A baked food, either dessert or entree, made light and fluffy by the addition of beaten egg whites before cooking.

**STEAM:** To cook by contact with steam in a covered container or in a perforated container placed over hot water. Sometimes foods are put into airtight molds, as in steamed puddings, and lowered into gently boiling water to cook. Also, food wrapped in tightly sealed foil and then baked will give a similar result to steaming.

**STEW:** To cook slowly in a liquid for an extended period of time.

**STRAIN:** To remove solids from liquids by pouring through a colander or sieve.

**THICKEN:** To add flour or cornstarch to a liquid to make it thicker. To make a thickening, measure the liquid to be thickened and for each cupful, mix 1 1/2 tablespoons flour with 3 tablespoons of water until smooth. Stir mixture into hot liquid; cook until thickened. One tablespoon of cornstarch will thicken 1 1/2 to 2 cups of liquid.

**TOAST:** To brown in a broiler, oven, toaster or over hot coals until crisp on the outside.

**TOSS:** To mix lightly with two forks or with a fork and spoon.

**WHIP:** To beat rapidly, with an electric mixer, hand beater or wire whisk, so as to incorporate air and to increase volume.

**WHISK:** To beat with a whisk or whip until well mixed.

**WHITE CHOCOLATE:** It is not really a true chocolate because it does not contain chocolate liquor. It's main ingredients are usually cocoa butter, milk and vanilla. In baking, be careful to use a true white chocolate and not a confectioners' coating type.

**VINAIGRETTE:** A dressing made from a mixture of vinegar, oil, salt and pepper. Mustard, garlic, shallots, anchovies, or other seasonings may be added. Use as dressing for salads and other cold or room temperature dishes.

**ZEST:** To remove in fine strips the outermost colored peel, or zest, of citrus fruits, being careful not to incorporate the bitter, white pith just underneath the surface.

# Index

# INDEX

# INDEX

# INDEX

# INDEX

# INDEX

## S

# INDEX

# INDEX

# ORDER FORM

**Please send me:**

_____ copies of **Back Home Again** @ $21.95 each ........ (IN residents + $1.10 tax = $23.05)    $_____

_____ copies of **Winners** @ $16.95 each........................ (IN residents + $.85 tax = $17.80)    $_____

Postage and Handling @ $3.00 each    $_____

Total enclosed    $_____

**Ship to:**

Name_____    Address _____

City_____    State _____    Zip _____

Make checks payable to **JLI Publications**

Charge to (circle one)    *VISA*    MasterCard    Signature _____

Account Number _____    Expiration _____

Credit card phone orders accepted: **1- 317-923-7004**

All proceeds from the cookbook sales will be returned to the
community through Junior League of Indianapolis, Inc. projects.

**Junior League of Indianapolis Publications**
**BACK HOME AGAIN**
**3050 N. Meridian**
**Indianapolis, Indiana 46208**

*Prices subject to change.*

---

# ORDER FORM

**Please send me:**

_____ copies of **Back Home Again** @ $21.95 each ........ (IN residents + $1.10 tax = $23.05)    $_____

_____ copies of **Winners** @ $16.95 each........................ (IN residents + $.85 tax = $17.80)    $_____

Postage and Handling @ $3.00 each    $_____

Total enclosed    $_____

**Ship to:**

Name_____    Address _____

City_____    State _____    Zip _____

Make checks payable to **JLI Publications**

Charge to (circle one)    *VISA*    MasterCard    Signature _____

Account Number _____    Expiration _____

Credit card phone orders accepted: **1- 317-923-7004**

All proceeds from the cookbook sales will be returned to the
community through Junior League of Indianapolis, Inc. projects.

**Junior League of Indianapolis Publications**
**BACK HOME AGAIN**
**3050 N. Meridian**
**Indianapolis, Indiana 46208**

*Prices subject to change.*